Postcards
from the
Trailer Park

Postcards
from the
Trailer Park

The Secret Lives of Climbers

CAMERON M. BURNS

THE LYONS PRESS
Guilford, Connecticut
An imprint of The Globe Pequot Press

The Lyons Press is an imprint of The Globe Pequot Press.

10 9 8 7 6 5 4 3 2 1

Printed in the United States of America

Designed by Maggie Peterson

ISBN 1-59228-540-6

Library of Congress Cataloging-in-Publication data is available on file.

Dedication

To five guys who put up with
one hell of a lot of nonsense and thrived:
Benny Bach (founder, Team Rio de Caca Climbing Team),
Jordan Campbell (a.k.a. Joradaño du Telemark),
Charley "P&G" French (cofounder of the FBI[1] Climbing Team),
Luke "El Hoopsticker" Laeser,
and Steve "Buffy" Porcella.

---

[1] *Fat Bastards International, a.k.a. FBI. See* Rock Climbing Dessert Rock III, *by Eric Bjørnstad, for the recipe.*

Table of Contents

Foreword

I first encountered Cam Burns in 1989, whilst collating an article for *Mountain* magazine on climbing on the Colorado Plateau, an area of desert in the lower part of the Rocky Mountains taking in pieces of Utah, Arizona, New Mexico, and Colorado. At that time I asked magazine contributors to provide a mug shot of themselves to go with their articles. Typically, as I later discovered, Cam came up with a slide of himself and Steve Porcella dressed in very shiny tight-fitting Lycra climbing tights in front of the Moab city landfill—"the world's most scenic dump," as the sign proclaimed. My juvenile sense of humor provided the obvious caption: "Steve Porcella and Cameron Burns: prominent members of the desert climbing community." Over the following years, Cam sent in many fine dispatches about climbing all over the West and interviews with some of America's most significant climbers of the period. And he reported on all sorts of things—mostly wisely, occasionally not so wisely.

Some years after the demise of *Mountain* I became editor of *Climber*, a mainstream British magazine. As part of my grand plan to give the thing a more international feel, I immediately recruited Cam to provide a monthly snapshot of the climbing scene in America. Cam had other ideas. His imagination is far too wide-ranging for a mere news slot, and his monthly columns provide a vivid, engaging, informative, humorous but strictly off-center commentary of climbing life in the USA: I decided to call the column "Postcards from the Trailer Park." Seven years later, he still completely misses (or ignores) the point of the original assignment, but we are the richer for it.

Cam's subject matter varies accordingly: personality profiles, adventures on remote crags, world travel, comment, anecdote, etc.

This collection is based primarily on Cam's column for *Climber*, but it includes much more material than has appeared in the column. For example, his 1993 journalistic profile of Fred Beckey first appeared in a short-lived British publication called *Mountain Review*. The article "Bright Lights, Cuidad Grande" appeared in the American magazine *Rock & Ice*. Others have appeared in various forms in *Climbing*, *American Alpine Journal*, *Ascent*, *Outdoor Australia*, *Outpost*, *Aspen Times* (where Cam was a staff writer for four years), *Mountain Gazette*, *Vertical*, *Apex*, and many other newspapers and magazines. The writing within this volume ranges from straightforward third-person journalism to completely off-the-wall essays, and it reflects his growth as a writer, a journalist, and a person. Dates attached to the stories represent the year of the adventure, not the year the story was written.

Cam's writing is not about being the strongest climber and climbing the world's toughest walls and mountains; rather, it's about being a regular guy and finding the strangeness, the meaning, the joy, and the humor in everything related to the world of ascent—but mostly the humor.

Humor is the soul of climbing and that follows for its literature, and Cam's writing never allows his subjects to take themselves too seriously. And so this compilation of *Postcards from the Trailer Park* is an important body of work, which I'm sure will take its rightful place in the extraordinarily rich and extensive literature of climbing.

Bernard Newman
Bingley, West Yorkshire, July 2004

Postcards

from the

Trailer Park

Climbing's baddest boys ride Harleys.

The Legend of Los Banditos (2000)

Stan Mish is giggling at slides.

Dan Langmade is rambling on about his now-defunct Harley-Davidson.

And Glenn "L. B." Rink is sipping tequila on the couch.

Welcome to Rink's pad in Flagstaff, Arizona, the unofficial reunion site for three members of Los Banditos, a rowdy motorcycle gang-cum-climbing club whose existence has eluded the history books and whose activities are ingrained into the psyche of every climber in the American West.

It's a chilly weekend in January, and three of the five Banditos have gathered here for two reasons: one, Mish is scheduled to give a Saturday night lecture at the local climbing gym, Vertical Relief (which, incidentally, he owns), about the Banditos; and two, because I've been assigned to write about the Banditos for *Climbing* magazine and have urged them to be present for interviews. (Unfortunately, the story never even makes it out of my word processor because, as the editor and I will later agree, the Banditos are just too far outside the limits of what's legal, what's publishable, and what's appropriate. In other words, these are the kinds of guys you want to read about.)

Around Rink's place are stacks of books, on everything from anarchy to the various uses of hemp. It's a perfect reflection of the countercultural trappings of Los Banditos themselves.

Every climber in the States can give you a quick rundown on Los Banditos. "They climb illegal towers, they ride Harleys, and they leave copies of *Easyriders* magazine on the summits of everything they climb," is how one person I queried summed it up. That's true, but there are a lot of other little details, as I was soon to learn.

The Banditos, as they're more commonly called, are a group of friends who began climbing in the early 1970s on the crags around Phoenix, Arizona. Long before they created the Banditos name, Mish, Rink, and Langmade, along with Jeff Bowman and Dave Hodson, were just a group of high school buddies, seeking climbing partners with similar mindsets, energy, and ways of expressing it.

The name *Banditos* came about in the fall of 1977, when members of the informal group began visiting and climbing on the Navajo Indian Reservation—an activity that is still in legal and social limbo and that is outwardly shunned in modern, politically correct America.

Really, it was Bowman who got the ball rolling because he wanted to climb Shiprock. Lacking a partner, he convinced Rink and Mish to do the climb.

"He really wanted to do Shiprock," recalled Mish. "He was a very motivated climber. He conned L. B. ("Little Buddy," a reference to

Rink's diminutive size) and me into going out there. We were kind of going 'Yeah, right, Jeff. Don't you know that's illegal?' Our theory was that we would park the car, leave the doors and windows open, and spread empty wine bottles all over the place, and it would never be known as a climber's car. It's actually been a motif ever since."

Rink and Mish were immediately hooked on Navajo lands climbing and returned with Bowman to Monument Valley in the fall of 1977, where Bowman had seen the now famous "Never Never Land" route on the Four Corners' most elegant spire, the Totem Pole.

Things picked up steam when the lanky, soft-spoken Langmade became more involved in the late 1970s. He soon became the driving force behind many Bandito routes, while at the same time cultivating and refining the group's image.

"In 1978, I saw the film *Easy Rider*," Langmade recalls, "and I decided, I gotta get a Harley. I thought that was the quintessential expression of freedom."

A short time after Langmade showed up at Mish's house on a thundering Hog, Mish bought a bike, as did Hodson. The bikes were never a steadfast element of Bandito culture, as they were ridden hard and were constantly falling to bits. But the bikes made such an impression on Phoenix climbers that, by the late 1970s, most climbers in Arizona had heard of the quirky group.

"One of the cheap tricks that we'd do, at a couple of Phoenix crags," says Mish, "is we'd ride out there on our bikes dressed in biker clothing, leathers, and fairly greasy-looking outfits. We'd play this game of being a bunch of bikers learning to climb. We'd start climbing in street shoes, soloing 5.4s and easy routes. It really made an impression on some people. A few people probably got their stories from that."

The word spread, gossip circulated, and the legend blossomed: Los Banditos went from being a few directionless young men with interests in climbing and motorcycles to being leather-clad heathens dragging their women around by the hair and hosting LSD-laden orgies under the desert moon. Honorary membership in the group was usually just a matter of knowing Mish or Langmade and doing a climb and/or a lot of drinking with them. Honorary members over the years have included John Middendorf, Bill Hatcher, Mimi DeGravila, John Matsen, and Jason Keith (now an upstanding lawyerly type), to name a few.

While the Banditos were simply "being young people having fun," as Mish describes it, they soon found they lacked an antagonist, and as the small gang evolved, they turned to the staid members of the Arizona Mountain Club, most notably Arizona legend Jim Waugh, for their own brand of entertainment.

Waugh, one of the most talented climbers Arizona has produced, has long held a role as the ethical conscience of Arizona climbing—a sort of Royal Robbins of the desert. So, they zeroed in on "Marshal Good" and made him the target of endless pranks. They bolted the front door of his Phoenix home closed; they sneaked up behind him while he was on stage at the Phoenix bouldering competition and yanked down his pants (twice); they stamped their homemade bolt hangers with the phrases "No Gud" in reference to their relationship with Waugh; and they let it be known that they, at least, weren't subject to the tight ethical considerations that Waugh and other AMC members hoped local climbers would uphold.

While a pure motorcycle gang can earn a name for itself on wacky antics and wild parties alone, a group devoted to hard riding and hard climbing has to do a little of both. And when it came to bold climbing, the Banditos weren't shy.

With the exception of perhaps Colorado climber Layton Kor, between the late 1970s and the mid-1980s, the Banditos picked off more of the major virgin towers on the Navajo reservation than any other climbers in history. They also gravitated to other areas, like the

Black Canyon of the Gunnison, and Yosemite Valley, repeating hard routes in fast times. And, of course, the legend grew some more.

All this Banditoing is explained to me Friday night at Rink's hippyesque pad, while he, Mish, and Langmade sort through a heap of dusty slides. They're drinking a lot and gobbling scraps of food off Rink's cluttered kitchen counter like wolves at a fresh kill, but all in all, they're not too different from most climbers I know. But I must quiz them about climbing on the Navajo reservation, an activity that some American climbers consider sacrilege.

"The big reason I didn't want to get caught," explains Mish, "was because I didn't want to deal with the cultural differences. I felt like I really wanted to climb those things, but I didn't want to offend anyone. That's why we were so secretive. It's even a little touchy giving slideshows because I don't want to offend anyone now."

Saturday afternoon, after a few hours cragging near Sedona, Mish, Rink, and Langmade make plans to meet at the gym, and we all pile into various automobiles. Sitting in the passenger seat of Langmade's Landshark, Mish is greeted by several young Flagstaff climbers who know him through the gym.

"Hey, I hear *Outside* magazine is in town to do a story on you guys," calls one youngster. Mish shrugs, looks over his shoulder at me, and smiles. The pinnacle of infamy in America is having your somewhat questionable activities written up in *Outside*. Ironically, the young man has a Banditos bolt hanger dangling from his rearview mirror. Banditos hangers and motorcycle magazines (notably, the ones featuring topless women posing with Harleys) are the gang's two best-known trademarks.

The hangers were all handmade in Langmade's father's metal shop, and they were always printed with a few irreverent communiqués, such as "Banditos," "Oh Shit," or "No Gud." The tiny scraps of metal have become collectors' items, as coveted as bits of rope from the first ascent of the Nose. Magazines are the other trademark. Banditos members have left copies of *Easyriders* (a highly cultural men's magazine) and *Gallery* (a super-low-budget yet still highly cultural men's magazine) on top of dozens of Southwestern spires.

At Mish's gym, Vertical Relief, a crowd has congregated half an hour before showtime. Mish, not certain of how to tell the story of the Banditos, wanders out front and awkwardly begins introducing the two other Banditos who are in the audience. He doesn't want to get into a full-blown discussion of what's right or wrong, legal or illegal, so he does his best to meld together a collection of anecdotes and images that, by the end of the night, has the young crowd laughing wildly.

And it truly is a satisfying story. Sure, the Banditos did a number of "illegal" climbs; they indulged in a lot of illicit substances; they drag raced through the streets of Phoenix with the cops close on their heels; and they stirred up the Arizona crags with their greaser tricks. But despite their bad-boy reputation, the Banditos' most important contribution to the climbing community has been to embody the free spirit that we all pursued when we began climbing—to show that life is meant to be lived to its fullest, even if the politically correct world around wrinkles its nose in disgust.

These days the Banditos are aging and have serious weekday careers that have scattered them far and wide. Mish is still in Flagstaff, working as an engineer; Langmade runs his father's metal fabrication facility in Phoenix and has raised several kids; and Rink recently earned a master's degree in botany and has a good lifestyle studying plants around the Colorado Plateau (it's reported that he has rediscovered many of the ancient trails in Canyon de Chelly). Bowman is high up in the Cascade Designs corporation in Seattle and lives there with wife and family; and Hodson works in the construction business somewhere (I couldn't find him for this article).

But don't let this little Norman-Rockwell-type collection of scenes involving our upstanding boys fool you about the Banditos. They all still going climbing, and when they do, it appears that the high life— i.e., pranks, parties, motorcycles, and the like—isn't quite out of their systems yet.

"I ride a BMW 1150 GS motorcycle to work every day, and after years of serving on the Access Fund board, including being the VP, I have given up political correctness and now climb everything that catches my eye, regardless of its legal status," Bowman told me recently. Mish and Rink still climb hard, and as often as possible. And Dan— perhaps the most devious of the group—still jabs the fine line between respectability and outright anarchy (like kayaking through the city of Phoenix several years ago, which landed him in court—"at least I got another line on my arrest record!").

Clearly, for the wild bunch, a good ride never ends.

One of the 50 Classics (1994)

A few years back, a friend and I decided to visit Canada. The mountains to our north, my friend Benny Bach assured me, "made the mountains of Colorado look like a flat, dry sticker patch." Up in Canada would be a true alpine environment and real mountaineering, he assured me. We might even have to wear down jackets. We loaded up the Team Rio de Caca climbing team bus (Benny's Subaru station wagon) and aimed the beast north, toward Wyoming, Montana, and other regions infested with tantalizingly pretty sheep.

Our original plan was to visit the Bugaboos, but somehow we took a wrong turn and ended up in Lake Louise, a sort of Canadian version of Disneyland in the mountains. Five-star hotels and fancy restaurants kept the never-ending busloads of arriving tourists happy and well-stocked. Short, flat nature trails led off in every direction, and there were paddleboats for rent on the lake. We bought T-shirts and ice-cream cones and sat on benches next to a gargantuan shopping mall, enjoying our climbing vacation and pondering our next objectives (hot dogs, hamburgers, and a six-pack of Molson beer).

Then, Benny had to go and ruin the trip by noticing a huge mountain looming over the candy floss/hot dog/ice-cream stand near our bench. It was, we later read, Mt. Temple, and it was a stunning piece of geologic work. Strangely, the only climbing book we had brought was a beat-up copy of Steve Roper and Allen Steck's *50 Classic Climbs,* a book that gets laughed out of most climbing conversations quicker than you can say "Baaah!" Coincidentally, Mt. Temple was in the book.

50 Classic Climbs, in case you've been living in jar contained in a lockbox inside a sealed hole underneath a rock for the past twenty-five years, describes fifty of the most crowded routes on the North American continent (or does the name give it away?). Many climbers don't realize that the 1978 guidebook is heavily based upon a book that came out in 1976, called *Climbing in North America,* which British author Chris Jones had originally titled *Crowded Climbing Routes of North America.* Clearly, Mr. Jones—coming from an island of heavily trod crags—wanted to divert the masses away from any good climbing in his new homeland, and hence reworked the title. (I'm currently writing an immigration guide to Antarctica for Californians.)

Anyway, the routes in *50 Classic Climbs* are some of today's most popular American routes, ranging from the Nose on El Cap, to the Cassin Ridge on Denali, to D1 on the Diamond.

So, generally speaking, when you hike up to the base of one of the fifty "classics," you're likely to be standing in a crowd resembling the gang at Madison Square Garden when the Rolling Stones play—you know, thousands and thousands of people.

(Many people prefer the popular nickname for the book, *50 Crowded Climbs*. I prefer *50 Classic Lines of People Waiting, 50 Classic Mob Scenes,* and *50 Places an Opportunist Like Me Can Borrow Money and Gear*.)

You rarely ever read about the routes in American magazines because there's an unspoken rule among magazine editors when it comes to routes described in *50 Classic Climbs*—the rule is: they're crowded enough.

"Personally, I'm reluctant to write about the fifty classics," said Dougald MacDonald, the former editor of *Rock & Ice* magazine, in the token interview I did for this column. "Not because they are too crowded but because there are so many other great classics that are lesser-known. Roper and Steck created an appetite for coverage of classic climbs that we try to fill with previously unknown routes."

Anyway, Benny and I, hoping we could find a mob at the base— you know, to borrow money and gear from—hiked up the next morning to the base of the "classic" route on Mt. Temple, the east ridge. There wasn't a soul around. Hmmm . . . what to do?

"Well, we could climb it," Benny suggested.

"Okay," I thought. "Since we're here. Although I had been hoping to sell a few hot dogs and T-shirts."

Though straightforward and easy, the climb turned out to be one of the best mountain routes I've ever done. The north face of Mt. Temple gets more interest from the Big-Trousered Club because of its difficult ice routes, but the east ridge is classic because it's fun. Roughly two miles long, and gaining almost six thousand feet in height, the climb involves rock climbing, mixed climbing, and glacier travel (over the summit and back down the other side), along with thousands upon thousands of feet of exposed scrambling—not to mention hot-dog-hucking off the north face when you realize you've brought way too many for a civilized lunch.

The climb was first done in August 1931 by professional mountain guide Hans Wittich and his client Otto Stegmaier. The pair managed to do the entire east ridge in fifteen hours, a fantastic achievement for the day. Indeed, when Jones repeated the route in 1977, he and his partner spent parts of three days completing the route (albeit during poor weather). "Never underestimate a route done in the 1930s," Jones later wrote. "Mountaineers back then were often fast and competent."

Benny and I, though thoroughly incompetent, were moderately quick—hot dogs and all. We struggled up the east ridge in sixteen hours and were back at the car by 5:00 A.M. We hadn't seen a single other person during our entire nighttime tour of the peak, and we often couldn't see each other. Crowded, it wasn't; classic it certainly was.

I decided then and there that some of the other fifty classics might be worth a look. Lost in the Canadian roadway system once again, we somehow stumbled upon the Selkirk Mountains, Rogers Pass, and Mt. Sir Donald. The northwest ridge of Mt. Sir Donald—a sort of steep hike—is another "fifty classic," and at 1:00 A.M., we parked the car and began our approach march.

For some reason, we had come down with a rare and incurable form of Canadian jet lag, even though we live in nearly the same time zone and had been nowhere near a plane. By the time the sun came up, we were ready to bivouac. At 2:00 P.M., after six hours of sleep, we began climbing the route. Though just a mountain scramble, and scoffed at by the Heavy-Breathers crowd, it was another classic: steep, direct, and with a light dusting of snow. We reached the summit at sunset and began our descent. By 6:00 A.M., we had reached terra firma, so we bivouacked again.

It had been a fun three nights, climbing routes that had loomed large on our bookshelf, and finding out that even inclusion in the ultimate American guidebook—a tome that creates mass hysteria and mob mentality whenever it's brought forth at the dinner table—didn't mean all the routes were ruined. Both Benny and I had learned a valuable lesson from our Canadian sojourn: If you're looking to scrounge money and gear, forget the mountains and go to the nearest bus station or hotel lobby.

We aimed the Team Rio de Caca climbing team bus southward, and headed for warm sheep.

Bright ideas in the crusade against gear thievery. The wife in action.

Promiscuous Racks and Gear Thievery on the Titan (1998)

One of the toughest things about the climbing life is the never-ending sharing of gear. The never-ending exchange of gear between myself and my partners—the rack-making, the swapping and sorting of cam-ming units, nuts, screws, pitons, what have you—always results in me schlepping home a selection of metal stuff that never looks quite right, prompting a few comments of "Gear thief!" from my friends.

Nineteen ninety-seven was a typical year for my promiscuous rack. I managed to get to East Africa, where I was confused on many inter-esting routes on Kili and Mount Kenya (for which I later wrote a guide-book). Closer to home, I managed to shimmy up a few classic Tetons approaches, I did a minor new scramble in the Wind Rivers, I grunted my way up a few new desert towers (as well as a bunch of repeats), and I fell off a smattering of alpine and ice routes throughout Colorado.

The route tally was okay, but it's the gear tally that made an indelible impression.

Gearwise, I accidentally took Boulder climber Benny Bach's No. 1 Camalot, two carabiners, and two slings after a trip into Rocky Mountain National Park. Accounting for the horrible state of the gear, that's a retail value of about US$50. Spring climbing in the desert, I wound up with four mangled 'biners belonging to my pal Jesse Harvey (total retail value about US$30). While rummaging about in the Winds with *The Fred*, I inadvertently wound up with his A5 rope bag (total retail value about US$30). In September, Briton Charlie French and I pulled a pile of stuck gear (a No. 0.5 Camalot, a 0.5 TCU, and four fixed hexes) out of the Kor Route on Standing Rock (total retail value about US$50) and he left it all to me. On Dark Angel, someone had rapped off the summit and left a fuzzy rope hanging. I kept it for rap slings (total retail value about US$50).

All told, a $210 year.

But I also lost a few things.

I gave Jesse his 'biners back, slightly more mangled than when I stole them (minus $30); Benny knows I've got some of his gear (minus $50); I later went on another excursion with Beckey and returned his rope bag (minus $30). Plus, I had to replace the trigger bar on Benny's Camalot (minus $8) because I've been using it as a kitchen hammer and it fell apart, and someone who remains at-large ended up with my brand new No. 4 Friend (minus $50) and a handful of 'biners (minus $30). Also, one of the porters on Kilimanjaro swiped my expensive pocketknife (minus $25). My 1997 total was a sobering negative $13. In short, I'm worse at thieving than I am at writing.

What's remarkable about sharing climbs is that, as climbers, we are always trading gear. Say, for example, there are one hundred thousand climbers in the United States. On each climbing trip you undertake (be it a day trip or a three-month expedition), you lose one piece of gear to your partner's rack. Now, again for the sake of example, each climber goes out fifty times a year. That's five million pieces of gear lost each year, and that's probably a conservative estimate.

But then there's the flip side of this marvelous equation—because, after all, there are always two sides to any equation. If your partner is ending up with something of yours after each trip, you're likely getting away with something of his. Another five million 'biners, camming units, and stoppers change hands. Ten million bits of gear being swapped annually from climber to climber, partner to partner—and again, that's a conservative calculation. It makes venereal diseases look a bit like couch potatoes.

With all this gear swapping going on, the smart objective is to try and create a positive trade deficit. If you lose a 'biner on a route, fine. But you want to try and pick up a camming unit. If you wind up with a chum's old rope, good. But make sure the most he gets is your weathered cordelette.

I've been exchanging equipment with partners for years, and now, everyone I climb with has a rack filled with carabiners, stoppers, and cams curiously similar to the millions I've lost over the years. In the spring of 1998, I decided it had to stop.

While I was arming myself for some desert climbing, I decided a little spray paint might not be unwise. So, I went down to the local supermarket and bought several cans of the brightest spray paint I could find: highway-construction-project orange. Ghastly stuff, but recognizable from outer space. Certainly the kind of paint that doesn't let gear get mixed up.

I returned home with the dozen cans of paint and got to work. I spread newspaper all over my patio, then dumped everything—from my No. 6 Big Dudes down to my nut tool—onto the pages. I carefully separated the carabiners from the protection, and sprayed everything with traffic-cone orange. I sprayed my iron and my camming units. I sprayed my stoppers and my carabiners. I sprayed my nailing gloves and my rock shoes. I sprayed my jumars and my harness.

As the morning went by, I found the chore becoming more and more enjoyable. The sound of paint whooshing from the nozzle lifted my spirits in a strange, spiritual way. The sight of disaster orange splattering all over our new patio furniture satisfied a certain crooked part of my brain.

With most of my gear already campfire orange and piled high on top of our iron patio table, I looked around for a blank concrete wall. Finding none, I contented myself with spray painting my sneakers and my helmet. Sure, I was going to look like an absolute dork the next time I went climbing, but at least I'd know I wasn't losing any gear to the International Conspiracy of Climbing Partners.

I sprayed the wife and the dog. I sprayed the milkman and the FedEx guy (we have a milkman?). I sprayed the neighbors, I sprayed the neighborhood. I sprayed far, I sprayed wide (I was, after all, *the Spraymaster*). It was one big glorious orange moment.

The following weekend—a cold weekend in March—Jesse called, urging me to do the Finger of Fate Route on the Titan, a lumpy bit of mud in Utah. I'd always loved lolling about in mud, and Jesse was persuasive: "C'mon, Cam, we'll bring a garden hose up there and see if we can erode the thing to nothing." It sounded like a fun way to spend a couple of days, and get a bath in, so I agreed.

We rolled up to the Fisher Towers parking lot late on a Saturday night. We wandered around the other campsites, asking fellow climbers if any parties were on the Finger, or who wanted the Finger, or who had been Fingered, and other inane questions at which I giggled but nobody else did.

"I gotta ask," said a polite young fellow from Gunnison, who was huddled around a stove with four of his friends, "what's up with the orange sneakers? You been working road construction or something?"

I shrugged off the enquiry, telling him my "emergency" orange footwear was the latest in big wall shoes from Europe: "The color helps with rescues in the Alps, in case the climber needs one. They're all the rage in France." This seemed to satisfy the young upstart. Jesse and I skulked back to our tent.

We wandered over to the route the next morning, carrying a load of orange metal and clothing. I tied in and began up the first pitch. As I slotted a stopper in a thin crack, a small scrape of orange paint came off on the rock. I moved up, and placed a Friend. Another small flake of orange paint came off. Oh boy, I thought: bad *juju*.

I continued up. Tiny flakes of orange paint came off with every gear placement, every move, every foot of altitude gained. I was leaving a tiny yet wonderfully obnoxious trail. At the first belay, I handed all the gear to Jesse.

"Umm, Cam," he said, looking at the rack. "We're sort of leaving tracks."

"Well, maybe if I start beating pitons into completely unnecessary places, bolting large scraps of iron into unusual positions, and hanging enormous Christo-esque pieces of fabric in thoughtful, clever locations, no one will notice the paint," I suggested.

"Hmm." Jesse seemed unconvinced. I thought perhaps the flakes were too small to cause concern, but Jesse—always the environmentalist and now reportedly a fur trapper in Alaska—had spotted them as soon as he yanked out the first stopper, and he alerted me to his concern. I led the second pitch, up to a sling belay, and, thoroughly overexercised for one day, called it quits and headed for camp.

The following day we were up around noon—what climbers call an "alpine start." We jugged to our high point and carried on. Meanwhile, a party of three had arrived. One of them (whom we nicknamed "Speed God") loudly announced that he and his partner (whom we called "F. G.") intended to make a "speed ascent" of the Mud Heap. He announced that he had made speed ascents of everything from Snotts Nose in Zimbabwe to Retched Shyting in Norway to Knobblyhump in California and he asked—not politely, mind you—if we would allow his zippy team to go sailing past when they caught up to us. We said fine, go sailing.

As Speedy lumbered up the first two pitches slower than a boring climbing story like this one, Jesse and I examined his gear. It was color-coded with electrical tape. Not just one color of tape, mind you, but five different bands of colored tape: yellow, red, yellow again, then black, and finally white. A sort of Morse code of colors, saying, "Hey, this is my gear. Don't take it!"

Cunning, I thought—very cunning. Most climbers use red tape, and their gear inevitably gets lost simply because everyone uses red tape. Five bands of tape and Speedy was sure to keep his kit.

Meanwhile, Speedy's partner had stamped all his carabiners and protection with his initials. "F. G." was printed everywhere. At one of the belays, F. G. himself explained that the letters appeared on both sides of every carabiner, on at least two of the cams in every one of his camming units, and on the shaft of every piton he owned (and I asked if he knew the term *compulsive obnoxious*).

After a few more hours of the silly climbing business, we descended the Rappel Gully and returned to camp. Speedy and F. G., who were apparently camped nearby, came over and asked about the route above their high point (which wasn't really very high for a pair of "speed climbers"). They eyed my orange gear. I studied Speedy's Morse code and the huge gouges in F. G.'s gear. We would, I surmised, have made a good team. No mixed racks whatsoever, although climbing together we would have required roughly three years to get up the Mud Heap.

Speed God's collection of colored tapes, however, had cost him about $30, since he'd had to buy two rolls of each color in order to label all his gear. My spray paint was only $12.50 all told, a several-carabiner difference.

Meanwhile, F. G. explained that for a more positive stamp, he heated his equipment first in his mother's electronic, state-of-the-art pottery kiln. The cost of each firing, he said, was about $50, and F. G. had to be very careful not to heat the metal to the point where it would be compromised.

No kidding, I thought (. . . "Jesse, did I hear that guy right?").

We chatted casually about the route, our gear markings, and the morrow, and how the Speed Team was going to flash past us and run up to the top. Of course, they never did. All talk as usual. Instead, I just kept inching up the tower, leaving flakes of orange, while the glacial Speed Team left a pile of tattered tape and tiny slivers of metal and grumbled because they weren't keeping up with us. After basking on the summit for a few minutes, Jesse and I scrambled back over to the top of the final steep pitch, and began our rappels.

Back at camp, we sorted gear. It quickly became apparent that whatever gear we'd brought had been scraped almost clean of my fiery, orange paint, and we spent hours in the waning light trying to assess who owned what. My clever scheme of spray painting everything had backfired. I picked up a huge pile of gear—our entire rack—and dumped it on the tarp in front of Jesse.

"Recognize anything?" I asked.

"Does it have orange paint on it?" he asked.

"Ummm . . . . Some of it. Why?" I said.

"Well, remember I bought Jon's rack off him, and he'd spray painted all his gear orange?"

"Yeah, but I brought the whole rack for this route, *didn't I?*"

"Are you sure? I remember on that trip to Arches you brought the entire rack. And that trip in to Monster Tower. Are you sure you did here, too?"

Heck, I couldn't remember—I'm a dithering old man. Every week another trip, every time a different partner, every day a different route, always a mix of gear.

I loaded all the equipment into Jesse's bag, then looked at the tiny rack I was left with: a few stoppers and a couple of cams. I squished it all in my day pack, feeling strangely naked. If you're a climber, losing gear is like losing a part of yourself. That #10 Stopper that you took your first leader fall on holds precious memories. That mangled Birdbeak that brought your first aid zipper to an end is a great conversation piece. And the tattered shreds of rope you cart around to use as a cordelette represented the first time you had prusiked.

I felt as though I'd been castrated, and drove home.

The Black Canyon of the Gunnison.

Scared of the Dark (2003)

One adjective you rarely hear in the climbing world is *scared*. I'm not certain whether that has to do with the fact that climbers genuinely do get scared and think that by acknowledging it they'll ruin their own performance (who can concentrate when they're scared, right?) or whether it's just not cool to acknowledge it. Then there's the possibility that some are mistaking adrenaline for fear—which is an easy thing to do.

Anyway, I don't mind admitting to an acquaintance with fear. It's one hell of a motivator.

One place that fear has always motivated me to stay away from is a place called the Black Canyon of the Gunnison, even though it's about an hour and a half from my home. The Black, as it's known, is one of the geologic marvels of North America. It slices a deep, fourteen-mile-long crack that ranges in depth from eighteen hundred to twenty-seven hundred feet through a plateau on the western side of Colorado.

The Black is special to geographers because its depth-to-narrowness ratio sets some kind of obscure but impressive geographical record—you know, like the world's biggest lump of asbestos or China's most popular shopping mall, or something like that. It's almost three thousand feet deep in places, yet as narrow as one thousand feet. The only canyons that are "deeper" in the Continental United States are Hells Canyon, in Idaho and Oregon (dubbed by some the deepest canyon in North America at 7,913 feet deep), and the Grand Canyon (six thousand feet deep). Certainly, the Black Canyon's Painted Wall is the highest cliff in Colorado. From river to rim it stands 2,250 feet.[1] But, even if geographers are being sweet, honest, and genuinely impressed by this mighty crack, the dimensions are so magnificent that they prompt a few weirdos to report phenomena such as being able to see the stars from the bottom of the canyon in the middle of the day and other questionable stuff.

Despite its menacing physical shape and color, the climbing in the Black is also scary. The rock is notoriously loose. There are dozens of stories of climbers pulling or knocking off huge blocks and small stones on even the most popular routes. (There's a picture in an old *Climbing* magazine of Jeff Achey holding a block the size of a basketball that he'd just pulled off a route; on one side of the block is a bolt with a carabiner attached.) The routes all feature huge roofs, overhanging slots, and circuitous sections where you worm your way from climbable rock to climbable rock. The routes are also very long, and should something go wrong—say, a huge block falls and cracks both your femurs and your skull—descent is extremely difficult because of the undulating nature of the warped vertical walls. Oh, and there appear to be absolutely zero fixed anchors—other than those on the Acheyan loose blocks.

In the spring of 2003, the famed Black Canyon pioneer Leonard Coyne and a friend took a novice climber on a long route there and the man, Doug McQueen, in his sixties, suffered a heart attack. Legendary American climber Jimmy Dunn has speculated that he died of fright. This suggests the drama that is the Black Canyon.

Nicely frightened for many years, I stayed away. Then my ever-enthusiastic friend Luke Laeser recently suggested that we go climb something called the Russian Arête, a roughly eighteen-hundred-foot doddle that was a strenuous forty-five-minute walk from the car. (When you reach midlife and go climbing two days per year, a forty-five-minute walk is considered fairly extreme. I suggest it be included in the next X Games.)

On a chilly late-October morning, we descended into the canyon. Even scrambling down the trail, the Black is an ominous place. Sunlight doesn't penetrate the deeper parts of it in fall and spring (the climbing season here), and the cliffs are so confusing that even finding a route is a bit of a crapshoot. But what got me was the absolute nonexistence of anything human: no climbers visible anywhere, no happy shouts from nearby parties surmounting a crux, no smiling tourists anywhere, above or below. It was just dark, silent, and scary. It reminded me of a mausoleum, a taxation department office, or a dentist's surgery.

At the base of the climb, I thought a division of labor might be in order: Luke would lead everything and winch me up, and I would drink all the water and eat all the food (one liter and eight chocolate Power Bars). Before I could even explain this nice arrangement to Luke, he was off, flying up the first pitch, a gorgeous left-facing corner that sucked in fingers and hands like car doors at school yards. Soon he was off up the second pitch too, flying up a slot of rotten rock with ease and grace, to a belay stance above a bomb bay slot—the kind of belay in which you can't really relax. You have to balance on one foot for three minutes, then switch feet.

According to a series of guidebooks, the Russian Arête was first climbed by Layton Kor and Dick Dorworth in 1970. Although the climb would be considered a semiclassic Black route today, it's hard to imagine what it was like in Kor's day. There was so much loose rock, and whole sections seemed to be built out of the stacked, rubbly pegmatite blocks (some clearly still anxious to get to the bottom of the canyon), that it was hard to imagine how much stuff would've fallen off during the first ascent.

Dorworth, an acquaintance, told me a little about the climb. "I have no idea what it was like on the first ascent," he wrote in a 2003 e-mail, "because I didn't do the first ascent with Kor. In fact, I went down there with Michael Kennedy in 1990 to climb the route simply because I was listed on the first ascent with Kor, but I have no idea who he climbed with or what it was like."

In many ways, Dick sums up the Black Canyon well: It is one great big dark mysterious cleft. For the most part, it's hard to tell who did what, when they did it, and whether you're on their route or a variation of it. There are, to put it mildly, some major holes in most climbers' knowledge of the place.

The weirdest thing about the Black, however, was the stuff floating around in the air. At every belay, I could look out into the yawning gap and see long, straight strands of spiders' silk and small pieces of bush drifting upward on thermal currents. The canyon created a dark, subtle background behind the floating objects. It was like standing over an enormous three-dimensional petri dish watching microscopic animals doing their thing.

The length of the climb was surprising. Luke has long a rope—seventy meters—and only after five rope-length pitches of sustained climbing did the route finally ease off (two easy lower-fifth-class pitches, followed by several hundred feet of scrambling).

At the top of the climb we sat and put on shoes for the forty-five-minute walk out. The route had been everything I'd expected—loose, scary, committing, and dangerous—but my fear had been supplanted by a greater feeling: that of wonder and surprise, challenge and fulfillment. There are a lot of emotions that crowd into the climbing life, so a little fear, I think, is natural.

I can't wait to explore the big dark crack some more.

---

1 *Yosemite doesn't really classify as a canyon, although the big stones there do beat out some of these numbers for height.*

The Black Ice Couloir, Grand Teton.

Bob the Builder in Valhalla (1997)

There are loads of great long ice climbs in North America, but one of the most famous lies on the backside of the Grand Teton. A twelve-hundred-foot ribbon of thick, seventy- to eighty-degree ice, lying in the folds of rock on the west side of the mountain, the Black Ice Couloir is a striking line that has made it into the hallowed halls of legendary status in North America. Not simply because it's an incredibly continuous chunk of frozen H_2O, and that when in condition, the climbing is superb, but because it's one of the most majestic of American peaks (the "Big Boob," for you non-French-speakers).

There's also another reason the Black Ice Couloir has acquired legendary status: the objective hazards. Sitting directly below the single most popular route on the Grand (the Owen-Spaulding Route), the Black Ice Couloir is often rattled by rockfall, knocked down by unsuspecting tourists clambering to the top of the mountain.

The third reason for writing about the climb is because of its approach—it's a quarter-pounder in a regular-burger kind of world and brings up something I've wondered for years: Why aren't really demanding approaches as heralded as the oftentimes easier climb?

"The history of ice climbing in the Teton Range very nearly begins with the ascent of the Black Ice Couloir," wrote Renny Jackson and the late Leigh Ortenburger in their exceptional guidebook, the *Climber's Guide to the Teton Range*. "Numerous climbers had peered down into the upper reaches of the Black Ice Couloir from the Upper Saddle, but it was long believed that the couloir was too dangerous to be considered seriously as a climbing route. The first attempt, on July 7, 1958, seemed to verify this opinion: Kenneth Weeks, Yvon Chouinard, and Frank Garneau started at the very bottom but retreated from just above the first section because of significant fall of rock and ice fragments. A second attempt, on June 26, 1961, by Fred Beckey and Charlie Bell, also failed."

In July 1961, a month after the Beckey-Bell attempt, Ray Jacquot and Herb Swedlund made an ascent of the couloir. While the pair "bypassed a considerable portion of the ice," they climbed the crux section of the route, about two-thirds up. Through the 1960s, several parties climbed more and more of the couloir, until finally, in 1969, George Lowe and Yvon Chouinard climbed the couloir in its entirety, creating a modern classic route.

In early September 1997, a close friend and sometime climbing partner Jeff Widen called and talked me into driving up to Wyoming to meet him for the Black Ice Couloir.

Jeff is a professional environmentalist, the kind of guy who fights logging, mining, road building, and anything else that can destroy

America's wild places. He does this by attending boring meetings held by government officials and, as he puts it, "by lobbying pompous members of Congress scared to death of the ire of the right-wingers (but don't quote me on that)"—and for this he deserves our praise.

I was, for many years, an environment correspondent for various Colorado newspapers, and what's genuinely strange about environmental-issues meetings is that they are so incredibly dull. They are more dull than should be legal. They are more boring than belaying anyone on anything. You'd think meetings about environmental issues would be big exciting events, like sit-ins or rallies, or forty-footers in the Fisher Towers where you rip out loads of gear. Nope—not even close.

Here's a typical meeting: a group of citizens show up at some ghastly office with flickering fluorescent lights that hum and sputter and make alien-invasion noises (I'm convinced you go crazy after a few hours' exposure). Then several bureaucrats in white shirts arrive and unfurl big colorful maps of areas no one recognizes and pin them to a board at the front of the room. Then they erect a tripodlike device and mount an oversized notepad on it. Then, one of the bureaucrats pulls out a collection of fat markers and writes something like "stakeholders" across the top of the first sheet in the pad. He rips this sheet off and tapes it to the wall. Then he writes "issues" across the next page, and tapes that to the wall. The he writes "scenarios" across another page, and "outcomes" across another, and "next steps" across another, and so on, until the room is encircled by huge pages with terms that people only vaguely understand.

Usually, there's another bureaucrat who wasn't given a set of markers, so this person's only means of having any fun is by talking. Thus begins a multi-hour-long drone about whatever it is we're here for, be it a new dirt bike trail or a timber sale. A gang of impeccably dressed old ladies asks questions (because, after all, a community's old ladies are the only ones willing to do the hard work of giving a crap about anything) and offers a few comments, while one young man with dreadlocks and a beard lingers about the periphery, not saying anything. After a few hours of this, the bureaucrats gather up their big notepad pages and we all say goodnight and go quietly on our way.

I came away from hundreds of meetings about environmental issues in the early 1990s wondering what the hell to write for the morning paper. I'd get back to my desk and very quickly think up headlines like: "Most Boring Meeting Ever Held" and "Forget the Forest: Billions of Brain Cells Decimated at Exceptionally Awful Meeting" and "Don't Read This Story If You Have to Operate Heavy Machinery Today."

Of course, I never wanted to let my readers down, so by the time the morning paper came out I'd crafted something much more entertaining like "Enviros Clash with Forest Service Officials" or "Radicals Fire Off Against Ski Area Plan" or even "Bureaucrats Cut Down Forest to Have Enough Oversized Notepads for Meetings with Enviros."

What's weirder than all this environmental-meeting stuff I'm describing is that many climbers consider themselves environmentalists. Climbing, by its very nature, is all about trampling something that's extremely tricky to get to and that can't be trampled by non-climbers. For example, a roof crack three thousand feet off the ground, or a high campsite that requires several sets of lungs to get to, or a mountain ridge that no sensible person would ever drive his Hummer up.

Even more strange is how climbers consider trampling. If we do it as a group, on a Saturday morning, with coffee and doughnuts, and the object is, say, to build a trail to a crag, that's okay—and our entire group is lauded in the pages of mountaineering-related magazines ("Yippee: Local Smurtzville Climbers Build New Fourlaned Tromper Trail to Crag"). But if we do it after rapelling down a ne'er-before-touched cliff and slamming a line of bolts into the rock, it's considered completely awful, and you are given endless grief by your peers—even if it becomes the most popular route in the state.

It's sort of like a brothel owner considering himself a member of the clergy and shagging the ladies in public, and having everyone think it's okay; then, when he does it on the sly, he's a bad guy. I've seen more plants yanked out by people establishing rock climbs than I could imagine a logger clearing away with a bulldozer, and if they do it with the encouragement of a few fellow climbers, it's okay. If they do it as individuals, God help them.

As usual, I digress.

Jeff goes to these meetings so we climber-environmentalists don't have to. He travels all over the nation, listening to bad plans and then trying to convince forest managers and other sorts of desk jockeys to reject them, all for a salary so paltry it would make Bill Gates gassy. He's a modern-day David Brower without the Sierra Club's publicity machine, an unknown Edward Abbey fighting behind the scenes, a modest David tackling corporate Goliaths—the kind of guy I wish I were, but am not selfless enough to be—after all, I need my trampling time.

Jeff's also a very motivated climber, and he had the Black Ice Couloir (and its approach) in his sights.

Besides his work as an environmentalist, one thing about Jeff that's always fascinated me is his collection of old gear: first-generation Kastinger double boots (we're talking the late 1960s here), old ice tools (the kind you see in etchings of Whymper), and nylon shell gear that had been around since the invention of the loom. It's scary when he pulls it out of his patched Johnny-Appleseed backpack; but it's truly uplifting to see him climb with the stuff. Apparently, no one has ever told him that fighting for the environment does not mean you have to subject yourself to outdated gear. I had a feeling that Jeff used his gear as long as possible because he felt guilty about the vast amount of materials, water, and energy that go into manufacturing things like ice tools and plastic boots; but later he told me he was just cheap—apparently a like-minded soul.

My September '97 scheduling was all weird, like a gang of airport lay-overs combined with a series of Mexican beach holidays. Two days prior to meeting Jeff, I was getting lost on the last pitch of a route on a mountain called Notchtop in Rocky Mountain National Park in Colorado. One day before meeting Jeff, I was hauling a client up a couloir between the Maroon Bells, two fourteen-thousand-foot mountains near my home. The twelve hours before I met Jeff were spent driving to Jackson Hole and then humping up the trail into Garnet Canyon. By the time I found him at the Grand's Lower Saddle around 9:00 P.M., I was ready to sleep for three weeks.

Not to be.

Jeff roused me using a mountaineering technique called *swift posterior boot placement* (his 1960s Kastinger boots leaving an indelible physical mark this time) and at 3:00 A.M. we set off, scrambling around a mess of loose rock and scree on the southwestern side of the Grand Teton, peering down into great dark depths, wondering where we were supposed to go next.

The sloppy trip from the Lower Saddle on the south side of the Grand to the start of the Black Ice Couloir is called the Valhalla Traverse, and while it is reported to be nothing more than a leisurely scramble, it's easily the crux of the route, perhaps the crux of life. Loose rock, body-bending drop-offs, the grogginess of sleep, and pitch-blackness make it one of the all-time worst route approaches I've ever heard of. It rambles around the southwestern side of the mountain like a drunken steam shovel, and crashes off ledges in some places while wobbling over hummocks of mud in others (or was that me?).

In fact, the Valhalla Traverse is so incredibly awful that I don't understand why its pioneers and history are not recorded in Jackson and Ortenburger's book. For that matter, why are totally awful approaches—regularly the toughest part of any mountain-situated exercise—not recorded the same way that the oftentimes easier climb is? I mean, the pioneers of the Valhalla Traverse are, to my way of thinking, far more important than the guys who climbed a bit of ice above its northerly end.

I could just imagine such a historical description: "The Valhalla Traverse was first attempted by Bob the Builder (BTB) in a dump truck in 1901. His vehicle fell twenty thousand feet into the center of the Earth and he was later memorialized in a 1990s children's television program. In the fifty years following BTB's attempt, there were 367 attempts to get across the Valhalla Traverse, none of which was successful. Seventy-nine of the world's most talented mountain athletes died trying, while most aspirants went running home with their mud-moving machinery between their legs. Finally, in 1952, a heavy equipment operator named Fred Beckey (because you know it'll be Fred) burrowed through a section of the mountain leading to the base of the Black Ice Couloir. . . ."

These ideas flooded my sleep-starved brain as Jeff and I wended our way between teetering towers of rubble and fallen-away sections of trail. Everything I touched seemed to disintegrate, then go crashing down into the black void. I longed for the whizzing rocks, tumbling ice, and falling tourists in the couloir. We reached the end of the traverse as night gave way to dawn; then, it was on to the ice.

Jeff took off on the first lead, swinging his prehistoric axes through the sky with the grace of our Neander Valley ancestors killing a shrew. I followed and quickly realized that my wife's 1997 mountaineering crampons with their horizontal metal front points—which I'd grabbed in a packing rush—weren't working anywhere near as well as Jeff's early '70s Footfangs. They bounced off the bulletproof ice with most kicks.

The climbing, we found, wasn't at all difficult—a cruise, in fact—but the weird angle at which the couloir sits, plus the sideways slant of the rock walls above, made for a disorienting experience. It reminded me of those tilted buildings that you walk around in at carnivals and circuses. The ghostly sounds of distant tourists clambering to the top of the Grand Teton floated down to us; and occasionally, a handful of pebbles would rattle our alpine world, adding to the strangeness. Rock anchors were impossible to find, so we had to rely on ice-screw-only belays. Luckily, we are both good at screwing around.

We moved into a sort of rhythm, as pitch after pitch of perfect water ice flew by. By the fifth pitch, I began to feel the past few days creep up on me. I stopped fifty feet below a steepish bulge and, as usual, found only ice anchors. I placed a screw, dropped several small but very important items, then called Jeff up. He looked at my belay; handed me back my gloves, tools, shoes, and clothes; and then moved on, quickly through the crux, which turned out to be in perfect condition and only slightly steeper than the entire eight hundred feet we'd already climbed. We had inadvertently scheduled our climb just right.

Jeff and I crept up three more pitches to the top, cresting the Upper Saddle early in the afternoon, as dozens of tourists were descending the Owen-Spaulding Route. They asked us where we'd come from and if we'd seen Bob the Builder. We pointed down into the dark, cold cleft, which seemed so uninviting compared with the warm, sunny rock we were now sitting on.

As is typical with most of my friends (who are all perverts), Jeff pulled out a pair of delicate lace panties and slung them over the top of his ancient ice axe for a photo, a special kind of ritual he goes through after every climb. Lingerie historians who see the photo will undoubtedly wonder about the juxtaposition of modern lace with Stone Age tools—and they will wonder, of course, which came first.

The Black Ice Couloir hadn't dropped a huge shower of stones on us, and the ice had been in perfect form. And it was a real cruise. The weird, disconcerting otherworldliness, though, must be how the climb gets its reputation. Sort of like being in a huge, tilted refrigerator, where carnival-goers lob stones in your direction—or something like that.

I dozed in the sun for a while, then Jeff roused me and we started walking down the trail. Apparently, he had to get to another environmental-issues meeting. I understood; I had to get home and start working on my new book, *Deadly Approaches for the Half-Asleep and Fully Incompetent.*

Charlie French and his support group.

In Patagonian Therapy (1995)

It took me three weeks of sitting in a smelly, dirty tent that looked like the interior of a broken washing machine to learn that mountaineering in Patagonia has little to do with climbing.

To be sure, there are the days when the sky dawns bright and clear and the wind stops howling for a few hours, when you run out and snatch a summit if you're very, very lucky. More than likely, you climb about half a route, then have to retreat in the soggiest, windiest blizzard you can remember, empty-handed. Then you sit and wait a couple of weeks for whatever comes next. Often, it's nothing. Patagonia is that way—it has the worst weather on the planet and some of the most beautiful mountains.

Nope, I'm convinced, climbing in Patagonia is about something else. Although everyone's planning to climb something—talking about it, dreaming about it, eating, sleeping, and breathing climbing—not a whole lot of climbing is getting done. In reality, the hundred or so young men who dwell in the beech forests below the world's most spectacular peaks for the four months of the austral summer are simply looking for something to do.

In December 1995, two English buddies, Julian Fisher and Charlie French, and I headed south to Argentine Patagonia for a six-week attempt to climb Cerro Fitzroy. Fitzroy and its neighbor, Cerro Torre, are the two most famous mountains in this southern area of the Andes, and climbers from all over the world head there to try their luck on the peaks. The mountains are under twelve thousand feet tall (paltry, really, compared even with our mountains in the western United States), but what they lack in height is more than made up for in technical difficulty. Both peaks combined have been climbed fewer times than Everest.

More onerous than the technical difficulties, however, is the weather. Unhampered by terra firma, winds whip around the lower portions of the Southern Hemisphere with the fury of a hurricane, meaning that in order to climb, you have to wait for a clear day. Sometimes, for months on end. Most climbers end up biding their time in the Rio Blanco camp (below Fitzroy) or the Campo Bridwell (below Cerro Torre), and as Julian, Charlie, and I were soon to learn, these base camps are truly weird places.

When the three of us arrived around mid-December, our first thoughts were that we'd stumbled into a refugee camp. Dozens of scraggly young men, clad in filthy long underwear and sporting patchy beards, moped about a cluster of ruinous shacks that looked like piles of construction debris set amid a beech forest. Mental asylums, Jonestown, Guyana, and William Golding's classic story *Lord of the*

Flies all came to mind at once. I had flashbacks to every Greyhound bus station I'd ever slept in.

It was an anarchic society, a fringe civilization dwelling between the Neanderthal epoch and present day. Scary monobrows and descending hairlines complemented the latest in high technology. Gizmos of all kinds were strapped to the scruffiest of Missing Links. With every patch of blue sky that floated overhead, dozens of wrists would be bared and excited consultations with barometer watches would ensue. Everyone who had a watch—even if the watch's most advanced feature was an alarm—became an instant meteorologist, and speculation on what the weather would do next ran the gamut from full-blown optimism (i.e., packing up gear and strapping on boots) to downright disgust, which was expressed, for the most part, by crawling back into a tent.

All the excited speculation would last only until the next set of white clouds floated overhead. Then everyone would sulk back into the weird daydream of being in a lush wilderness, thousands of miles from home, with no real purpose for the day. Thus, you begin to look for one—a purpose, that is. (An employment office would do brisk business here.)

Take Gunnar, a clock maker from Germany, for example. He spent the first two weeks of his visit to Argentina hauling more than fifty pounds of potatoes between the nearby village of Chalten and the Rio Blanco base camp at the foot of Fitzroy. Certainly, hauling fifty pounds of potatoes can be done in a couple of days, but Gunnar felt the task needed his full attention for about fourteen. On several clear mornings, as Julian, Charlie, and I humped gear and food to Paso Superior for a night in a snow cave and a crack at the mountain, we passed Gunnar.

"Gunnar, aren't you going to try some climbing?" we'd ask.

"Oh no," he'd say, dropping a sack of potatoes on the ground near his tent. "I must return to Chalten to pick up some more potatoes. I think if I go down again tonight, I can bring them all up by the end of the week."

Gunnar spent the bulk of his time wrangling his precious potatoes, counting them, then recounting them, scrubbing and peeling, boiling and baking. The Fitz was reportedly his climbing objective, but apparently there was nothing nearly as satisfying as having spent a day washing and primping seventy potatoes. If he grew bored with his potatoes, he'd start cooking other things. Gunnar could charm the socks off the local gauchos, and about once a week he'd wander back into Rio Blanco with a lamb he'd extracted from one of the local cowboys. Then, he'd set about organizing a party.

Gunnar loved parties. He organized a party for Christmas, for New Year's Eve, and several parties because he was bored. But his real coup de grâce was his twenty-eighth birthday party, a wild feast held in a farmyard outside Chalten, where he took reservations and a $6 contribution from any climber who wanted to attend. Needless to say, potatoes were the featured side dish. But Gunnar was happy—he'd found his purpose, and he cherished his role as party host-cum-restauranteur-cum-chef.

Then there was Jim. Jim was in Patagonia with one of Europe's best-known climbers but felt he shouldn't be there, since he hadn't the skills or experience for serious mountaineering. He'd never even walked across a glacier. Jim was a nervous, insecure wreck.

Jim and his introspective misgivings allowed us all to play psychologist, and he gave us the platform from which we could offer tidbits of wisdom and positive thoughts. He was the patient, and we were the doctors, nursing his bruised mind back, we hoped, to normal health without losing our own stable mental ground.

If, God forbid, we ever woke up in the morning and wondered what the hell we were doing there, it was easy to focus on Jim. We'd get up, have our morning coffee and oatmeal, and casually sprint over to Jim's tent so we could begin offering observations and insights. If two of the camp's budding psychologists arrived at Jim's tent at the same time, it was usually not a problem. Most of us in the newly formed Rio Blanco Psychological Association (and Ward) seemed to be in agreement, and so double-teaming Jim was essentially the same thing as getting a second opinion.

"Dr. Charlie, what do you think?"

"I think Jim will do fine on that crevasse-riddled glacier, Dr. Cam."

"Just got to step over all the bodies, eh, Dr. Charlie?"

"And outrun the avalanches, Dr. Cam."

"Say, Jim. Mind if we borrow some of your gear since you don't quite know how it works anyway? Those are some lovely new crampons."

And so it went.

I remember one time, in late December, when a disagreement did occur between two psychologists, but a third happened to be wandering back from washing his underwear and was able to break the tie fairly promptly. Like Gunnar, Jim, in his own way, had his niche. Others found their own roles to play.

Julian, a dentist from Newcastle, became the local news service. He had both an irrepressible restlessness about him and a wonderful, funny ability to socialize in multiple languages, so he'd spend each day wandering around camp gathering the news and distributing it— often simultaneously. Back in the tent, Charlie and I would grill him into the wee hours on what the Italians were doing, or how high the French had fixed their ropes on the north pillar.

Harry and Kari (their real names) were from Finland, and were trying to make the first Finnish ascent of Fitzroy. They were the Finnish version of the Two Ronnies.[1] Harry was a bricklayer, and he told us all about cheating the Finnish government, from dodging taxes to getting unemployment benefits. Kari, meanwhile, worked for the government and explained how the government was continually developing new techniques for catching tax evaders and welfare cheats. Had their complementary strengths been in terms of climbing ability, they would have been mountain supermen. As it was, they seemed to spend a lot of time in their tent talking about Finnish government policies.

Jay, a professional climber from the States, had so much experience actually reaching the summits of these hard Patagonian peaks that he became, essentially, a consultant to every other Rio Blanco resident, a Yoda among pubescent Jedi warriors. His tent—a bright yellow The North Face version of a circus tent, which we affectionately called "the big top"—only confirmed his massive status.

There were gourmet chefs and talented carpenters, gear repairmen and musicians, photographers and videographers, message carriers and dishwashers, and, of course, comedians of all sorts. As the weeks dragged by, everyone slowly settled into a role, no matter how ill-defined the role. In short, we'd all escaped to Patagonia, but we needed an escape from the escape. The roles were often muddled. Gunnar was the best cook for miles, but we each took a shot at making some tasty gem. Some of the more experimental culinary creations remained experiments.

I spent days mulling over my own skills and wondering how I could put them to community service. My contribution was a ratty collection of guidebooks, topos, maps, and the spiral notebook I'd bought for $8 in Rio Gallegos (this was back when the Argentine peso was pegged to the U.S. dollar). The topos, photocopied from the pages of Buscaini and Metzeltin's famous book *Patagonia,* held precious information that every Rio Blanco resident wanted to know. It didn't matter that the topos were a decade old and were printed with Italian climbing ratings, and that a zillion new routes had been established since they were drawn. All that mattered was that the topo looked vaguely like a mountain someone was thinking about climbing.

With each curious visitor to the tent, I'd hem and haw over their request, dig through reams of photocopies, and finally pull out the desired route diagram and a clean sheet of white paper on which it could be drawn. I felt vastly satisfied every time a would-be ascensionist wandered away from the tent with a shred of white paper in hand, ready to take on Patagonia's finest. My pile of information became my domain, the one place within base camp where I ruled supreme. I had nautical maps showing the Patagonian coastline, books about trekking around the mountains, informal sketches of the peaks copied from tourist maps, and photocopied pages from every *American Alpine Journal* published in the past ten years. It could take me days to find a topo that was in my pile. Occasionally, I would hike down to Chalten, where a popular pub had vast reams of notes on routes, peaks, and ascents, to update my files.

Of course, in Patagonia, the weather destroys everyone's life and their escape from it. When it cleared up for a couple of days in mid-January, Gunnar couldn't sit around base camp peeling potatoes. He had to go climbing. Jim couldn't sit around feeling out of place on a glacier after a hundred eager psychologists had found him fit for mountaineering. He had to go climbing. We all did, and with varying degrees of success we managed to become Patagonian climbers for one great historical day.

After that, the skies turned on us, and moisture of all classification sputtered out of the heavens in a never-ending drizzle. Everything in camp received a slow, thorough soaking, and my precious library was reduced to a soggy heap of pulp. As each day dragged toward our imminent departure, I spent despondent afternoons picking out the most destroyed maps, carefully wadding them up, and tossing them into a fire pit.

On the last day, I handed over the remaining pages and books to Kari, who promised he would take over the role of camp librarian. Of course, with all the text in English and Italian, and the ratings in French and Italian, and most of the pages utterly soaked, he was looking at either a hell of a lot of sorting work, or rolling a record-breaking spitball.

At the end of January, we went home. Julian returned to England and his dentistry; Charlie went back to his computers and winter climbing in Scotland; Jay packed up and went back to his professional climbing adventures; Harry and Kari returned to Finland and their government; Gunnar went back to Germany and his clock making; and Jim went back to California and checked himself into a clinic. I returned to my newspaper's deadlines, headlines, and high stress. But for a few precious weeks, I had been the best librarian in Patagonia. Able to pull information out of a disorganized heap of paper at the drop of a hat. Able to steer a disoriented climber to the foot of his proposed goal. Able to shed a little light on the mysteries of the peaks around us.

Maybe mountaineering in Patagonia really isn't about climbing at all. Maybe it's about something more basic. Escaping from the escape. Finding a role, no matter how trivial. Pretending to be a contributing member of society even when you don't know what that means. If I had a little more time, I might try to solve the mysterious lure of Patagonia's famed peaks and the weird, social and antisocial side effects.

As for right now, I've got to start digging. An Italian friend wants a diagram of Fitzroy's Cassarotto Route.

---

1 *A phenomenally popular English comedy series that aired from 1966 to 1987, starring Ronnie Corbett and Ronnie Barker.*

Erik Weihenmayer helps a kid learn to climb blind.

CARDS FROM THE TRAILER 2004

Seeing Straight with Erik Weihenmayer (2001)

If you've never tried it, next time you're at the local climbing gym, do this: Put on a blindfold and climb a wall on top rope.

Sounds easy? I thought so, while watching the then-thirty-two-year-old Erik Weihenmayer ("wine-mayor"), who is blind, cruise casually and confidently up a forty-foot wall in downtown Aspen, Colorado. With a little of Erik's enthusiastic guidance, and a really tight belay, I jerked, wobbled, and barn-doored my way up forty feet of mind-opening terrain. Everything I'd been told by my mountaineering class instructors in high school came flooding back: "Burns, you idiot! Keep your feet on the rock!" "Burns, you idiot! Don't pull on the rope!"

"Burns, you idiot! Don't dangle there like a lifeless butt of ham."

High school was no fun.

Meeting Erik at an outdoor festival in Aspen in 2001 was, however, lots of fun.

I'd heard about Erik for years, through a mutual friend I'd met in the Himalaya, and I was so curious about Erik that I enrolled for his bouldering clinic, held on a small artificial wall in a downtown Aspen park. He had recently climbed Everest with a team of friends and was swarmed by little kids and fascinated adults, many of whom wanted books, T-shirts, and body parts autographed.

Erik suffers from retinoschisis, a degenerative eye disorder that had taken his sight by the time he was thirteen. Although he fumbled awkwardly through a few years of adolescence (who doesn't?), at the ripe old age of sixteen he was introduced to rock climbing at a camp for blind kids. He quickly found that he excelled at climbing because, as we all know (at least those of us paying attention), climbing is not just about seeing holds.

"It was a great sport for me because it's all about your body and how to use your balance," Erik told me, "It seemed to work [for me] and it seemed to work pretty well. And I especially liked that problem-solving aspect of climbing. Reading the rock with your hands is a lot like reading a road map."

Erik is a tall, strong, muscular fellow with a casual, confident air and a manner that says, "Welcome." Erik is no "disabled" person either. He leads up to 5.10, and when he did the Nose with Hans Florine, he led seven pitches—including the first, fourth, Stovelegs, and Pancake Flake pitches.

"It's hard to imagine," he said of leading, "because you can't see into a crack. But if I'm able to jam a finger, even a pinkie, in there and feel the gear, I can pretty much tell where the cams of a camming unit are or if something's going to stay."

After his first rock climbing outings, Erik moved on to bigger and bigger adventures. He's climbed McKinley (Denali), Kilimanjaro, Aconcagua, and Mt. Vinson, not to mention more technical stuff, like Polar Circus, El Cap, dozens of routes in Eldorado Canyon, and spires in the desert. He also runs marathons, skis, and does acrobatic skydiving and long-distance cycling.

In late 1998, Erik was scheduled to go to the Himalaya to run in the grueling hundred-mile Himalayan Run & Trek event in West Darjeeling, as part of a team of "disabled" athletes. Erik couldn't go, but his acquaintance Doug Ullman, a three-time cancer survivor, ran in the race. I mentioned this to Erik, as I'd had the opportunity to photograph Doug in the race. "Now that guy really impresses me," Erik said. "I respect people who go beyond the norm and go beyond peoples' expectations—who create their own expectations and limits. That's what it's all about."

Erik has received praise from 99 percent of the climbing community and general public for his mountaineering activities, but it's the few critics who irk him.

One criticism Erik heard from the U.K. came from a Mike Trueman, who wrote in the *London Sunday Times,* ". . . To his credit he reached the summit, but not just with the aid of two ski poles, as the BBC reported. There were also eleven Sherpas and twelve other climbers assisting him and the venture cost £1.4m. He did well, but the motives of those who placed him in such danger and made money from it must be questioned."

Actually, Erik says, "The climb cost about $250,000. It was the documentary made of the climb that cost over $1.5 million. Besides, my small group of friends and I were climbing as a group of friends, nothing more. I asked my friend Chris [Morris] about that letter and Chris said, 'Ignore it. You climbed every inch of that mountain and don't let that letter belittle it.' Certainly I was never short-roped."

While Everest might today be a cocktail party topic and something of a weird joke to the climbing world, Erik has his own ideas. "People say Everest isn't pure anymore. The current trends have actually opened it up more. It doesn't take the resources of a nation or nationalistic interests to get a team to and up Everest anymore."

Erik became the first blind person to complete the fabled Seven Summits in 2002, when he reached the top of both Mt. Elbrus in Europe and Australia's Kosciusko—in sum, a great series of accomplishments.

But before I left the clinic, I did have to ask Erik about the loss of the view, something I've always cherished as a part of climbing.

"Admittedly, I'm biased," he said. "I think it's almost overemphasized. A lot of times, you get to a summit and it's during a whiteout or dark or something. To me, the climbing experience is something much more elemental. It's about the internal feeling and a connection to your body. But it's also about a connection to the world. When I climb, I hear the crampons crunch on the snow beneath my feet, and feel the rush of wind when I get into an exposed area, the sunlight when I pop up onto a ridge. There's a whole lot more to it than looking at the view."

Visionary words from an inspirational man—we could all do well to see things so clearly.

Petit Piton, St. Lucia.

The Best Base Camp on Earth
(2003)

Ever since I first wrapped a loosely fitting rope around my waist and secured it with Sellotape[1] and a sheepshank, my parents have been encouraging me to climb the north face of the Eiger. "We could have a lovely holiday sitting on that famous balcony at Kleine Scheidegg, behind a telescope and with a mug of tea in each hand," my dad keeps reminding me. "You know, Son, that balcony where the tourists watch all the climbers fall to early, bloody, and horrible deaths, and where those who do live are either awfully maimed or live the rest of their lives with an overwhelming sense of inadequacy?"

"Yes, Father, I know the spot."

I've never been to Kleine Scheidegg, but the thought of my parents having a lovely holiday on a balcony while I dodge whizzing stones and tumbling Continentals has never been particularly appealing. So after a hunt through other great hotels of the world (sitting below Eiger-shaped mountains, that is), I finally decided I could probably talk them into a family holiday in St. Lucia, a former colony in the Windward Islands of the Caribbean.

The Windward Islands are a volcanic chain arching from Venezuela in the south to the Leeward Islands and the Greater Antilles in the north. They are mostly former French and British colonies, some of which still retain ties to European motherlands.[2] Because of their volcanic nature, many of these islands are essentially big mountains sticking up thousands of feet out of the sea. For mountain climbers, their huge vertical gains from sea level offer great hiking, scrambling, and, in places, rock climbing—though it appears the extensive rock climbing is almost wholly undeveloped.

The Pitons of St. Lucia are possibly the most famous of all the Windward Islands' mountains, primarily due to their shape. Twin, perfectly shaped conical spires, they appear regularly in Caribbean brochures and on the cover of high-dollar travel magazines.

The mountains themselves are barely a half-mile apart, separated by a small valley and a bay. Gros Piton is the taller of the two; it sticks 2,620 feet out of the ocean and culminates in a round but highly overgrown summit. Petit Piton is steeper, rockier, and, though only 160 feet shorter than Gros Piton, more appealing. You can hike up Gros Piton, whereas you've got to climb quite a bit of rock to get up the Petit Piton. While selecting a couple of mountains to climb was easy, selecting the Caribbean's version of Kleine Scheidegg was difficult. There are only a few nice hotels along the mountainous southwest coast of St. Lucia, and most of them have limited views of the Pitons because they're either too close to the mountains (e.g., directly underneath them) or blocked by hills.

One beautiful and rustic hotel, Stonefield Estate, was an exception. Like Kleine Scheidegg, it boasts a huge, perfectly flat balcony staring straight at the north face of the Petit Piton. You can lazily sit here and trace the entire route on the shaded face with your tea-soaked finger. Best of all, the balcony has a pool, so the sweaty work of watching tumbling offspring can be offset by the occasional refreshing dip. I figure Stonefield Estate is about the best base camp on Earth.

I packed up the family and we flew to St. Lucia. It was teatime. After arriving at St. Lucia's capital's airport in the middle of the night, my parents, wife, and children grabbed the sole, very sleepy cabbie and directed him to a hotel on the northern tip of the thirty-mile-long island, where we had a room waiting: the Hotel Capri. The Hotel Capri, we soon learned, was sort of an informal hangout for Europeans and Brits wanting to experience some of the local flavor—things like "jump-ups" (street parties) and Caribbean yoga. We bumbled in around 1:00 A.M. with loads of luggage and were met—much to the delight of my Commonwealth-bred parents and me—with huge mugs of tea. Andrew Davies, the hotel's owner, was a young Brit who had traded London stock exchange ticker-tape watching for linen washing and had established the Hotel Capri in the former Taiwanese embassy. (Okay, why Taiwan had an embassy in St. Lucia is beyond me, but when you book yourself in, ask Andrew.)

We slept soundly, then awoke to a gorgeous view across the northern shores of St. Lucia—and a full English breakfast, with huge pots of tea and many types of baked goods that readily absorbed marmalade as a sweetener. Clearly, if you're of Commonwealth lineage, there are solid arguments for traveling to former British colonies, a decent cup of tea being at the top of my list.

We spent the next day in a taxi riding to the bottom end of the island, where the Pitons are located. There, we found lodging in a gorgeous, rambling hotel (Stonefield Estate), unpacked our bags, and prepared for an assault on the Pitons . . . or, at least, I did. My parents, wife, and children had little interest in scaling these lumps of the Earth's crust but, being of the Earth-lump-climbing mindset, I was raring to go.

I decided I should climb the Gros Piton first, as a warm-up, and my dad decided to accompany me. Weirdly, even though the mountain itself was about a mile and a half away from Stonefield (as the crow flies), it took us about forty-five minutes to get there by land-based vehicle. The road turned back on itself hundreds of times every quarter mile or so, climbed roller-coaster-steep hills randomly, and rumbled along in more directions than most horizontal-plane-dwelling mammals should ever experience (clearly, the French were in charge during the road-building periods). At a tiny village called *Fond Gens Libre* ("Valley of the Free People"), we acquired our requisite government guide, a tiny woman named Merle, and we set off on a trail through the jungle. After just a half-mile of lush, green forest, we came to a cave, which was the cultural highlight of the day.

The cave—well, a rock, really—has a fascinating story. It was used as a dwelling by black "brigands" during their freedom fighting in the late eighteenth century. After the French Revolution, French Republicans abolished slavery, giving the blacks their freedom. When it appeared the British would repossess the island shortly thereafter (bringing back slavery), the brigands formed a militia and traveled about the island fighting for freedom. They were no match for the British military, and by the end of the eighteenth century, they were all but quashed. In 1798 they cut a deal with British forces, saving their own lives but in exchange returning themselves to slavery.

Culture aside, this one "cave" had possibly the best bouldering on the entire island. As I intimated, this wasn't really a cave; rather, it was a massive block filled with huge pockets on its downhill, overhanging side. The rock itself is a volcanic tuff, very much like Shiprock and a few other desert plugs (a bit like gritstone)—but better: rougher and stronger. With Merle and Father egging me on ("Go for it, Cam . . . there are probably no hairy spiders in those giant, web- and dead-insect-filled buckets . . ."), I figured out most of a stunning traverse—the "Mango Tango," about easy 5.10—in my sandals. Still, I reckon with a good wire brush and a little exploration, Fond Gens Libre could be a bit of a bouldering mecca. Of course, when Merle wanted to know the cultural background for bouldering ("Why do you do that?") I, a man used to filling every ear within farting-shot with tedious tales of irrelevant stuff, was a tad lost for words.

"Why not?" I responded.

We then hiked the peak, which was straightforward enough and culminated in some lovely views.

Later that day, I signed up for the Petit Piton at the hotel reception desk. As with the Gros Piton, a guide is required. As it turned out, two other folks from Stonefield Estate were slated for the ascent: Lindsay and Russ, a husband-wife team of lawyers from Alabama. The three of us were to go with a local resident named Jah-I, a Rastafarian man who had climbed Petit Piton 2,876 times. Now, this is pretty cool—how many mountain climbing guides do you know who are full-blown Rastafarians?

As we tromped off into the hazy morning light, Dad tossed me a bright red T-shirt: "Nice red shirt," he said. "Make it easier to see you dropping off that huge face. I'll go set up my telescope at the pool." "Okay, Dad. Thanks. I see the blood-colored T-shirt has been soaked in tea...."

Our small group headed off into the jungle around 7:30 A.M., Jah-I out in front, me next, then Lindsay, then Russ, and finally Jah's son, Livingstone, who was on his 106th ascent of the Petit Piton.

The Petit Piton was much more enjoyable than the Gros. Pulling up on roots and boulders was sort of like climbing on the easy section of the local climbing wall, but a lot more fun (Jah-I climbed barefoot, of course). Sections of roots were interspersed with sections of rock, many of which were equipped with fixed ropes. In fact, there were loads of ropes on the Petit Piton, a few strangely dangling from tree limbs, obviously the tattered remains of ascents gone bad. There was a spot where we swung from one rope to another, a sort of Hinterstoisser Traverse of the Jungle (just call me George). The crux was a low-angled offwidth crack, about forty feet tall, which would've been a lot harder without the fixed rope. In fact, I was hard-pressed to imagine how one might've climbed it in the rain, had it been raining. I guess we would've climbed the spiny plants.

We arrived at the summit drenched with sweat.

I looked for my parents sitting in beach chairs, sipping buckets of tea and watching through binoculars at the Stonefield Estate's pool. Of course, it was only 9:00 A.M. and they weren't there. No one was. It was too early. My parents were still sleeping, as were my daughters and wife. I was no one's hero, and the fantastically mediocre trajectory of my life retained its sinking arc—headed, I assumed, toward an inauspicious conclusion. Our mini-expedition descended without incident.

Later that morning, as the entire Burns Family Traveling Circus sat on the balcony and had needles stuck in our arms for continuous intravenous tea supply, I outlined the route on the Petit Piton while my Dad videotaped me.

"Pretty nifty, Son. That's a big Petit Piton," he said. "And you didn't fall to an early, bloody, and horrible death, and you're not awfully maimed."

"Nope, and no overwhelming sense of inadequacy," I said. "The fantastically mediocre trajectory retains its sinking arc."

"Well, better get out some Sellotape and the sheepshank manual," Dad said. "Time for some loosely fitting rope and some misdirected, balcony-based encouragement."

"Good idea, Dad. Pass the tea."

1 An Australian (and European) brand of cellophane ("scotch") tape.
2 St. Lucia itself was fought over quite a bit by the French and British, and the island changed ownership fourteen times.

Inside the Big Outdoor Industry (1999)

In late 1999, on a whim, I decided to attend one of the premier American outdoor industry trade shows, this one in particular dubbed "OR" for *Outdoor Retailer*—the magazine that sponsors the event, in Salt Lake City. This was not the "hook-and-bullet" crowd, as journos call it—hunters, anglers, etc.—rather, this was the adrenaline side of the outdoors: people who climb mountains and paddle through tsunamis, the so-called "self-propelled" crowd, which generally doesn't carry a gun.

My plans were to take a good, hard, serious look at the outdoor industry and how it is growing and changing in America. I had several newspapers and magazines interested in a report and, no doubt, after reading this, every one of you will be baking up indoor-wall handholds in your faulty old kitchen ovens (OSHA folks, are you listening?).

After all, in the United States, outdoor stuff crested the $5 billion mark in 1999—something of a milestone that most of us dirtbag types will never properly fathom. (For the record, in 1999, apparel led at $1.7 billion; followed closely by "gear" at $1.5 billion; "accessories" at $957 million; and, finally, footwear, at $806 million, according to *Outdoor Retailer.*)

If you've never been to an outdoor industry trade show, I highly recommend it.

Simply put, they are big conventions where thousands of manufacturers of tents, backpacks, shoes, clothes, kayaks, ropes, freeze-dried food, and other stuff display said stuff to several thousand underpaid and over-harried retail outlet operators in the hope that the retail outlet operators will suddenly become interested and buy a boodle of whatever it is they make and then mark it up by 100 percent and sell it to a well-heeled sector of the populace more commonly dubbed "consumers."

And to lure the unsuspecting store owners into their midst, the manufacturers have a few tricks up their sleeves (known as "cunning stunts," in the business).

First, the booths themselves are very colorful and highly decorated. If you're a retailer who has just stepped off a fifteen-hour journey from far away and you wander past one of these booths, it's a safe bet the colors and pretty pictures of mountains with climbers and kayakers and runners doing their thing will slow you up. As you stand there trying to figure out where the photo was taken, two sales representatives mysteriously appear at either arm and gingerly assist you inside the booth, where you'll be seated in a comfortable chair, offered a refreshment of some kind (say, organic soda or spiced cider—something fairly P.C.), then bombarded with information about whatever it is they make. If the firm makes clothing, you will get your own version of a runway show, your own sample article of clothing to take home (hopefully they've picked something that looks good on you), and a Library of Congress–sized pile of literature.

The sample jacket is always nice, and you sure needed that glass of juice, but the literature is completely inane—because it's all, absolutely, 100 percent identical.

Here is the standard pitch for a marketing plan delivered by most outdoor equipment and clothing firms' marketing people: "Hey, I know, let's get some young, very beautiful, very athletic models, put them in a dramatic and beautiful mountain setting—I'm thinking the right side of El Cap or the Dru at dusk or some exotic place in Tibet— have them wearing *your clothes* (that was my assistant Sierra-Brook's idea—good one, huh?), and photograph them. Maybe get some of those really cheery native folks in the pictures. Then we'll put all these photos in a colorful and lavishly illustrated catalog and the general public will go berserk over your gear and buy truckloads of it and you'll get filthy rich. Great idea, huh?"

Certainly, the Glossy Catalog Marketing Plan has worked for many years, but, then again, *it's the only outdoor industry marketing plan that's ever been tried.*

Aren't marketing people supposed to be creative?

Just once, I'd like to see an outdoor-gear maker decorate a catalog with pictures of old people who are losing their hair, have bad teeth (or better yet, no teeth), wear at least two pairs of glasses at a time when reading *anything*, couldn't climb a set of stairs without a noisy hydraulic device, and have various types of un-Photoshoppable medical machinery attached to nostrils, mouths, ears, and other body cavities. And, because they're outside all day, they'd have very wrinkly and blotchy skin. Now, that kind of catalog would get some attention. (Note to self: Start Old Blotchy Person Marketing Firm. Hmmm . . . www.obpmf.com seems to be free. . . .)

Not only are the individuals in most outdoor gear catalogs all wrong, but most of us don't spend our lives running rivers in Chile, wandering through Honduran villages with surfboards, or scaling cliffs in Alaska, so I'd very much appreciate a catalog filled with images of people using outdoor equipment the way they normally use it: say, wearing a Gore-Tex shell while waiting for the 8:05 to Hoboken, scraping cobwebs out of an attic corner with a tent pole, pounding in picture hangers with an ice tool, or aerating the lawn with the latest crampons (which is actually what most people do with crampons). Heck, even an old gummer dumping bottles and cans along the side of the road while wearing high-tech polyunmethylated boxer shorts designed for climbing Everest would be a more accurate depiction of what really happens with all that gear (and I volunteer to model).

What about really fat people? How about incompetent people—with broken arms and legs after big outdoor-activity-related accidents? How about people without limbs (Aaron Ralston aside for a moment)? How about really thin handsome people who look sort of in shape but never actually get off the couch? How about the *very*—wait, the *severely*—incontinent?

I digress, but you get the point. One of us—you or me, or perhaps both of us together—needs to start a union of unemployed fat, old, ugly, incompetent (and incontinent), unoutdoorsy people who would like to pose mostly nude halfway up the side of Annapurna so that they can appear in outdoor gear catalogs.

What's worse is that a lot of the marketeers selling these products have only the faintest notion of how they're used, or, for that matter, what the outdoors are anyway. They work at big firms like Pissstupid & Peespot, LLC in New York, Eatchunder & Hoikings, LLC in Los Angeles, and Frick & Crunch, LLC in Boston. The most "out" they've ever been is by train to Hoboken (for the www.obpmf.com Gore-Tex shell shoot, of course). Thus, to the characters writing the press releases, catalog copy, and sometimes vital technical information about a down suit you might take into a deadly, high-altitude environment, the outdoors means horny squirrels in Bryant Park and dying trees along the Santa Monica freeway.

I can picture Messrs. Frick & Crunch working on a press release about a new tent:

"Fricky, whaddyou think? Should we say it comes in a lovely blue that matches your eyes?"

"No, no. Real mountain men are possibly really going to use this thing, although I can't understand what the hell they'd do with these skinny aluminum tubes. These are people who daily challenge the hardest campsites on the Earth's crust and they have big heaving chests and ferocious Germanic expressions on their faces."

"Did you say ferocious crusts on their expressions?"

"No, Crunchy, ferocious crusts on their feces . . . oh hell, it's all the same thing, I guess."

"What are they expressing?"

"Oh, Crunchy, never mind. We've got to come up with some tremendously inane language that appeals to these numb-brained heathens."

"But there are women doing it, too."

"Okay, you're right. Let's make it even more numb-brained—just kidding! How about this: 'The all-new model AF1005 tent from The Western Front is the only tent you'll ever need, whether you're'...hmm, what should I say here Crunchy?"

"How about: 'Whether you're climbing *up* a new bolted-on sport route on Everest or making a first *descent* of the Cashew Face via helicopter assisted camel-kayak.'"

"What the hell is a camel-kayak?"

"No idea, but I overheard a chappie talking about one at last year's trade show. Apparently they're all the rage."

"Bloody brilliant then. How about 'Whether you're climbing *up* a new sport route on K2'—yes, let's go with K2; it's reportedly more treacherous to canoe down than Everest—'or making a first *descent* of the Cashew Face via helicopter-assisted camel-kayak—or perhaps just looking to start a cultlike place in the jungle serving Kool-Aid, the all-new model AF1005 tent from The National Front'—"

"TNF."

"Right, TNF! 'Whether you're climbing *up* a new sport route on K2 or making a first *descent* of the crunchy Cashew Face via helicopter-assisted camel-kayak—or perhaps just looking to start a cultlike place in the jungle serving Kool-Aid, the all-new model AF1005 tent from TNF is the only tent you'll ever need!'"

"Fricky, that's the bee's knees. Do you think we should still mention that it matches your eyes?"

What's arguably worse are those times when people who really use outdoor gear start running the PR campaigns because they go to great lengths to make certain *they are the campaign.*

I used to hang about with a climber from Boulder—Jim Diddly, or thereabouts—with his own marketing firm called Gneiss Guys Marketing or Rock Solid Marketing or Hold On Marketing or Over the Top Sales ... or something even more clever than I can dribble up endlessly onto the keyboard. Jim was the marketing "guru" for about twenty outdoor-equipment makers. During the mid-1990s, in every one of these twenty firms' campaigns were pictures of him on his latest outing, whether climbing in Pakistan or gumming a bagel at Moe's. To wit:

• Page 33 of the 1997 Pristinemountaincrush Gear twice-annual socks catalog: "Jim Diddly gluing together his suppurating toe—smashed by rockfall on the north face of Stiffmoaning IV—in a soggy camp in the Karakoram";

• Page 27 of the 1999 Natureplunder Designs biweekly catalog: "Little Dribbly Diddly [Jim's daughter] eating a strawberry and cream cheese muffin while having her face painted by Hard Harry, a clown who regularly boulders V98a+, at the farmer's market on Pearl Street"; and

• Page 2 of the 2002 Wildplacesdestructo Outerwear quarter-daily e-catalog: "Randy Diddly [Jim's brother] pissing off the locals in some never-before-visited-by-white-people part of the world by shoving a teal Himalayan Designs T-shirt on a wrinkly old lady with brown teeth despite the fact that this never-before-encountered culture believes all teal-colored things are evil deities."

I don't know about you, but when I pick up a catalog of outdoor gear and see these pictures—and I'm sure the people in such images are really wonderful, upbeat folks—I don't give a stuff what they're doing, what they're eating, where they are, *who they are*, and how loud they dress in previously unadultered foreign lands (even though, ironically, I have adulterated many a foreign land myself and work in marketing as well). I'd much rather see pictures of a middle-aged pot-bellied guy straining to bend over so he can put on crampons than a young beautiful athlete being nimble in the woods.

I think the majority of outdoor industry marketing folks' creative energy goes into naming their kids. Ever met a child named Sierra Rain or Shasta Sunset? Sure you have. River Eddy or Hairboat Harry? You betcha. Mountain Sequoia or Alpine Summer? Maybe. Alpenglow Moon or Serac Storm? Possibly. These kids seem to show up in every one of the catalogs, and it's oftentimes a good bet they're the children, especially the daughters, of outdoor marketing folks. (I must admit, though, I very much like people who use animal names: Bear, Wolf, Fawn, Samoyed, Duck, Heifer, etc.)

If you've been alive since the 1960s, you might remember the quasi-back-to-nature-sounding names given to children by their hippie parents: Wildflower Harvest, Spirit Sky, Mountain Song, and other appellations that were as much statements of freedom as they were about the out-of-doors. The names of today seem to speak directly to the parents' favorite parts of the outdoors. I think this trend should be taken a step further—I'd love to meet a kid named Gnarly Offwidth or A5 Nailup.

What'll be infinitely more confusing is when all these youngsters marry, and we have a whole western nomenclature revolution on our hands. Imagine a local newspaper announcement when a couple of these youngsters get hitched: "Gnarly Offwidth, whose outdoor gear company on Fourth Street was recently named 'Only Outdoor Gear Company on Fourth Street' by the *Smurtzville Times,* and Alpenglow Moon were married June 1; they are now expecting a child, Gnarly Moon."

Fortunately, to facilitate the coming Nomenclature Revolution of the Mountain West, most outdoor goods trade shows have a strong "opposite sex element," as a friend recently pointed out, "like Whole Foods on a Saturday night." Many of the folks who arrive with one young athletic partner go home with another (and they sometimes make a quick switch from bouldering to play-boating). For a convention attended by vast numbers of vegetarians, it's one of the grandest meat markets on the planet.

If you haven't met the outdoor industry marketing folks themselves, you've met their dogs. Walk around any mountain town in the modern West and every dog you meet will own a name that is a jumble of the letter *k*, the letter *l*, an *a* and an *o*, and possibly several others, and it will sound like either an Eskimo term or something generated by a Jamaican, as a few quick suggestions suggest: Kaya, Makalu, Chinook, Nanook, Balto, Kibo, Pisco, etc. (The list of super-P.C.

dog names is somewhere downloadable and it is not debatable—you are not allowed to call your dog *Rex*.)

By now you're getting a mental picture (or a picture that's mental): the outdoor gear industry and its shows are a cross between a flea market and a used-car lot—a bit like a Vegas production in which the audience is invited to participate in the dancing and puppetry.

But remember, the OR show is better than most. It's miles more fun and it's certainly a lot less technologically confusing than any hook-and-bullet show ("Whaddya reckon, Vern? Is the four-aught-six guud with a four-by-seven thousand scope and a round of plastic squirrel shot, or shuud I go with the double-action bolt clever model with the 458 millimeter cannon rounds?") and the people running it are really good, dedicated people. You are given free samples of *everything*, all the manufacturers are happy to see you, and you do have a good time, so you should go.

I arrived at the 1999 OR show late, just in time to catch the tail end of a lecture by U.K. climber Paul Pritchard. He was giving a talk about smashing his head during an ascent of the Totem Pole in Tasmania. As a result of all the surgeries (and the fact that his head was shaved) one could actually peer inside his volcano-shaped noggin where, Paul was happy to point out, there was a several-inch square of flesh that pulsated. It was one of the most disturbing things I've ever seen, but Paul was quite proud of it.

"Yeah, and you know the best thing?" he asked smiling. "When you come out of 'ospital in Tasmania, they let you take the nurse 'ome." (Very nice, Paul; now get that heaving wound away from me.)

Next stop was a trade show booth where a firm I'll call Mega Gear Company (a.k.a. Grey Rhombus) had all its wares on display. One of the firm's reps took me on a tour through the company's 2000 product line: awesome new ice tools, fantastic new boots, super-cool new camming units. I was drooling like a dog in the cat box until I realized that this exact process had been repeated the year before, and the year before that, and the year before that. Indeed, every time I come to these trade shows and am wowed by the latest and greatest—then go out and buy some—I find myself horribly out of date within six months. ("Jeez, Cam. You're not still using that old piece-of-junk harness from February '02, are you? The March '02s are already out and they're so much better. Look, the March '02s have this useless little tab of nylon here that the February '02s don't have....") Clearly, those outdoor industry marketing guys are onto something.

Anyway, at the Mega Gear Company equipment booth, all the gear was shiny and new and very impressive. And, it goes without saying, they were doing a brisk trade, which brings up the other trick employed by outdoor equipment manufacturers at the outdoor industry trade shows: *booze*. Manufacturers are so eager to sell their wares that they start serving beer, often fairly early in the morning.

This actually suited me rather well, and as I quaffed several lagers and wondered how I might afford a new ice tool (or, more importantly, what I was going to eat for breakfast), it seemed that the crowd was thinning out—and rather quickly. Indeed, by the time I'd finished my beer and burped noisily, there was no one else in the booth. My gear-scrounging brethren had disappeared.

I wandered over to The North Face booth, where typically you'd find a crowd of climbing bums lined up schmoozing for various tidbits of nylon outerwear or expedition cash. No one was there. Then I went over to the Patagonia booth, where they'd normally be seen trying to wangle a few pairs of really spongy underpants. No one to be seen.

Then a fellow I knew from a neighborhood climbing shop wandered by holding a short, red, deformed plastic stick, which sort of curved one way and had a lump on the end.

"Look, Cam. I just got a free Chuckit!"

"A Chuckit!?" I asked.

"Yeah. Everyone's trying to get one. They're the shit."

The OR Media Kit provided to reporters summed it up better than I ever could: "The Chuckit! is the new, must-have piece of gear for the millennium. The Chuckit! allows you to pick up a tennis ball without having to touch the potentially drool-covered ball. What's more, you can throw the ball a long, long way."

Grey Rhombus ice tools aside, I had to go look at the Chuckit!

Inventor Mark Oblack explained he owned a great big drooling Cheasapeake Bay retriever named Chester who slobbered on tennis balls the way the seats in most aquatic theme parks moisten ticket buyers' trousers.

Mark hated the gooey, sloppy mess required of each orb launch, so he invented the Chuckit!, a sticklike, ball-throwing device. How this coveted piece of equipment ended up at a trade show with tents, backpacks, and ice tools was quite the mystery, until Oblack explained he'd simply dumped some off at REI's Seattle headquarters and they'd begun selling Chuckit!s by the thousands.

After the Chuckit!, I decided to look around the trade show some more. While Oblack and I were wrestling over whether or not I could get a sample Chuckit!, a climbing buddy told me to go check out "those Porta Potty guys in the Pavilion."

"Don't take the Chuckit! over to those Porta Potty guys!" Mark warned, finally relinquishing one of the spherical-object-launching devices.

The "Porta Potty guys in the Pavilion" turned out to be two brothers, Brian and Aaron Phillips, who were selling their dad, William's, design for a folding, portable backwoods toilet. It was a simple plastic device, strong enough to hold 750 pounds (the Phillips brothers offered to pose standing on the unit with two of their friends). Once you did your business into a regular household garbage bag fitted under the seat, you dumped in some "Pooh Powder," a chemical mixture designed to solidify everything and start breaking it down. Then you tied it all up and dropped it off in the nearest trash can.

Being a failed chemist, I had to ask, "What's in Pooh Powder?"

"Ahh. That's a family secret," Brian said. "It's been patented. We call it Eleven Herbs and Spices."

The brochure promised "personal solutions for extreme situations." Obviously, the Phillips boys were onto something good. At that particular moment in history, the nation of Venezuela was thinking about buying 200,000 of the toilets for their earthquake-ravaged nation, and Turkey and Egypt were both interested, too, and the Phillips had recently won a contract to supply 250,000 American Marines with the devices. You had to wonder what the Colonel would've thought. At least the Phillips brothers probably would've been open to using a fat guy in their marketing materials.

The OR Media Kit was the most illuminating piece of literature I'd ever read. One gear company entry stated this: "We took the Splog a step further. The Splog+ keeps the integrity of our Apex-Award-winning Splog, adding an overlayed waterproof Nubuk leather vamp and mudguard, plus a higher back. The Splog+ has the same layering concept of the original Splog, + a little more."

Buzzing with curiosity, I bypassed Lynn Hill and Beth Rodden signing posters and headed off to see the company's booth. The Splog turned out to be a "sports clog," a simple but comfortable shoe with a low back-of-the-foot covering. "It's more for après ski, or a hard day at work," Michelle, the "Splog Lady," explained. She slipped a pair on my feet, and I was sold—although I probably would've been *more* sold if her name had been Inuit Buttress.

This, of course, brings up another fascinating thing about selling outdoor gear: the names that manufacturers attach to normal everyday items, like shoes. The Splog—though a lovely shoe—was just the tip of the silly name iceberg, and I was suddenly seized by a desire to find as many oddball names given to shorts, pants, shoes, hats, gloves, and other commonplace stuff that I could.

As roughly one minute of research uncovered, the names of all outdoor clothing fits into one of three categories: (1) a big pointy mountain (Cerro Torre is good for starters, but it's too common nowadays—better to offer up names that are a bit more obscure, like Rakaposhi or Trisul); (2) a particular climbing route (the Zodiac on El Cap comes up quite a bit, no doubt because it's also the name of a company that makes toilet brushes); or (3) some *wah* thing, like the children's names mentioned above: Mandala, Yogi, Seeker, Bodhi—pretty much any term from yoga can work as the name for a piece of clothing these days (what's better still is when you can combine some big mountain with a yoga term, like Rainier-sutra or Longs-asana).[1]

The thing is, while there are yonks of companies that offer very colorful, very nice-looking clothes with some mountain or climbing route title, there's absolutely no way in hell I'd actually wear this over-priced "outdoors" clothing on a climb. In fact, I think I'd strictly *avoid* taking nice outdoorsy clothes anywhere near the mountains for fear they'd be destroyed. I can just picture the wife when I got home:

"Oh, no! I bought you that poser shirt so you didn't *have* to go out and run around with your idiot friends, and now look—you've gone and splattered blood all over it!"

"Sorry, dear. We were just chopping up the dead Italian guy so we could get him out of our way while we climbed the thing. I forgot I was wearing the $185 Chichi-Gear shirt. . . ."

Sure, that happens all the time.

If I were in business, which I hope to be soon, I'd offer both clothing and names for said clothing that would be true to the cause: the Psycho Peak Coveralls (like mechanics' coveralls but with a built-in hatchet holder for your ice tools); the Bigwall Bucket Pants (because everyone needs a bucket on a big wall); and the Superkickass Bouldering Thong (after all, more people should be bouldering in thongs).

Of course, the outdoor industry is changing.

As I cruised around the aisles of camp chaise lounges and hand-cranked flashlights, the "extra-chafing bijou-bouncer tights" and the "Tibetan-cut toploader shorts" (with the extra-long dongwallet accessory), the hand-sewn ear warmers and the "elimination-oriented spandex hooded frumplebags," it was obvious that pretty much any regular household item can be marketed as an "outdoor" product. And once you go into massive production in China (which sends its manufacturing emissions and pollutants west, to pristine outdoorsy places like Oregon, and California—where the people in the catalogs are being photographed while huffing and puffing up mountains), you become part of "the outdoor industry." Whether you're making it better or not, I'm not certain, but you're certainly a part of it. (I wonder where the pollution from the production of this book goes.)

Eight years ago, there were no companies making outdoor doggie booties. In 1999, I counted five. With the economic rise of the American consumer, pretty much everything is going to be considered when they're walking down the aisles at REI with a pile of shekels to spend. And once Chinese and Indian consumers learn the intrinsic value of having Fido's feet not touch raw ground, a few of these firms will be headed into the multinational stratosphere.

But many argue that this crazy proliferation of products is a bad thing. I've heard critics say we're getting too convenience-ized, too luxury-ized, too *easy*-ized.

I guess I'll take the Splogs. But for now, I'm going to leave the "self-heat-in-a-bag" cappuccinos, the backpacker Barcaloungers, and the super-lightweight backpacker's doggie stand-up dining table. After all, as my friend Bob Ward remarked at the show, "What kind of outdoorsy person is afraid of picking up a potentially drool-covered ball?"

---

1 *Okay, a fourth category is the Greek letter, like the Gamma pants or the Delta undies.*

Me in my cheap tent on Aconcagua's Normal Route.

On Aconcagua with the Wal-Mart Climbing Team (1996)

While I was attending an outdoor industry trade show in 1994, a neo-phyte climber came up to me and asked, "Hey, Cam, how do you get free gear?"

I pondered the query: "Good question. Let me know when you've got the answer."

He wandered off into the crowd, aiming more or less for the nearest equipment company's booth, and I watched curiously as he window-shopped among the displays of shiny new camming gear.

I don't know if he ever landed any free gear, but somehow I doubt it. Every climber wants free gear. Every climber wants free clothes, too, with bright logos and expensive, trendy labels. Every climber wants to be paid for going climbing. (And it goes without saying: every climber wants free food.)

The pinnacle of success in American climbing is being on The North Face's climbing team. This small, elite group of climbers has been everywhere and done, pretty much, everything. Their names are permanently emblazoned in the skulls of the huddled masses the way a hot fire-poker jab in the eye leaves a big black hole and singed eyelashes.

Here at the Trailer Park, in sunny Colorado, I waited throughout the early 1990s for a call from The North Face and the inevitable invitation to come join the gods. But, by about 1995, it was becoming apparent that they'd either lost my number or noticed my wooden leg ("great firewood during cold bivouacs," I wrote in a letter recommending myself).

So, I called them.

"Who? What? I think you have the wrong number—click," came the response. Not exactly what I'd expected. Anyway, still wanting to be a part of something big and elite, I formed my own climbing team: the Wal-Mart Climbing Team.

In the off chance you've been living in jar contained in a lock box inside a sealed hole underneath a rock for the past twenty years, I should probably explain: Wal-Mart is a preeminent chain of retail stores that specializes in selling huge volumes of cheap crap. The company erects gigantic, Hindenburgesque buildings on the outskirts of cities and towns (where land is cheap), and then drives prices so low that downtown businesses go under—or at least that's the business model. It's worked quite well, actually, and now America is exporting the Wal-Mart business model to many other nations, including China and Mexico, and I'm sure they are pleased to receive it.

Many Americans go to Wal-Mart for stuff like toilet paper, laundry detergent, sticky tape, motor oil, underwear, and three-ring binders, but they also sell TVs, furniture, clothes, toys, food, camping gear, guns and ammo—you name it. Many Americans attack Wal-Mart for its policies toward employees, manufacturers, resources, politics—(but this is not an article about *that* Wal-Mart discussion).

Anyway, a few years back, my sister Penny was visiting from Australia. With no camping gear of her own, she went to Wal-Mart and bought a Wal-Mart tent, a hideous blue and yellow thing that had the words *Wilderness Trails* stamped across the exterior. She brought it back to my parents' house and we set it up in the backyard. We immediately noticed that the rain fly was tiny, only three square feet or thereabouts. We strapped it to the roof of the tent, where it covered only a small portion of the dome—a sort of half a fly, if you will. I crawled in. The floor material was paper-thin and the guy lines were a kind of thin black string that you might find attached to a crummy child's toy.

Still, for $45 it wasn't a bad deal. It lasted for Penny's entire stay, then wound up in my parent's basement after she left.

In February 1995, I found myself loitering around the Buenos Aires airport, waiting for my old pal Benny Bach to show up so we could go "do" (i.e., walk up) Aconcagua, a big pile of rocks near the Argentinian-Chilean border. Benny didn't own a tent and I didn't own a tent, and the only solution we could come up with was borrowing my sister's Wilderness Trails tent, which he'd picked up before jetting south.

To get to Aconcagua, you take a bus from Mendoza, Argentina, west toward Chile. Before reaching Chile, you get off the bus. I'm not quite sure how to describe the spot where you get off the bus, except to say it's smack dab in the middle of nowhere. From this point, you cart a not-very-polite pile of gear about twenty-five miles up a rough, dry valley.

Well, we did. Most sensible people get a donkey to haul the gear; we were more than a bit broke after the exorbitant airfare to Buenos Aires. That's why we did our own carrying and why, for goodness' sake, we had a cheaper-than-heck tent. (But a better question yet: Why are the most polluted cities on Earth are called "good air" or some such nonsense?)

Anyway, this twenty-five-mile approach march would have taken a fit man two short days. It took us about three long ones. I came down with dysentery about fifteen miles into the jaunt, and had to spend the better part of a day lolling about in the dirt beside the trail, while my body processed some of the vilest creatures that have ever lived in a Mendoza hamburger. Late that evening, I struggled into Aconcagua's base camp, called Plaza de Mulas, and started searching for the Wilderness Trails tent.

If you have never been to Plaza of the Mules, it is not recommended unless you are a social scientist, a pervert, or you have a very well developed sense of humor. (For the record, I am the second.) Aconcagua, according to the statistics, is the tallest mountain in the Western Hemisphere (at 22,840 feet) and it is labeled by many as the "tallest trekking peak on Earth,"[1] meaning that the average Joe, with little or no mountaineering experience, can go and walk up it, or at least try to walk up it.

The base camp for Aconcagua's regular route, Plaza de Mulas is the highest circus in the Western Hemisphere. This doesn't mean there are chihuahuas riding bicycles along tightropes and clowns juggling bowling pins and acrobats doing flips, although if you encountered them here they would not seem out of place. When I say *circus* I mean that Aconcagua has, on its flanks, a mighty huge collection of some of the most unconventional *Homo sapiens* the world has ever seen, and they are all performing completely bizarre acts that frankly make sword-swallowing look like a walk in the park.

For example: water gathering. In most Western communities, this is done via a vast basin-based rainwater gathering system that collects precipitation, sends it first through various filters (some good, some not so good) and then into homes as potable liquid. On Aconcagua, it is done by a leaky pipe in a poopy stream, and the subsequent drinkees act a tad like chihuahuas on trikes and clowns juggling peanuts— which, of course, they're not. They're just sick from the altitude and drinking bad water, which is giving them the runs. I guess the only way Plaza de Mulas did not exactly match the dictionary definition of the term *circus* was the simple fact that it lacked a "big top." And arguably, that was looming above in the form of the mountain.

The other thing about circuses is they tend to involve a lot of people. I guessed there were well over one hundred tents in base camp, and that was a conservative estimate. According to the Aconcagua National Park people, during the 2001–2002 season 3,378 people[2] attempted to reach the summit of Aconcagua. That is, to put it mildly, a staggering mass of humanity. I don't know where you live, but that is about twice the number of people who live in my town, and I couldn't fathom seeing all my neighbors, coworkers, friends, family members, and various passersby (and their alter egos) wandering about on any mountain—even a big one—at the same time.

The vast majority of these people attempt to climb to Aconcagua during the austral summer, December to February, when the mountain is at its warmest (you know, forty below or thereabouts), and when places like Antwerp and Manchester and Cleveland are really gray and awful. And they all gather at the Plaza of the Mules, sometimes for months, living in a tent city.

The Plaza isn't really a plaza, as you might find in an Italian Renaissance village. Rather, it's just a huge, flat, ugly area of rocky moraine that's close to the start of the trail up the mountain. I later took several pictures of it, which the publishers of this book (Random House . . . or The Mountaineers Books . . . or maybe Sharp End Publishing . . . or possibly The Bumslop County Weed-Pulling Society

Press) have hopefully printed somewhere left or right of this text (and if they didn't, I don't blame them). What impressed me more than anything was not how many tents and people there were, but how dreary the whole place was—like an unattractive pile of mine tailings or a Superfund site of tremendous proportions.

I staggered up the last few steps to the Plaza and crested the edge of the moraine to be confronted by more than one hundred tents—every one of which was blue, yellow, or a combination thereof, but all in all very similar to the Wilderness Trails tent. I wandered (*lumbered,* really) around looking for Benny's tent until, blundering between several close-in tents where I tripped over a web of guy lines, I fell almost on top of it. I apologized to the several people whom I had fallen upon, crawled inside, and within no time was fast asleep. I woke a short while later, and Benny suggested we find some water for cooking. There was a stream trickling through the middle of the "plaza," but the water it carried looked strangely milky. Near it was a pipe, carrying, we assumed, cleaner water down to somewhere dirtier.

We started wandering uphill, following the stream and the pipe. About ten people each year die on Aconcagua, according to the official statistics. That is quite a lot, and I'm certain the dying process begins at Plaza de Mulas. As Benny and I wandered through the tent city, we saw lots of people who seemed at odds with their environment. Certainly, there were a lot of individuals in recumbent positions, most fully clothed and with their legs and booted feet sticking out tent doors. Most looked as if they were drunk, or as if they had just been punched and fallen, or as if they'd just woken up *in* a bad dream—possibly all three. Sprawled out on the rocky ground, not one of them looked the least bit happy. It reminded me of a POW camp, but in this instance the inhabitants had chosen—in fact, had spent thousands of dollars and committed months of time—to be there, in this dreary Superfund site, boiling milky water to drink and lolling around in the dirt.

Above the small city, Benny and I found the end of the pipe. It had a cut-in-half plastic barrel attached to it, and water from the stream was entering the pipe. We filled several pots with water, then ambled back through the tents. We cooked a milky dinner, then went to bed and slept soundly.

The next day was a "rest day."

Rest days are mountaineering's finest invention.[3] These are twenty-four-hour periods when climbers recuperate from a strenuous previous day's exercise. Generally, they involve remaining in a horizontal position, usually deep among the baffles of a cozy sleeping bag with a great volume of soft items (sometimes fellow climbers) wedged under the cranium, while lazily cooking things that are subsequently chewed and digested in bed, followed by bouts of reading, more cooking, more eating, and more sloppy dribbling. A few noodle-juice stains on a mummy bag is a small price to pay for a resplendent rest day amongst the peaks.

Mountain climbing seems to be the only sporting activity that offers rest days. I think rest days should be established across all sectors of life, like Christmas or Ramadan. The Spanish certainly come close with the *siesta,* but that's a scant few hours; and the fact that the Spanish don't get to spend the entire day in bed takes the shine off their reclined sojourn.

What if every other morning we all decided to stay in bed for, say, twelve hours, eating and reading and dribbling noodle juice down our fronts? My kids would love it; so would my wife. My dog would go nuts—even my cat would tolerate it. I have no idea what my employer might say, but then again, if he was *rest-daying* too, there might not be a problem (but I cannot picture him dribbling noodles . . . wait—got it).

And the nice thing about rest days is you don't actually have to stay in bed if you don't want to. You can get up and walk around. You can check out the scene, do a bit of washing, plan the coming days, and even socialize (although you're stuck with a bunch of sad weirdos who've spent thousands of dollars to fly halfway round the world to live at a high-altitude Superfund site, but don't tell them I said so). Thus it was that we met our English neighbors.

On Aconcagua, as on any mountain, you become aware of the world's nationalities and their wonderfully odd quirks. During the 1995–96 season, there seemed to be a lot of Brits and Germans on the mountain, but there was the usual collection of Americans, Argentines, and Chileans, also.

The Brits we met, most notably a father-son team camped near us at Plaza de Mulas, kept saying they were *cream-crackered*, a Spoonerism for *knackered*, which means tired. Of course, I just thought they were an alternative-lifestyle couple, and I didn't ask about the lad's mother. After talking to them for several minutes, I was *cream-crackered* myself and felt a level of empathy for the mother I've not felt for any English mother before or since. But there you go; that's how big mountains are.

As our rest day drifted by, Benny and I did a little bit of packing, a little bit of planning, then some considerable noodle dribbling. While we were futzing around over something inconsequential, we met a Catalonian climber named Jordi and his girlfriend, Beatrice. Jordi wanted to climb Aconcagua in a day from about the sixteen-thousand-foot level, while he trained for Everest, which is a fairly ambitious goal. He asked if he could overnight with us at Camp Alaska, a small area of flat ground on the west side of the mountain, before trying for the top. We said sure, but warned him that our tent was rather small.

He looked at the Wilderness Trails tent curiously.

"Where is zee roof?" Jordi asked.

"You mean the fly?" I pointed out the small patch of light blue nylon on top.

"Ahh, I zee. Very small. Thees is a good tent?"

"Si, si, señor," I explained. "Inexpensivo! Muy!"

"American tent?"

"Ummm, I'd say China is a safer bet."

"Sheena? Hmmm."

"That or one of the Koreas possibly. Maybe Hong Kong. Maybe Indonesia."

"Zay make good tents zere?"

"Well, they *manufacture* Wilderness Trails tents there."

Jordi studied the tent a while longer, staring at it the way children stare at other kids' birth defects. Then his concentration eased and he turned to me: "Okay. I zee you in ze morning."

He wandered off and Benny and I studied our birth defect. During the repacking process it had started disgorging dirty clothes and equipment, so that now, many vital pieces of gear were either out on the gravel getting stepped on or, if the items were lighter, blowing away in the incessant wind. I couldn't decide whether it looked more like a yard sale or a plane crash.

Benny and I spent the next day walking up to Camp Alaska and back, to acclimatize. The day after that, we moved up to Camp Alaska and stayed the night. Jordi came with us. There were a half-dozen other tents—serious, professional-looking things—and a group of people who were obviously part of some guided, well-funded group. They all had matching jackets and hats, matching gloves and boots. They looked quite smart, but in a cultish sort of way, yet I saw no Kool-Aid decanters.

In our group, Benny looked like a mountain climber. He was wearing some fairly coordinated colors, mostly black, but with splashes of orange. I was wearing a hideous turquoise and maroon jacket, blue pants, a light blue hat, dark blue gloves, and black boots. I looked like a doll that had been dressed by a color-blind (and possibly retarded) child—and, in a way, I had been.

At Camp Alaska, we found a small spot between several maroon tents and got to work building a ring of rocks that would act as a windbreak. Then we set up the Wilderness Trails tent. To make sure we could all fit, the three of us squeezed inside and lay down. It was very tight, but cozy in a weird sort of "you're-not-my-girlfriend-but-you're-warm-and-you're-soft-and-you're-here" kind of way. (Don't worry, nothing off-color happened; it was too damned cold.)

It really was very cold. One of the things that makes walking up big mountains like Aconcagua so tricky are those times when you need to go to the bathroom. It's so cold that any exposed flesh risks being frost-bitten, thus the acreage of skin exposed must be kept to a minimum. Problem is, number twos require considerable flesh exposure. Heck, even number one can be tricky at times.

I was well aware of this, and before I journeyed to Argentina I had asked my poor mother to cut slits into the several layers of fleece I usually wore in the mountains, in the exact same place on each. Into these she had sewn zippers, so that when completely clad in my "assault suit," as I like to call it, the zippers lined up and allowed easy access for taking a piss. (I remember watching her perform the sewing, and she had a remarkable expression of disgust the entire time, as if she were riding in a taxi with a farting driver. That's why I advocate you hug your mother this instant and tell her how wonderful she is.)

Anyway, this new system of aligned zippers worked well for peeing. For the other business, I just prayed I wouldn't have to go often if at all. I mulled over all these strange high-mountain adaptations as we assembled, then ate, dinner: a big, soggy lump of noodles. After dinner, the sun came out from behind some clouds and put on a dazzling show. We found ourselves standing among the big, professional-looking Kool-Aid group ooohing and aawing at the sunset, and as we did so, we struck up a conversation with a German doctor.

I love German names. They're so rich and colorful, and they make their owners sound like real mountain men. I can't remember his name exactly, but it was very mountainy—something like Rheinhold Mein Helmutt or Musterschitz Indermilkecreek or Wolfgang Upondawg or Handhold Uhnder Ubercling or Vornamen Nachamen.

Anyway, he was bloody well brilliant. One of us went off to pee (can't remember who), and this German doctor asked why we didn't rig something so we didn't need to go anywhere to pee.

"Huh?" I asked.

"Luuk," he said, pointing at his big green and white mountaineering boot.

"Yes, nice boots," I suggested.

"No, luuk ut zee schmall pipe, nixt to zee boot." He pointed at his foot and I could just see the bottom of a narrow clear plastic tube that exited his pant leg and ended an inch above the gravel. Suddenly, a stream of yellowish liquid squirted out.

I shot him a querying glance.

"Zi? I don't need to get undrized to pee. You shud du thiz."

He reached into his pocket, then handed me a small plastic packet with a rubber thing inside. On closer inspection I found the rubber thing was a sort of funnel that fitted onto the average penis, presumably for hospital patients who couldn't get up and go to the bathroom. The bottom of the funnel had a ridged fitting, where you could attach tubing and, presumably, remove liquid output to some distant location. The clever doctor had rigged his device so that he could just wander around and pee at any time.

"That's awesome," Benny said.

"That is pretty smart," I agreed.

And it really was. Just imagine being able to wander around all day without once pulling down your pants and exposing a great deal of flesh (or in my case, a very small amount of flesh). In fact, here was another climbing world invention that, like the rest day, would be welcomed in the regular world. Picture us all going to work each day wearing one of these devices. It would do away with unnecessary bathroom breaks and we could chug coffee all day long until we shook like aspen leaves in a breeze. As I was lost in thought about my new mountaineering product line, the sun set and the mountain grew even colder, so we all turned in.

Inside the tent, we were so wedged together that it was hard to roll over. Strangely, Jordi got the middle position, which was the most comfortable. Every time he made even the slightest movement, my face was mashed into blue nylon. When he rolled toward me, my face was mashed into the rock ring we'd built as a windbreak.

One thing that we noticed in our sleepless discomfort was that it was getting windier as the night dragged on. The Wilderness Trails tent shook and flapped. The poles strained and the seams bulged. The entire thing appeared ready to explode. We lay still and quiet, and listened to the flapping.

To our great surprise, the tent survived the night. Jordi took off for the summit at first light, and Benny and I loaded up our stuff and continued up the mountain, marching around in the gravel with serious high-altitude buzzes.

Our next camp on the mountain was at a place called *Nido de Condores* (17,600 feet), which, roughly translated, means "hundreds of piles of human excrement," I think (*Nido*, ironically, is also the most common brand of dried milk in South America, making one wonder about its contents).

On Aconcagua with the Wal-Mart Climbing Team (1996)

Anyway, the night at Nido was most uncomfortable. I estimated the wind speed at easily five hundred miles per hour, and the old "WT" was under so much pressure that all night long it performed magical gymnastic feats that—like these stories—defied rational logic (you know, as opposed to *irrational logic*). With every mighty gust, the WT would spiral in on itself and squash flat against our chests. Then, when the gust had passed, the entire dome would spring back into shape, like a balloon that's had pressure taken off of it. This compression and expansion was so dramatic that—when I got up to pee—the old WT looked more like a hyperactive, blue-nylon iron lung than a form of temporary dwelling.

At around 3:00 A.M., the wind got so powerful that Benny and I decided we'd better do a status check. A seam near the door looked ready to pop, and the prospect of sitting among the excrement with no tent to shield us from the view meant this was serious. Outside, in a howling gale, we found that the tiny strings holding down corners of the tent were breaking. The tent was ready for liftoff and a fast ride to Africa.

"We better get back in and weigh it down!" Benny screamed.

The rest of the night was spent with us sprawled out inside, pushing down as much floor area as we could touch. We prayed for the WT and sang songs to keep our spirits high. A form of bizarre exorcism was underway. Finally, after an eternity, dawn broke to the east, and the wind died down. By this point I was so maladjusted from the altitude that I wanted to go down. I had spent two nights without sleeping a wink and I was hallucinating like crazy—I think.

"This serious business of walking around in the gravel will have to wait a day or two," I suggested.

Benny agreed, and we left the bulk of our gear and descended to Plaza de Mulas, where we spent two nights in the Plaza's big, square hotel, which had no heating system whatsoever. The odd thing about this hotel is that it has a rule (or at least it had a rule back then) that you couldn't wear boots inside it. Most of the other occupants seemed to have camp booties, or slippers, or other footgear. I had cheap wool socks from (you guessed it) Wal-Mart, and my feet froze. This place was so cold I could see my breath while I unsuccessfully pleaded for the heat to be turned up.

Still, it was an interesting place. In the "lounge" part of the hotel—a meat locker with no meat but with some armchairs and a coffee table and about four Europeans dressed in enough clothing to outfit an arctic assault unit—Benny and I met two guys trying to do the first Greek ascent of Aconcagua.[4] They told us about flying to Chile with Aeroflot, the infamous Russian airline with confusing flight routes. They had boarded their flight in Athens and flown to Frankfurt. From there they flew to Shannon, Ireland, and from there to New York. From New York they had flown to Chicago, Chicago to Miami, and from Miami to Caracas, and from Caracas to Lima, then finally on to Santiago. All told, the "flight" had taken them three days. They had had to load their luggage themselves, and they had been given coupons for cafeterias in various airports—there was no onboard food. Still, it seemed like a nice warm-up misadventure for the gravel-stomping of Aconcagua.

In the morning, feeling fit as fiddles, we walked back up to Nido de Condores, packed up the tent and gear, and carried on to Berlin Camp. This section of the march was sort of strange because we passed the carcasses of several horses (is *that* why it's called Plaza de Mulas?), making one wonder what had happened to their owners. Berlin Camp was an ugly place, strewn with trash and frozen human excrement in just about every place we looked. There were several huts at Berlin Camp, all extremely disgusting erections, so we came up with the clever idea of setting up the Wilderness Trails tent inside one of the huts, a sort of condom for the muck.

We overcooked another pot of noodles and went to bed. I wasn't bothered by the altitude this time, but I was bothered by the cold. It was freezing. In the morning, an American chap we met told us the temperature had dipped to forty below. Considering we had fiber-filled sleeping bags, fleece clothing, and leather boots (and not a lick of down), it was somewhat remarkable we hadn't just frozen in place, like one of the thousands of turds we had passed.

The next day, about our seventeenth on the mountain, was to see our summit bid. We packed up our frozen water bottles (I have no idea why, they certainly weren't going to be of any use to us in minus-forty conditions), pulled on our leather boots and shell gear, and trudged off into the wind.

As I pointed out earlier, Aconcagua is considered by many the highest "trekking peak" on Earth. But I found stomping up a gravel trail at over twenty thousand feet on Aconcagua to be the coldest, most monotonous, and frankly, the strangest "climbing" experience I've ever had. Don't get me wrong, I enjoy walking—whether on gravel, snow, mud, grass, cement, or young coworkers—and think it a fine expenditure of time, and I'll do it any day of the week. But on Aconcagua, walking to the summit is the entire experience. There is no "journey," as over-philosophizing wankers like to pretend. There's no challenge in getting there. There's no enjoying *the experience* over *the summit,* as a lot of goofy spiritual shucksters describe mountain climbing. Aconcagua is about walking around in gravel, finding tent sites that are not atop piles of human waste, and getting to the tallest damned summit in the Western Hemisphere. Period.

My problem during our summit bid (and why the heck is it called a *bid?* This isn't a darn auction.) was the simple fact that my feet were freezing. I couldn't feel them any longer, and I was getting scared that I was really screwing them up. I expressed all this to Benny, who looked as miserable as I felt. He suggested we stop and attempt to warm up my feet. We halted at a place that was out of the fiercest blasts of wind (no place was out of the gale altogether) and he unzipped the front of his jacket, fleece linings, and shirts. I pulled my feet out of my boots and stuck them against his bare chest.

Now, I doubt that you've ever pressed your four-week-dirty feet against another man's chest, but it was my first time and I found the whole thing bizarre. Benny did too, I'm certain. People just don't do this sort of thing in polite company. People who are polite wear plastic boots and keep their feet warm and don't go pulling them out at critical life junctures. And they certainly wouldn't ask to press them close to another's bosom without thoroughly washing them. All this reaffirmed my feeling that climbers are flat-out self-absorbed.

The other point about the whole feet-on-bare-chest thing is that it's absolutely bonkers. My feet were already deep inside three pairs of wool socks, then inside some sturdy (though admittedly thin) leather boots. Yet somehow I believed taking off all those socks, exposing them to minus-forty temperatures and Hurricane Aconcagua before sticking them on my dying friend's frozen chest would warm them up.

My judgment has always been questionable, but the toes-on-tits idea seemed exceedingly rational at the time because it's what you learn about people doing on very big mountains when they get very cold tootsies. In fact, anyone who's ever read old mountaineering books knows—because it's an unstated law—that putting malodorous dogs on a fairly clean abdomen is how you address severely butt-numbing temperatures (warming the butt is a different issue). In hindsight, it was the most cockamamie thing I could have ever schemed up, and, as Benny winced at first the coldness of my feet and then their scent, an expression that said "never-believe-anything-you-read-about-climbing" came over his strained face.

Predictably, it didn't work. Benny's chest felt colder than my feet, and as I put two stumps of ice back into my thin leather boots, I realized I had to go down.

"Even one toe ain't worth it to me," I screamed at Benny in the gale. "I'm going back to Berlin to warm 'em up. Okay?"

"Okay. I'm going to keep going."

I started down and within an hour was back at Camp Berlin. I climbed into my plus-forty-degree-rated sleeping bag and did thirty-five minutes' worth of Richard Simmons. I still couldn't get warm. I stood up, in my sleeping bag inside the tent, and jumped. That didn't work. I ran in place. That didn't work. I did sit-ups, which I hate, and that didn't work. I was freezing, and there was no amount of mummy-bag athleticism that would get rid of the cold.

After an hour and a half of mad wriggling, Benny showed up.

"It's too frickin' cold," he said. "Let's get out of here."

We did a hasty pack—the kind Richard Simmons might've done—and were on the descent in no time. After about three hours' marching, I was finally warm.

As we trudged down the trail, I thought about our summit attempt and failure, about our thin fleece gear, and the boots we'd brought, about our inadequate noodle-soaked sleeping bags and about the Greeks and their climb (one of them had succeeded in the first Greek ascent but he had suffered frostbitten toes). I thought about the German doctor with the dick catheter; about Jordi and his attempt at the summit (he had turned around about where we had); and about the Thai man and his failed attempt on the first Thai ascent.

Strangely, the one thing that hadn't gone wrong, misbehaved, or simply shut us down was our tent—the mighty WT. The Wilderness Trail tent, our old pal WT, despite its humble beginnings, had proven our point, whatever that might be.

The pinnacle of success in American climbing might be membership on The North Face's climbing team, but the pinnacle of fun—always a goal of mine—is climbing a big mountain and having a really good laugh afterward. My sister's tent guaranteed us that.

1 *There are taller trekking peaks in Asia.*
2 *See www.rudyparra.com/stats.htm.*
3 *For the record, the worst invention in mountaineering is something called the "alpine start," in which you get up shortly after going to bed and proceed straight to undertake a ghastly amount of exercise.*
4 *While we were back down at the fourteen-thousand-foot level, we also befriended a man attempting the first Thai ascent.*

Luke Laeser on the north buttress of Capitol Peak.

"Chosseneering" on Capitol Peak's Big Buttress (2003)

In the spring of 2003, a friend of mine named Luke Laeser went with several other chaps to Mexico, where he established the world's biggest sport climb, called Logical Progression, on a rock called El Gigante. I wrote a brief article about it for a magazine and then began receiving all sorts of comments, criticisms, and suggestions—from the mundane to the extreme—from our climbing brethren in the non-English-speaking world, and, in particular, in the Spanish-speaking world.

I have no idea how people get other people's e-mail addresses, but a lot of very angry people seem to have mine, and all of them who were critics of the route e-mailed me.

"My stomach was ill of listening [to] what you were doing" came from a Mexican critic. It instantly became my favorite comment because, after all, that's what happens when you go to Mexico—your stomach gets very ill and you get a bout of Mexican Gravy Leg. But it went on: "I am so sad about the persons like you, because [you] don't respect other climbers and countries. You only confirm the image of the U.S.A.'s people (*ignorants*)."

I thought that was a pretty good comment, too—especially since I'm an ignorant Australian, a "Double Colonial" as one Brit recently described me, which leads, I might add, to the obvious—a Double Ignorant, if you will. Being a Double Colonial means you're allowed all sorts of freedoms not afforded a Single Colonial: things like mucking up the tea when you make it, and not caring whether you're serving watercress sandwiches or *waterlogged* sandwiches at your next swimming-pool-croquet luncheon.

But what these lively comments really prompt is the ultimate admission that the English language is troublesome—hundreds of thousands of words, many of which mean close to the same thing and have no rhyme or reason as to pronunciation. Spanish, as you well know, is delightfully well-ordered and sensible. Every written letter makes a sound, and there are very few double or triple (or more) meanings for words.

After I had received all these wonderful commentaries via my e-mail (and forwarded them to Luke) and apologized to the aforementioned Spanish brethren that our language was a shambles, we decided we should go and look at bigger potential bolting projects. Near my home is a wonderful chunk of falling-to-bits rock called Capitol Peak. We thought we'd go explore.

Capitol Peak has made a few Colorado climbers famous—at least in part. Capitol Peak is a lovely bit of topography, rising on its north side a couple thousand feet above a lake of the same name. The northern aspect of Capitol is a warped, undulating wall of sorts, a forty-five-degree washboard of gullies, buttresses, and couloirs where rockfall is constant and route-finding is a matter of following protection, or avoiding choss.

This face has been the object of desire for several generations of climbers. In 1936, the famed Colorado mountaineer Carl Blaurock, along with Walter Scott, Evelyn Runnette, and Dudley Smith, attempted a "couloir filled with loose and rotten rock" and gained the 12,600-foot level, then retreated. Blaurock returned the next summer and completed the route with Elwyn Arps and Harold Popham. In 1952, another route was pioneered by local climber Bob Craig (author of *Storm and Sorrow*), along with Sandro Sabbatini and Richard Wright. The late George Bell, along with David Michael and Michael Cohen, climbed a new route on the face in 1963—as did others in those Golden Years of Colorado mountaineering.

How Capitol became *most* famous, though, is for the winter ascents. The first recorded winter ascent was in 1966, by Matthew Wells, Karl Arndt, William Roos, and Charles Carlin via the regular route. In 1972, legendary German-born ski-mountaineer Fritz Stammberger and Gordon Whitmer made the first winter ascent of the north face of Capitol, taking "eleven hours of face climbing— twenty-two-hundred feet of ice, packed snow, wet and dry rock to the summit. A bivouac on top."

Bivouacked at the base of the mountain, we ran into several other folks climbing the peak. One of them, who claimed to be a beginning climber named Jeff, seemed to know everything about mountaineering there was to know. He also suggested Capitol was so loose that we should take a crowbar up and pry off the loose bits.

Up on the climb, we admitted Jeff was correct and that a crowbar would've been the best bit of gear to have—beginning climbers seem to know a lot these days. The only problem with prying off the loose bits would be the time required: several millennia. Climbing on big mountain faces really is a sport unto itself, especially if said faces are falling apart like plastic surgery in a horror flick.

As we lumbered away, Luke coined the English-language term *chosseneering,* but it seemed there were many other words to describe our activity: *trundleering, rockeneering, taluseneering.* In fact, any word describing questionable geology that works with the suffix "-neering"—*crapeneering, crudeneering, junkeneering, pileneering, heapeneering*—seemed a fairly appropriate description of whatever it was we were doing. Had the mountain been made of slate, we could've been *slateneering.*

Then again, that's the beauty, so to speak, of English. Although Spanish and other tongues are well-ordered, what Spanish climber can say he went *junkeneering* last weekend? If I submit this piece to the folks at the *Oxford English Dictionary* (OED), it's possible they might add some of these terms to the always expanding collection of nutty English-language words. I bet if I submitted it to the folks at the *Oxford Spanish Dictionary* (OSD), just down the street, they'd laugh me out of the language business altogether.

The toughest aspect of the subcategory of *chosseneering* is not so much the climbing but the delicate art of *not knocking things over,* a collective term that likely has no Spanish equal except, maybe, *peligroso.*

On Capitol's north face there are many teetering, gravity-excited parts of the mountain all too eager to make contact with your partner's head. Dunno about you, but I'm like a bull in a china shop. If it's delicate, and if it can be knocked over and broken, I'll back my Unimog into it. Helmets are the most underappreciated bit of gear.

On the summit, Luke found he'd dropped his hiking boots, so he walked off in climbing shoes. We arrived back at the bivouac, and he did a fast deal with one of Jeff's friends by buying a pair of his hiking boots (he, oddly, had two pairs) for the several-mile walk out.

We humped our way back along the track, sweating in the stifling heat and laughing at the idea of prying all the loose rock off Capitol. It had been a good day out—not climbing, not mountaineering. Not hiking, camping, or experiencing wilderness. It had been a good day *chosseneering.* I might be a Double Ignorant, but at least I have the luxury to tell the wife I wasn't actually out *climbing* this weekend.

Overhangs and Hangovers at California's Real 'Trad' Area (1990)

My fingers trembled and my feet skated about. My head pounded. I reached up to clip a rusty old bolt hanger that looked about as solid as a newspaper yacht in a gale. I snagged it with the 'biner and skooched my waist up against the bolt: "Take . . . err, no, don't take. Just take out the slack. I'm going to barf."

My belayer Dan McCollum and I were trying to get up a short route called Post Orgasmic Depression, or POD, a short rock climb at Pinnacles National Monument. Our problem was that we had spent the entire previous evening imbibing inappropriate volumes of alcohol, in celebration of our friend Steve Porcella's impending marriage to a gal named Sandy.

The Alcoholics Anonymous people would've had a field day with us. Lacking any kind of organizational skills, Dan and I had decided that a few days cragging at Pinnacles would constitute Steve's bachelor party—actually wait! Let me clarify that. Lacking any kind of organizational skills, Dan and I had decided a few days cragging at Pinnacles while severely hungover would constitute a superb bachelor party—you know, because it does everywhere.

In November 1990, we loaded up Dan's half-seater Micro (a Japanese model, still not yet available in the rest of the known commuting world) with about forty crates of 15-percent beer for five people for two days, climbed onto the roof, and aimed the Micro north from our then-homes in the suburban bliss of Los Angeles. We spent two days with some of the worst hangovers the world has ever seen, clinging gingerly to the edges of Pinnacle's crumbling boulders and trying not to fall off of them. But during those moments when our heads did clear, we were rewarded with a magical climbing experience in a land of grottoes and caves and overhanging walls.

So, I was having a hard time focusing on POD, as it's known, to which I curtly introduced you at the beginning of this alleged piece of literature.

California has long had a ground-up climbing tradition,[1] not unlike many British and a few European crags. The heroes of the 1930s' golden era of California mountaineering (Brower, Eichorn, Bedayn, Dawson, Leonard, etc.) had set a standard that was built upon by Yosemite's pioneers of the late 1950s and '60s, creating the attitude that if it doesn't start at the bottom, it ain't real climbing.

But in the late 1980s, as rappel bolting swept across the North American continent the way sores from a venereal disease spread across the human nether regions (the similarities between the two processes are quite striking), many California climbers began experimenting with rappel bolting. Whole crags went up (often overnight) and even the venerated shrines of traditional climbing (Yosemite and Joshua Tree) saw the establishment of many, many rappel-bolted routes.

But tucked away in a backwoodsy area of California's Coast Range, Pinnacles National Monument missed out on that new wave of climbing styles and it remains, to this day, possibly California's most traditional climbing area. During our visit, we found out just how traditional.

The morning after we had arrived at Pinnacles, Dan and I stumbled into the ranger station to ask about potential closures on routes, and other such issues. The ranger, it turned out, was Dave Rubine, a local climber and guidebook author who was then putting the touches on his latest edition. He walked Dan and me over to the nearest route, which had about two bolts in eighty feet, and he studied my every tremble while I climbed it. (Luckily, Ranger Dave didn't notice the souvenir handhold I pulled off at about the forty-foot mark.) When I nervously reached the top, Rubine pronounced me fit to climb in Pinnacles and then walked away. I, of course, pronounced myself unfit for any more climbing at Pinnacles, and we beat a hasty retreat to the campsite, where several thousand bottles of beer eagerly awaited our return.

"The Pinnacles is a serious climbing area with many difficult routes," wrote Paul Gagner, author of the 1983 guidebook. "Not only will you find some long runouts, loose knobs and bad bolts, but Friend and nut placements can be marginal in the soft rock" (and thank you for an uplifting and inspiring call to arms, Paul).

But, of course, Paul's right. The history of Pinnacles climbing is as varied as the movements you make squirming into a pair of 1971 bell-bottoms. During the 1930s, Sierra Club members used the area for practice climbing. In 1947, a guy named John Salathé (hmm . . . that sounds familiar) climbed a formation called the Hand, a route that frightens parties today, despite the addition of several bolts. Yosemite climbers of the '50s and '60s came and went, including Jim Bridwell, Steve Roper, Al Steck, Chuck and Ellen Wilts, Mort Hempel, Joe Fitschen, and Glen Denny.

But it wasn't until the late 1970s that Pinnacles got its reputation. A group of Bay Area climbers, including Chris Vandiver, Tom Higgins, Frank Sarnquist, Barry Bates, and Rupert Kammerlander, established a handful of routes with horrifyingly long runouts and—for the period, before rock gyms in every basement—very hard climbing. Higgins's 1980 story in *Ascent*, "Anti-Climbing at Pinnacles" sealed the deal, making routes like Shake and Bake legends of mythic proportion.

Most of the bolts placed at Pinnacles were, until this decade, those little quarter-inchers you still find throughout much of California: scary, old, and miles apart. In the early '90s, a group of new route activists (Tom Davis, Kelly Rich, Rubine, and Gagner, among others) began using 3/8-inch bolts and, but for a very few exceptions, the routes still went in on lead, hand-drilled from hooks, making them "sporty" as Austin Powers's teeth, or the plot lines in these stories.

After suffering through another raucous all-nighter in the sub-zero temperatures, Dan and I awoke with renewed enthusiasm. Steve, the groom-to-be, had arrived the previous evening, and it was his turn to sweat.

We crawled through a tunnel and came out on the other side of something called the Monolith: a massive chunk of stone sitting squarely in the middle of one of Pinnacles' prettier valleys. Steve quickly climbed something called Foreplay, which we then all top-roped. That's how I got to POD, and my hangover came back. I moved past the spinning hanger and wobbled up the wall, pulling on huge knobs tilted at crazy angles and jutting from all over the place. With bile rising in my throat, I pulled the top of the Monolith and relaxed. Someone named this route sorta well. I lowered off, my eyes blurry, and Steve and Dan top-roped it.

We then wandered around to see what we could see, climbing routes where we could count the bolts from the ground and avoiding those that had "FA: Vandiver or Higgins" after the route description in the guidebook.

We ended up doing at least a couple climbs during our two-day visit. No one took any big whippers, but in the middle of our stay, the nearest town—Coalinga, California—opened a Pinnacles branch of the AA. They set up an office next to Rubine's and held hourly meetings. And I must say, despite some sordid confessions and desperate therapy sessions, Steve's last few days as a free man were some of the best of his climbing life. Maybe.

---

1 *A ground-up climbing tradition is not one that is shredded like hamburger meat; rather, it's one in which the local ethic requires one to climb from the bottom and worry about the protection as you go. That said, there are several places in the state with ground-up (i.e., a nonsensical mixture of styles existing side by side) climbing traditions.*

Balls to the Walls
with Warren Hollinger (1996)

"What's the matter?" inquired the voice.

"I don't know," I said, honestly, trying to figure out why I'd lost enthusiasm for the wall, especially since I was halfway up one of the prettiest pitches I'd ever led in my life. "I'm just not into it."

My partner, Warren Hollinger, sat patiently on the ledge below, wondering what was wrong. At Warren's urging, I worked up a little higher, drilled a hole for a bolt, one next to it for a pendulum, then strung the two together and set up a belay. Warren cleaned the pitch and dangled next to me.

"You okay?" he asked.

"Fine," I said. "Just not into *it* today, the way I should be. No motivation."

Warren took off up the crack above me, moving quickly and efficiently, not comprehending a lack of motivation for any reason. He'd never had to deal with that, and likely never would. That's just how Warren was: motivated to the core, no matter what the game.

It was late 1996, and Warren and I were four days out, on the west face of Mountain of the Sun, a two-thousand-foot sandstone face in Zion National Park. We had climbed and hauled roughly twelve hundred feet of beautiful crack systems and desperate "jungle pitches"—areas of the mountain that were part rock, part foliage, and a wholly logistical nightmare. We had cursed, laughed, and struggled our way up more than half the beautiful line we were climbing.

At the time, the then-31-year-old Warren was midway through becoming one of the most experienced and driven wall climbers on the planet, even though he had been climbing a mere seven years. He had already pioneered new routes on Baffin Island and in the Bugaboos, and he had spent countless months in Yosemite slugging away in the vertical world.

I stumbled into Warren at a trade show in early 1996 and struck up a conversation. I immediately liked him. He was warm, friendly, and enthusiastic about *everything*: a combination sweetheart to his friends and tiger to the mountains. We made plans to climb in Zion National Park the following fall.

After meeting at the Watchman Campground, Warren and I drove up and down the canyon, looking at formations and pondering crack systems. I pointed out a number of the small, red-colored thousand-foot walls and explained that the first thousand feet of rock had generally the best rock quality. Warren, of course, was looking at only the biggest formations, the really stunning mountains. At the visitor center, we scanned the route registry books and looked at what had recently been done, and what there was to do. Then he walked over to a scale model of the park.

"What's that?" he asked, pointing at what looked like the biggest wall on the most elegantly shaped formation.

"Er, Mountain of the Sun," I said, double-checking the key to the model.

"Well, then that's it, right there!" he said smiling. "That's what we'll do."

And so we were off, spending six days in the vertical realm.

Ordinarily, my a lack of motivation on Pitch 11 would've been a huge problem, as during that period I was generally climbing with several youngsters who left the bulk of the leading up to me. With Warren, this sort of thing wasn't even an issue. He took off and led four of the remaining five leads, even though it was his first time on sandstone. I just jugged and tried to make myself useful, and, I'll admit, under his razor-sharp gaze, I felt a bit like a kid who had no idea why we were there. He ordered me about during the descent and I withdrew into a shell. Warren was, without question, the most focused, most driven wall climber I've ever met—to the point where it almost felt as if demons were whipping him, propelling him onward whatever the situation.

We topped out and, as a massive storm began brewing on the western horizon, rapped back to Earth. The first drops of sleet hit us as we humped our loads back to the road. Just another two-thousand-foot, casual jaunt for Warren; a gut-busting drain on body fat for me.

In the larger scheme of things, Warren's climbing career was nothing short of amazing. He was born in Canada and raised there to the age of ten; then his family moved to Hawaii, where he grew up. Warren then made his way to California, where he became a stockbroker. His wild and creative personality called for thrills and, at one point in 1988, he tried skydiving. He loved it but found that the thrill of being up in the sky for only a few minutes wasn't enough. "I wanted to stay up there longer," he later told a fellow stockbroker. His business colleague suggested he try big wall climbing, and within months, Warren had quit his job and was climbing full-time.

That was in 1989. By the mid-1990s, Warren had done about twenty Yosemite walls and was a full-time Valley resident—and a very hardcore climber. He was also starting to adventure abroad, and in August 1994 he traveled to the Bugaboos, where he and British climber Jerry Gore established a new route on the west face of North Howser Tower. At the summit, the pair was struck by lightning; it's something of a miracle they survived.

In 1995, Warren went to Baffin Island with Mark Synnott and Gore and knocked off the first ascents of the 19-pitch *Crossfire* on the Great Cross Pillar and the 19-pitch *Nuvualik* on the Turret. The trip showed Warren at his finest: focused, driven, and not entirely tolerant of any sign of weakness.

Indeed, the British magazine *High,* with information from Gore, went on to report, "The climbing [on Great Cross Pillar] was immediately demanding and several hard aid pitches only fell to some inspired leading by the talented Canadian Hollinger. Several lengthy sections were climbed entirely on copperheads, sometimes a string of number ones."

After the Great Cross Pillar route, and with their pick-up date of June 24 rapidly approaching, the three climbers had only ten days to squeeze in another climb. They fixed five pitches on the Turret, then made a fast, lightweight ascent, reaching the summit and returning to the fjord in forty hours.

"The trio had no time for a proper rest on their return as the Inuit team arrived with some urgency to transport them . . . back to Clyde River," *High* reported. "The sea ice was already beginning to break up

. . . and the group had an epic escape. Bogged down in melting ice and without the manpower to effectively move their equipment and sinking skidoos, they were fortunate to run into a much bigger party of Inuits who came to their rescue."

Synnott later wrote about Warren's firey personality when, descending from the ascent of the Great Cross Pillar, the two had gotten into an argument over the line of descent. More telling was Synnott's time in base camp: "I wanted to milk the rest at base camp as long as possible," he wrote. "If we had let him, Warren would've probably started hiking loads [to Polar Sun Spire] immediately." The three did their second route, on the Turret, but Polar Sun Spire was already a done deal in Warren's eyes.

Polar Sun Spire is a boat-prow-shaped mountain that rises 4,400 feet above Sam Ford Fjord, a huge chunk of rock that has few equals on Earth. In the summer of 1996, Warren and Synnott returned to Baffin Island (with Californian Jeff Chapman) and, in late May, started up a route they thought would take them a whole month to complete.

"Though none of us could truly conceive of the depths we would have to dig to pull off such an ascent," Warren later wrote, "nor even understand our own motives for enduring such a stay on a wall three times longer than any of us had previously experienced, our belief in the mission was unshakeable."

What took place was one of the most impressive big wall ascents in American history, a route that required thirty-nine days to complete and that was hailed as possibly the biggest face climbed on Earth.

Warren's 1997 *American Alpine Journal* article about the climb is one of the most interesting reads in mountaineering literature. Written in diary format, it opens with the comment: "I have absolutely no idea what day it is today, or even whether it's morning or evening . . . twenty-four-hour light affords us strategies rarely contemplated in a more southern latitude. Climbing sessions of twenty to thirty hours become the norm; our clocks now run on a thirty-six-hour day."

Climbing capsule style (in which several pitches are fixed and a hanging camp is periodically moved upward), they crawled up the wall at a rate of about 113 feet per day, the three climbers taking turns with rest days. Every third day, one of them did nothing but recuperate from the hard work of leading, hauling, and establishing belays.

"Were all a bit edgy," Warren wrote on Day Nineteen, "and probably have one lightly heated argument every day or two. Everything gets resolved and we always go back to our usual routine. Generally, food (or lack of food, that is) seems to be the source of our disagreements. . . . we've upped our rations to have more snacking food. I hope this is a good strategy."

Still, heavy lifting, bone-chilling cold, and a lack of calories weren't the only challenges. The entire climb was fraught with rockfall: "It's a bit unnerving listening to all the avalanches hitting and ice around the ledge every thirty to sixty seconds," he wrote on Day Twenty-nine. "I hear the missiles coming, and for an eternity I can't decide whether it'll be a direct hit or a near miss."

Warren's article also showed something of his personality and his taste for the extreme: "I sometimes secretly wish I could stay up here longer. On the mellow days, there seems to be no place else in the world I would rather be. . . ." The three men survived the ascent (and more importantly the descent), and the route was lauded around the world in the climbing presses as one of the grandest adventures ever undertaken. It launched Synnott and Warren as big names in the climbing community, where Synnott remains to this day.

While we toiled under the Utah sun, Warren told me about his plans for the other two climbs of his Big Three: the south face of Cerro Torre and the north face of Great Trango Tower.

"After that, I'll probably quit climbing," he admitted. "Stay focused, get the job done, then you can move on to other things."

He wasn't sure what might come next in life, but he knew his climbing career had a horizon. He had met Tony Robbins, the world-famous motivational speaker, and he thought that might be the path for him. Just an idea in 1996, but there would be something really interesting, really wonderful, beyond climbing. I was envious not only of his motivation but also of the clarity with which he saw life.

By the time of our Zion trip, Warren was already a professional climber—that is, making his living from slide shows and through product endorsement. But he also knew (as do many others) that to remain a professional climber, everything he did had to be bigger, bolder, and better (i.e., more likely to kill him) than the last thing he did—one of the reasons Chris Bonington told me in a 1992 interview why he took up adventure journalism after his so-called "Everest years."

By 1996, climbing was already wreaking havoc with Warren's life: "I was able to put blinders on and I gained tremendous personal ground," he told me years later. "But at the same time it [climbing] was the most selfish endeavor I ever got involved with. I could share parts of it through slide shows and writing, but other than that it held no real value."

Regardless, he continued on like a young bull, hauling his demons around with him.

As I contented myself with minor climbs in the lesser ranges, I watched Warren's fame grow. It was nothing short of meteoric, and well deserved.

In the summer of 1997, Warren went to the Karakoram to attempt the second of his big goals: the north face of Great Trango Tower. When he got there, he quickly realized the route was a bad idea: a low-angled wall with seracs looming ominously above it.

Warren and his fellow climbers (Wally Barker, Brad Jarrett, and John Rzeczycki) dubbed it a death trap and turned their attention to a 3,750-foot new route on the north face of the nearby Nameless Tower. On the descent, as Barker noted in the 1998 *American Alpine Journal,* the climbers fought among themselves.

At the base of the climb, Warren was hit by a falling rock "that easily could have resulted in his death," Barker wrote. "The accident occurred in the dark at the bottom of the last rappel while pulling ropes and was indirectly caused by poor communication among quibbling expedition members."

By this point in time, Warren already knew that operating at the level at which he was operating was unsustainable.

In 1998, Warren went to Patagonia to attempt the third of his now-altered list of goals—the south face of Cerro Torre—via a new route. The glaciers below the peak were so choppy that it took Warren and his partners (Russel Mitrovich and Sean Easton) five weeks just to shuttle loads to the base of the wall. They used their ropes to string together a route across the glacier below the face, but even before they reached the wall, Warren was having reservations: "I felt like that was the route I was going to die on," he said recently. "It felt good to back off." The trio instead climbed the standard Compressor Route on Cerro Torre.

In February 1999, fresh off his Patagonian adventure, Warren had a serious accident in which he took a sixty-foot fall while climbing a new route on the Rainbow Wall at Red Rocks, Nevada. The fall smashed five vertebrae, two of which were completely crushed. Remarkably, only two weeks prior to the climb, Warren had decided to get a cell phone. The Rainbow Wall sits behind several other large rock formations, and is somewhat cut off from a direct line of sight to nearby Las Vegas. When Warren's partner, Brian McCray, pulled out the new phone to call for help, the phone's reception registered about one-tenth of its normal, in-city power. The two climbers were just high enough for McCray to make contact. Had they been only a pitch lower, the phone might not have worked at all. Warren thinks that if they hadn't taken the cell phone, he'd probably be dead.

About eight hours after the accident, he was helicoptered to a Las Vegas hospital and had surgery on his spine. The damage was so extensive that surgeons went in from the side.

"They cut through my side and broke ribs to get into the front of my spine and put in a titanium spacer to replace the vertebrae bodies," Warren recalled with fondness.

He spent weeks recuperating in Vegas before finally heading home to his mother's place in Hawaii.

There, he spent months sitting around on the couch, wearing a huge brace to keep his back in place. For a long time, he could only walk with a cane. He knew his climbing career was over—at the very least—and he had been told he might not walk again. As the months after the accident progressed, Warren realized this was his break from the self-fulfilling and destructive world of ascent.

He also knew that the second half of his life had begun, and that to get through it, he needed a body that could function. He began challenging himself, getting used to the foot-long titanium rods in his back and the way they acted as a support system for the rest of his frame. "I did a lot of intensive rehab," he said. "I did a lot of walking, then fast walking—on a treadmill, then on the road—and got myself used to the jarring."

Sixteen months after the 1999 accident, Warren even ran a marathon. Then a second one. "I used them as a direction for rehabilitation," he said. "But after a while, I burned out. The hard work of rebuilding my body was mostly over, and it was time to refocus my energies into what I was going to do with the rest of my life." A year and a half after the accident, he took a job in Lanai doing industrial rigging. It lasted a couple of months, but he was quick to move on to other things.

Recently, he's started his own company, gotten married, and bought his own house. He plans to live long and live well.

Not surprisingly, Warren, who was clearly on the ultimate climbing career track—that is, one in which the stakes get higher and higher with every route—doesn't miss climbing much.

"What I miss," he said in 2004, "is the camaraderie. I don't miss being cold, wet, and strung-out on some route. I don't miss nearly dying a dozen times on some climb in the middle of nowhere. I miss knowing people the way you get to know them when you climb with them. I miss the intense bonds that are created with people that only a sport like climbing can cultivate. I did a lot of soloing, but it was never as enjoyable as going with someone else."

Perhaps the most poignant argument Warren makes is in regard to his mother, who flew out to Las Vegas after his back-breaking accident. That incident, and the subsequent weeks and months, were a torturous period for her.

"When we tell our loved ones that 'if one day I die in the mountains, then at least you know that I died doing what I loved,' it is absolute bullshit," he said. "The only person I was fooling was myself, and I used ideas like that to rationalize heading into life-threatening situations with a clear conscience."

If you think about it, Warren is on the right track and always has been. Many of us keep on climbing because we don't have the audacity to quit. The thrill of ascent, even the small climbs, is like a drug we can't stop taking. I've heard of professional climbers being on expeditions when their children are born, or being away from home and family for ten, eleven months of the year. The burden carried by their families must be enormous.

In the months after his accident, news items about Warren appeared on various websites and in various magazines. I knew that Warren had taken a prominent place in the American climbing scene, but I had no idea that he was this prominent. Clearly, his truly exceptional big-wall climbing exploits placed him on the great climbing pedestal, which is as it should be. He's done outrageous things and pushed the boat out a heck of a lot farther than most.

But in many ways, I think his truly remarkable comprehension of climbing in the greater context of life was never fully appreciated. Too bad, because if Warren has a gift for the climbing world, it's probably got little to do with grades, routes, and walls.

Right: Mike Baker on Animas Spire.
Left: the author with the now-famous hoopstick.

The Desert's Softest Rock and the Invention of Hoopsticking (1992)

One of the most unfathomably useless things I've learned after nearly two decades of climbing in the desert is that the rock varies a great deal in color, strength, composition, and roughness from place to place. This knowledge takes on a great deal of import during times of precipitation. When you're anyplace close to sandstone and it rains, you start thinking bad thoughts. The fact that nearly every guidebook to climbing in Zion National Park matter-of-factly reports that the rock there loses 66 percent of its strength when hydrated makes it hard not to pee your pants with fright—just don't pee on the rock, thank you very much.

While many climbers might argue that the Fisher Towers and Arches National Park have the softest rock in the American Southwest—and understandably so—my vote goes to a tiny slice of yellow desert near the small town of Abiquiu, New Mexico.

The slice I'm thinking of is called Ghost Ranch, and it's where the famed artist Georgia O'Keefe spent considerable time painting soft-colored, round forms that many art fans agree look like bits of the female anatomy. Today the "ranch" is a sort of art school–slash–conference center, where aspiring painters of things that look like soft-colored female anatomy spend considerable sums of money to hone their skills.

In the early 1990s, after a climbing trip to Mexico with Fred Beckey rotted out like raw liver in a sauna, Mike Baker and I returned to our then-homes near Santa Fe and pondered other objectives. We struck upon the idea of climbing the never-before-tried spires at Ghost Ranch.

The border country of western New Mexico and eastern Arizona is well-known for its canyons, cliffs, and spires. In the 1960s, many of that area's more famous towers were climbed by the golden-agers of the day—including the Californians Jerry Gallwas, Bill Feuerer, Don Wilson, Mark Powell, Steve Roper, and Chuck Pratt; and their Colorado counterparts Layton Kor, Harvey Carter, Art Howells, Don Doucette, Steve Cheyney, and Michael Dudley. These two core groups from their respective states claimed the area's most impressive spires, including the Totem Pole, Venus Needle, Navajo Needle, and Spider Rock.

But farther east and south—in places like Ghost Ranch—the land, as Mike and I soon learned, is filled with unclimbed spires and walls.

After dumping (manhandling, really) Fred at the airport in Albuquerque in February 1991, our attention pretty quickly settled on a few of these towers—especially since one of them (we called it Ghost Spire, but some Abiquiu-area folks call it Chimney Rock) is on the cover of Ansel Adams's book *Photographs of Dirtpiles of the Southwest.*

We had to climb it.

We did, a few days after we found it. On a chilly February day we humped our "gear" to the base of the shaft and studied the thing with confusion. The tower was only about a rope-length tall, but it overhung on all sides—a bit like a frozen tornado or a giant yellow carrot. There was a tunnel piercing the entire thing, about halfway up (the "eye," we called it). The only feasible-looking way up the monolith was a disintegrating crack that widened as it rose then culminated in a steep offwidth below the eye. We figured we would aim for the tunnel and hope for the best. I offered Mike the lead, but he declined, and with that quick, nervous "No thanks, Cam," I was stuck.

One of the great subsports of climbing is an activity called the Partner Ploy (also known as the Leader Follies, the Climber Capers, the Hardman Hoax, and the Sharp End Shenanigans).

In most ranges and at most crags, the Partner Ploy is a straightforward little exercise. Here's how it's played: you offer your fellow climber (usually one of your dearest friends, with whom you've suffered great physical pain in pretty mountain settings, but sometimes a spouse, parent, or child) the opportunity to lead the next section of a climb in a soft but coolly unconcerned kind of way.

You do this by offering it to them the way you might offer them a shot at washing the dishes, scooping the cat box, or changing a really sopping diaper.

The response, which you don't even wait for and are impermeable to the utterance of, is mumbled in a whimper and is promptly ignored, and you continue racking up the many devices you'll need to prove yourself a hero. You start climbing while your partner—whomever he or she is—grumbles (and usually squats) into the semifrustrating position of being your belay slave for the better part of a day.

The Partner Ploy can also be done in a less subtle, more *Sergeant Rock* kind of way. In the *Sergeant Rock* routine, you simply start pointing out everything that can (and, of course, will) go wrong: "That block in the corner—which wobbled madly last time I did this route—is definitely going to plop in the leader's lap"; "Er, sorry this rope has a few chew holes—the dog got a bit out of hand last night while we were towing Mother's car to the garage"; "Those new cams had a bit of a recall last month, but no one has died using them yet." . . . Anyway, you get the general idea: without too much effort, the lead is yours.

In the American desert, things are slightly different because the rock is more unreliable than in other places. In a new area in the desert, where the rock drains out cracks the moment you put a cupped hand inside them—well, we were about to get our money's worth.

Thus it was that I found myself armed to the teeth with ropes and oddly shaped pieces of metal alloy in an area that never had been explored by climbers and likely never will be again, and Mike had just let slip the ultimate faux pas in the Partner Ploy. As I said, I was stuck.

There was no way I could do likewise, even though that might have proved the most sensible approach to the matter. I took the "nooselike end" of the rope (an infinitely better term than *sharp end*), tied it to my waist, and proceeded to swim my way up a crack that was disgorging sand faster than my swim fins could flap it out of the crevice.

I stopped two-thirds of the way to the tunnel, dragged up a zip line that had a hammer and a six-inch bong attached, and pounded the bong deep into the crack. Then rock was so soft that it was hard to see what I was hitting after just a few blows. With that, I excreted several Hail Marys through my pores and threw my soon-to-be-lifeless body into the offwidth, which turned out to be not as bad as I thought. Shortly thereafter, I hauled myself into the tunnel piercing the tower.

Once in the tunnel, I jammed several camming units into the

mud and told Mike that everything was under control—I've never been particularly generous with the truth. Mike swam up to me and we decided—again, by nonpositive reinforcement—that I should lead the second pitch, which I did, swearing all the way (". . . bells on bobbed-tails ring, making spirits high . . .").

At the summit I banged several large pieces of metal into a crack (was that a hubcap?), knotted them together with spindly twine, and rappelled off into the wind—with the exception of the actual climbing, a rather splendid day at the crag.

The next day, we returned to climb something we called Animas Spire. It was a small tower sitting underneath Ghost Tower, and we hadn't noticed it until we were bailing off the latter. Although only fifty feet tall, it was a real pole. A huge offwidth crack split the tower, like the prongs of a tuning fork. Mike, without a word, took the rack and threw his body at the rock in a sort of spastic prostration, which actually worked—more or less—most of the way up. On top, he drilled a hole for a piton, then I lowered him off the other side. I jugged up my side (now that Mike was anchor meat on the other side), slapped the summit, left a can of Budweiser there, then was lowered back down my side of the fork—frankly, a great game of yo-yo and not much more. But Mike had, at least, extricated himself from a humiliated position in the Hardman Follies. We were both back in form and ready for some real stupidity.

Our next job was the biggest of the area's towers, a chunk of mush I later named Mount Ethan Putterman—something of an inside joke that in later years would go horribly awry, much to my enjoyment.

Mike and I spent several days trying to figure out what kind of gear would make passage up the monolith safe, and we eventually hit upon the idea of snow anchors and gardening implements, the rock being more like loose corn than sandstone.

Mike managed a bike shop, so he had the bicycle technicians there build several strange pitonlike gadgets that we called "sharksteeth" and "splades." Sharksteeth, when one was handed to me during the hike toward the tower, appeared to be sort of big, flat aluminum scraps, with forward-facing prongs riveted on the sides, sort of like badly designed fishhooks. Imagine a fishhook designer taking a fishhook and instead of making the barb go the opposite direction to the hook (so the fish cannot wriggle free), the barb is placed going the same direction as the point of the hook so that, in fact, it makes getting off the hook easier than ever. This appeared to be the strategy behind the recently invented sharksteeth, and I shuddered at the thought of actually using them.

Splades were much better. I invented splades, and although I'm no Laszlo Biro or Sookie Bang, three-foot-long garden stakes drilled to take webbing seemed like the most obvious thing to bring along when climbing an oversized pile of muck. We threw in a handful of regular pitons, a bunch of camming units and stoppers, a wad of slings, and called it good. The rack looked absolutely idiotic, but the pieces of gear had proud names and we felt our pants bulging with testosterone—apparently just our brains dangling low.

By negative ex-inclusion, I was chosen to lead the pile. The yellow rock made the rock in Arches look like concrete and the stone in the Fisher Towers feel like marble. I started digging.

Our first attempt on the spire started on March 13—it ended in failure at the base of what appeared to be a band of gypsum. With our brains tucked between our legs, we retreated.

By March 17, after days of discussion about what kind of gear to use to get up the gypsum, we'd attracted a bit of an enthusiastic though morbid following. My dad was most keen to see how I'd ascend the flaky white rock, and he decided to come along and watch the action—as did my mother, my sister, and my sister's boyfriend, Archie. While the tribe grunted up the talus cone to the base of the spire, I jumared up my fixed rope to the gypsum. I redrove the high-est of several knifeblades and began studying the next stretch of rock.

Then, Mike—who was kindly belaying in the manner of someone very happy to lose the Leader Follies—screamed at me to stop every-thing. It seemed my dad needed a belay up the gentle hike to the base of the tower. Mike yanked on my zip line (and I nearly tumbled over backwards) then threw a loop of it to my father, whom he hauled up the hike. It was the single craziest thing I'd seen in my life, and I knew it was just the start of unfathomable silliness. As soon as Dad was comfortably ensconced sprawling buttside in a flat, sandy bowl at the bottom of the climb, my highest piton popped out. The second pin popped, too. The third piece of gear down was a large Lost Arrow. Miraculously for me, but to the chagrin of my sicko action-loving family, it stopped my fall. Then, as if on cue, my mother started yelling, "Come down this instant, you silly boy! Come down here, you silly boy! You're going to get yourself killed!"

This, of course, set my father laughing and he almost rolled out of the sprawling buttside sandy-bowl position Mike had worked so hard to put him in. Luckily, though, Mike was watching. He yanked on the zip line and quickly threw my dad a loop of it to keep him from tumbling downhill to Española. I, of course, nearly fell—but that didn't seem to bother the other members of the circus.

Anyway, defeated and befuddled, I lowered off and called it a day. The next day, I dragged a Bosch (I know; don't say it) up to the knifeblades, redrove them, then drilled a three-bolt belay station in the gypsum—*safe-ish* at last. On Day Four, I jugged to my high point on the fixed rope. I clipped a new lead rope through the three-bolt belay station and started anew.

The climbing mechanics of the next few hours are likely of little interest to the reader, but suffice it to say I fought a protracted battle with some of the most horrible stone I've ever met, working my up through tilting blocks and across and right on a ledge that I literally dug as I went, before gaining a crack system that led upward.

I moved vertically up (*climbed* does not fit as the verb here) the crack system on nuts, hexes, friends, and a huge aluminum stake. It was as loose as loose gets, even looser. I must've knocked down five thousand pounds' worth of rock and soil. My camera was crushed by falling rock, my sunglasses were ground to dust, and Mike was clobbered on the head dozens of times. A backpack disappeared under the sand. Mike disappeared under the sand. My dad dug him out. Mike let out slack and walked backward, away from the rock, in an attempt to dodge the rubble.

Finally, after four exceptionally weird days, I hauled myself onto the top. The summit was made up of a strange combination of stuff—as far as I could tell, a blend of gypsum, chert, and calcite. Weirdly, there was a ditch splitting the summit. I hammered a dozen three-foot-long gardening stakes around the perimeter for an anchor, placed a bolt in one wall of the ditch, and told Mike he could ascend. He cleaned the route, swearing all the way (". . . bells on bobbed-tails ring, making spirits high . . .").

For some strange reason, I had spent several hours preparing a summit register—strange because it was clear no one would ever climb the thing again and stranger still because I should have focused that creative energy on devising some real climbing equipment. Inside the register were placed a pair of women's panties, a piece of police crime tape, a notepad, and a photo of Mount Putterman with an ink arrow pointing to the top: "You are here." We rappelled off and headed for the car, lamenting our less-than-adequate abilities in the Gear Design Department.

About a year later, while hiking around Ghost Ranch, I found another tower. Set back in a canyon behind the conference center, it was as big as Ghost Tower and Mount Ethan Putterman and kind of leaned against a canyon wall—unclimbed, too, I assumed. I called a then-high school kid I knew named Luke Laeser and we got to work.

The first couple of pitches went fine, and we gained the notch between tower and wall. Then, things got weird. The last forty feet or thereabouts of the tower were crackless, so we began the slow process of placing a bolt ladder. The rock started getting soft, so soft that I thought the bolts would not hold my weight. Luke and I descended to the ground and pondered a solution. There was a nice, even block on the summit, and we decided to attach a long sling to a pole and try to drape it over the top.

We went home, bought several sections of aluminum pole at the hardware store, attached them to one another, tied a sling to the top, and tried it out. The limp sling flapped in the breeze—totally useless in its then-current form.

"We need the sling loop to be rigid," Luke suggested.

"Yeah, like a hoop," I agreed.

We looked at each other, both thinking the exact same thing: we needed a hoop on a stick.

Round Two saw me flailing away on the side of the tower with the newly invented hoopstick, eventually snagging the top, fixing the sling, and yarding my way to the summit. I placed an anchor and Luke came up. We balanced on the summit for a few minutes, then rapped off into a strong wind.

The wife—as usual, in tow against her will—called up: "That was the most ridiculous-looking thing I've ever seen."

"Yes, but did you snap a few photos?"

Apparently she had, and they are curious scenes indeed. Inventing new gear and climbing a handful of virgin towers that look like soft female forms is always fun. But when you invent new gear that really works, it's a special treat. The sharksteeth had let us down, as had several other scrappy pieces of junk I haven't mentioned, but the hoopstick turned out to be a real winner, a trusted friend, a proven tool that boasts simplicity of assemblage with ease of use. Most climbers will never need a reliable method for snaring the summits of loose dirt clods in the middle of nowhere in a strong wind, but for those who do, I predict the hoopstick will become the gold standard.

And this is where invention becomes exciting. Social change lies at the intersection of technological development and broad availability of that technology. Just look at what Alexander Graham Bell promulgated in a few short years: In 1876, he and fellow inventor Thomas Watson invented the telephone. Two years later, the first telephone exchange—with twenty-one customers—opened in New Haven, Connecticut. By 1893, Bell (the company) was providing telephone service to roughly 266,000 customers. By 1918, ten million Bell System telephones were in service. And today, there are hundreds of millions of telephones; arguably, the world could not function without them.

If hoopsticking takes off as a subsport of climbing—like bouldering and sport climbing—I predict great things for the hoopstick. Indeed, as I write this, I'm in negotiations with Black Diamond, the gear company, which wants to produce a modified version called a Loopstick™.

Currently, we are in the middle of a very exciting period in the history of soft rock climbing, and I can't wait to see what developments will occur next. The late, great American President Teddy Roosevelt once described his idea of foreign policy as being "to walk softly and carry a big stick."

Luke and I have learned that the best way to climb crappy towers is "to walk with bowed legs and carry a big hoopstick."

Left: The Cordillera Quimsa Cruz, Bolivia. Right: Mike Walker in front of the eponymous hotel (inset).

In Bolivia's
Secret Mountains (2002)

One of the best questions ever posed is, "What rock did *you* crawl out from under?" In the summer of 2002, I had the opportunity of being the askee of such a question during a trip to Bolivia—more specifically, to the Cordillera Quimsa Cruz.

The Cordillera Quimsa Cruz is a subrange of the Cordillera Real, in the central part of this small South American nation. The northern portion of this subrange (a *sub-subrange*, if you will) is sometimes called the Araca Group, and it's characterized by granodiorite spires that have been likened to the Chamonix Aiguilles and Pakistan's Karakorum.

Just as Patagonia has been somewhat dominated by Italian climbers, the northern Cordillera Quimsa Cruz has been dominated by Germans ever since the 1930s, when a guy named Hesse undertook the first real exploration. After that, the region didn't see much action until the late 1980s, when another German expedition (dubbed the *Bayreuther Andenexpedition 1987,* which in English means "Bayreuther Andenexpedition 1987") came and went. Several other expeditions visited the southern part of the range during the 1960s, notably a Japanese expedition that bagged many peaks.

These German guys, of which there were twenty-one, managed to get into the range and in a couple of short weeks pull off all kinds of fascinating first ascents. They had great weather, big Mercedes truck support, the ability to speak Spanish, and apparently some money. They climbed about twenty of the Quimsa Cruz's wild spires and walls and made the Fatherland proud (don't you hate German precision?). Mike Walker, Benny Bach, and I, during the summer of 2002, had the entirely converse experience: little money, no Spanish, no Mercedes trucks, and Scottish weather. Still, we managed to pull off a couple of new routes in the three sunny days that we did have.

Our saving grace became, of course, a rock—a big rock, located at about fifteen thousand feet. It had obviously been the saving grace for many of the local miners who regularly travel through the range.

After we'd trekked into the area we thought would offer sufficient climbing (an area overlooking the Amazon Basin), an ongoing storm prompted us to seek out this rock and cower under it for the bulk of our two-week excursion. We called it variously The Hotel Walker, The Hotel Excremente, and The Hotel of Allpoops: It was filled with cow manure, overrun by high-altitude mice on uppers, and generally pretty disgusting.

June 29 to July 7 was a depressing stretch of time. Benny and I climbed a minor rock peak above camp in a blizzard, then two days later attempted an almost-six-thousand-meter "slog peak," but we were turned around by gale-force winds. Cowering under the rock from 4:30 in the afternoon until 8:30 in the morning (when it was finally warm enough to get out of our sleeping bags) made the experience complete. Worse, whenever one of us stood up—perhaps eight times a day—we smashed our soft skulls on the underside of our beloved rock. It was like wandering around European ruins, which were surely inhabited by midgets when they were built.

On July 7, the skies parted and for the first time on this particular trip the daytime temperature wasn't below about ball-numbing, so we decided to try a rock climb. Located right above the Hotel Walker was a spire that the German lads had named (if I'm reading their published report correctly), "Nordostl Turm" (a.k.a. "Co. Gerhard"), at 5,304 meters. So, we started up this colorfully named hummock of stone, expecting to back off after an exploratory morning. Eight hours later, after Benny had led the single most disgusting piece of rock I've ever experienced (a chimney, sides coated with moss and lichen and ice, and no gear), we topped out on the eastern ridge. The descent was close to the ascent, a confusing procession of sand-filled chutes and crumbly ledges.

The following day, we lounged about under the rock, eating thin food, drinking supposedly clean water, and farting a lot—weird water down there in Latin America. I stayed in the pit, photographing the hyperactive mice to the blaring sounds of Mike's *National Geographic* theme-tune humming ("dah-da-da-DAH-da, dah-da-da-DAH-da").

On July 9, we were at it again, on yet another huge slab above camp—part of the Nordostl Turm complex. This time, the twelve-hundred-foot route offered easier climbing but harder living. We'd all been suffering from bouts of diarrhea, so energy levels were miniscule and nappy loads pretty large. We trudged back to the Hotel wasted, and passed out sub-rock.

The following morning, after another six inches of snow had dropped outta nowhere, a local caballero we'd hired to haul a few things (his skinny horses carried about thirty pounds of stuff while we hauled about ninety pounds apiece) came to take us home. We gladly bid adieu to one of the most interesting mountain ranges we'd ever seen, vowing to return with a Mercedes truck, a workable understanding of Spanish, money, and a few indentured German porters.

Nordostl Turm certainly could use a few more routes, and it was one of two dozen peaks within spitting distance that offered huge cliffs, unknown, unseen, and unexplored by the climbing world. This is a mountain range worth the hassle—despite the dented skulls.

It's me, Benny, and Paul.

Bright Lights, Ciudad Grande

I. It's Winter. Do You Know Where You Are?

You live in Los Angeles. You hate Los Angeles. In Los Angeles you spend every day and many hours of every day driving around. Driving is like television: it shrivels the brain. Everyone in Los Angeles is shriveled you are shriveling too. A small voice inside you insists you get out, get away, do something—"hey," the voice says, "how about a mountain climbing trip."

Good idea, you think. But where?

You head to the nearest climbing store for inspiration. This gear shop has many books. One of those is R.J. Secor's *Mexico's Volcanoes*. It sits on the edge of the shelf. You pick it up, not realizing that this will become a large mistake.

Mexico's volcanoes fascinate you. The climbing is easy and high, and the weather in January is sunny. There are wonderfully cozy huts on the mountains, and Popocatapetl has a lodge at thirteen thousand feet.

You buy the book and go home. At home, you think about the amount of mountain climbing you have done lately, which is none. Popo is a good idea for starters.

Traveling in Mexico alone is like playing Monopoly alone—very weird. You decide to enlist a companion. You call Benny in Boulder. Benny says yes, he'll climb volcanoes. Benny also suggests Nepal, China, and Ecuador because Benny is quite mad and is ready for anything. You want to believe that Benny will go to Mexico, but you are not sure. A brain like his can go through many shifts before it settles on a decision. You hate Benny's spontaneity. You wish you were spontaneous. You hate Benny.

You call Paul in San Diego. Paul says he'll definitely go, and that he's very excited about the Mexican volcanoes. You trust Paul. Paul is reliable. He will go if he says so. You wish you were reliable. You hate Paul.

You meet at your parents' house in New Mexico. Benny has brought a friend named Charles. Charles is skinny and tall and kind of strange, like you. For twenty minutes, while Charles repacks his backpack, you watch him out of the corner of your eye. Charles finishes repacking and asks you what you're staring at. You hate Charles.

The four of you ride to Santa Fe with your parents. Your mother asks you where you are going, why you are going, how long you'll be gone, when you'll be back, and whether or not you packed clean underwear.

"South. Because. Twelve days. In January. No."

The car swerves into the nearest department store. Your mother buys you a packet of BVDs. Your friends snicker. You hate your mother.

You arrive on schedule at the Greyhound bus station in Santa Fe. This is the first of many bus rides you will take over the next several weeks. You are traveling by bus because it is cheap and you are broke.

Benny suggests you bring refreshments on the bus ride. You and Benny walk to a nearby 7-Eleven. On the bus you break out the refreshments. Benny also breaks out a small round can of chewing tobacco. You've never had chewing tobacco but it looks like a bit like fibrous Vegemite, so it must be okay.

You take a handful. Now your mouth is full of chew and the bus crunches over a large object. You swallow. Hard. Your head goes numb. You try drinking some juice and your stomach churns. The bus crashes over another large object.

Now you are on your knees in the toilet compartment of the Greyhound. How did you get here? You feel an eruption. Lava. Quaking. Volcano-like. You are glad you have unflagging concentration on your mountain climbing objective. Still, you are an idiot and that's not likely to change in this lifetime. You wonder what comes after that.

When you get to El Paso, you revive. You get off the jostling bus. You almost remember what it means to not feel queasy. You exchange dollars for pesos. It's 2,200 pesos for every dollar. You feel rich.

Juarez is the first place you experience in Mexico. After you dis-embark, you find the bus to Mexico City and buy another bus ticket. It costs fifty-six thousand pesos. Pesos now don't seem like such a good idea.

After two more queasy days you reach Amecameca, a village east of Mexico City. Over the rooftops of the buildings are two enormous mountains. They disappear in the clouds. You stare at them, frozen. These are big mountains. You have hiked up fourteeners before, but these . . . . You feel queasy. You wish you were back on the bus.

Wandering around Amecameca is fun. Everyone smiles and calls out to you. Most of the townsfolk shout, *"Tlamacas!"* You think this means "hello." You shout back, *"Tlamacas!"* You like Mexicans. They are so friendly.

Out in the street Charles pulls out your guidebook. "Hey guys, Tlamacas is the name of a place." You wonder how Charles pilfered your guidebook. Apparently, the friendly locals are taxi drivers who want to take you to Tlamacas, the lodge on Popocatapetl at thirteen thousand feet. The locals need your pesos, not your friendship. You pay ten thousand pesos for a ride to Tlamacas. You hate pesos.

II. The Department of Ash and Gravel

At Tlamacas you can't breathe. You stagger into the lodge and rent a bunk. Paul, Charles and Benny follow. They can't breathe either. A Mexican ranger shows you the attic. He points to some cushions on the floor. You don't care where you are. You just want to lie down. You lie down. You stay down.

Two days later you are ready to climb the mountain. You worry that this isn't your day. You wish you could check your horoscope in the *Tlamacas Times.*

Benny and Paul are climbing Popo with you. Charles is too sick. You think he may die. Paul tucks Charles into bed and hands him your guidebook: "Here. You keep this for us." Paul has just given Charles a reason to live. Paul is clever. You hate Paul even more.

Outside, it is dark. Luckily you've remembered a headlamp. There are hundreds of small lights all over the mountain. Maybe thousands. This makes you hate mountain climbing. You thought you were a rugged individual because you climbed mountains. You aren't.

You catch up to another climber on the mountain. His name is Risto. Like you, Risto is from Los Angeles. He joins you and Benny and Paul as you climb up El Ventorillo.

El Ventorillo is the direct route up Popocatapetl. You like the idea of a direct route. Steep. Hard. Dangerous. El Ventorillo is not. It is a grunt up ash and gravel. You take one step forward and slide back thirty feet. You are climbing Popocatapetl several times in one trip. You feel like Sisyphus. You start pushing a rock.

At 9 A.M. you reach the Queretamo hut. Its placement on the slope is strange. You go inside and peer out. The hut is tilted. Queretamo, you decide, is designed to out-slide lava. You leave the hut quickly. Carefully, too. The Queretamo hut is surrounded by human excrement.

Another fifteen hundred feet and you reach the Teopixcalco hut. More poop. Above the Teopixcalco hut is a glacier. You pull out your crampons. Crampons are neat-looking. You feel tough owning crampons. You got yours cheap at a garage sale. They are very old and have long straps, but they were very cheap.

In forty minutes you still haven't got your crampons on properly. You want to huck them off the mountain. You try to remember you are a tough mountain climber.

You reach a crevasse. Now you really can't breathe. You are going to vomit up your lungs. Your crampons are falling off. You curse and complain, but cursing takes your breath away. You shut up. You crawl groggily up to the summit.

Paul arrives at the summit first. Benny second. You third. Lungless and groggy. Risto doesn't arrive. Risto has disappeared. You spend twenty minutes on the summit. Popo is a beautiful mountain. It is round and tall and you are on top. It has a massive crater. There is a small orange hut on the summit. The hut is in terrible condition. Benny tries to push the hut into the crater, but it is too heavy. You descend.

By 3 P.M., you are back at the Tlamacas lodge. Many other climbers are there. Several hundred are from Boulder. Several dozen are from Denver. A handful are from Salt Lake City. One is from Mexico. You left Boulder because there were too many climbers. Now you are back in Boulder, only it has moved. You wonder if Eldorado Canyon is full of Mexicans in January. You doubt it.

As much as you dislike the lodge, it has a bed in it. You climb the stairs to the attic. Charles is still there. Inside his sleeping bag. You think about your guidebook. It's somewhere in there too.

Charles and Benny go home after six days. Benny had to get back to his job in Boulder because he has a career. You tell Benny you are "between situations," which means you are unemployed. You have stayed around to climb since you have nothing else to do. You wish you had a career to return to. You hate Benny even more.

Two days later you climb Iztaccihuatl with Paul. A taxi picks you up at 4 A.M. By 5 A.M. you are exhausted. You have just spent an hour hiking the trailhead road, walking alongside a taxi that was supposed to carry you. Instead, you are carrying pieces of the taxi.

You say goodbye to the driver and begin walking. The trail crunches underfoot. At 10 A.M. you reach a hut. It has fallen to pieces over the years, torn to shreds by the incessant wind. You are being torn to shreds by the incessant wind. Your lips have lost their outer layer of skin three times already. Cold sores have formed on all four sides of your mouth. You look like a leper. You guess the wind is blowing one hundred fifty miles per hour. Paul suggests a bigger number. Maybe two hundred.

You pass two more huts. Like all the other huts you have passed, these are surrounded by human excrement and toilet paper. It is very important to watch your step when you climb the Mexican volcanoes. You haven't watched yours. Now you have poo on your shoe.

You climb to what you think is the summit of Izta. It is not. You climb to what you now think is the summit. It is not. You climb again to a point that you believe is the summit. Then you climb some more.

One crampon has fallen off and flops behind your foot. You are mad. You visualize a smelter and liquid crampons. Finally you reach what you think is the summit. It is and you are glad. It is a gorgeous, sunny day and the view is forever. Izta is a beautiful volcano, but its summit is covered with human excrement. As you stand in the two-hundred-mile-per-hour-negative-forty-degree-wind, you are awed by the skill and daring of mountain climbers. And their lack of taste.

You watch your lips' fourth layer of skin tear from your mouth and blow away, across the mountain. You wave goodbye.

Descending Arista Del Sol, you run into the Boulder herd. They have ropes and impressive looking gear and fancy clothes and other stuff. You have a flopping crampon and are wearing purple sweatpants. They have taken a different route. They try to belittle the one you climbed. You want to tell them to enjoy the feces on top. But you don't. You are a chickenshit.

You can see El Pico de Orizaba off to the east. It is a striking mountain. The thick pollution from Mexico City has turned it a pretty lavender color. The peak is topped with a shimmering cap of ice. El Pico de Orizaba is the tallest volcano of all the Mexican volcanoes. You hadn't planned to climb it, but now El Pico de Orizaba is all you can think about. You wonder if the pollution makes it like climbing much higher peak.

You plead with Paul to go. He says no, he won't climb Orizaba. He has to get back to school. Paul has a real life. You wish you had a real life. You hate Paul even more.

You go to Mexico City with Paul and leave him at the bus station. He is wearing an enormous backpack, ash-clogged boots, shorts and a tie-dyed Grateful Dead T-shirt. An ice axe and crampons are strapped to the backpack. You think he looks funny. You think he looks like he is thinking the same thing about you.

Four bus rides later, alone, you are wandering the streets in a town whose name you can't pronounce. It is very, very late. Luckily, you have your guidebook. You love your guidebook. You hold it close. You smell Charles.

Your guidebook suggests that you might be lost enough to be in Tlachichuca. It says to find Senor Reyes's bunkhouse. Four hours later and you are still lost. Then you meet Senor Reyes. He takes you to his bunkhouse. There are other climbers staying in the bunkhouse. One of them is Risto.

Risto!

"I narrowly escaped the death-like claws of the dangerous Mexican Yeti who chased me into a crevasse where I bivvied for 12 days and nights, eating only icicles and toe-jam." Risto bursts out laughing. You let out a nervous giggle. You wish Paul were around. You are getting weird. You hate Risto.

The next day Senor Reyes asks a guy named Leopoldo to drive you to Orizaba's hut at 13,800 feet, where you will spend the night. Leopoldo is funny. He teaches you Spanish. He makes rude gestures and then states the appropriate Spanish word. You repeat the word. Leopoldo corrects your pronunciation. You are learning Spanish. Leopoldo laughs riotously. Leopoldo's driving is also riot-like. By the time you reach the hut your tailbone is ground to powder.

Leopoldo stops the truck at the Octavio Alvarez hut on Orizaba's northeast side. Finally, you are here. So are dozens of others. You don't need to ask where they are from. You already know.

Leopoldo drives off with a fresh load of climbers. Another taxi arrives. Ten more climbers get out. Eight of the new climbers are from Boulder. The other two are German.

You befriend the Germans. They are great people. They are wonderful. They are different. More importantly, with the Germans, you are different.

III. Sometimes a Vague Mountain

At 3:30 A.M. one of the Boulder climbers shakes you awake. He tells you your alarm clock has been ringing for half an hour. He tells you to turn it off. He is sick of it.

At 7 A.M. you reach the Jamapa Glacier. It is cold. The wind is blowing harder than ever. You struggle with your crampons. They suck. You are ready to hammer the points into foil. You don't have a hammer. Too bad. You understand that life sucks and then you die. Perhaps heaven has a crampon smelter.

At 9 A.M. you stop for water. You are at sixteen thousand feet. The ice is steep. You take note of where a slip would deposit you. Probably at the bottom. Maybe on the hazy beach at Veracruz. You consider jumping.

Hiking. Hiking up Orizaba. And up. And up. The Jamapa Glacier is enormous and blinding white. Your corneas are peeling off. You are freaking out. You better wait for the Germans.

You summit El Pico de Orizaba with the Germans. You hate the summit. Your head aches and you can't breathe. You have climbed five thousand feet to sit in gravel and feel cold. You are an idiot. What did you expect?

The Germans enjoy themselves and snap many photos. You take one photo: your feet in gravel. It is all you will remember. That and the restroom on the bus.

You descend with the Germans. It takes only three hours. It is easy. You like easy. Back at the Octavio Alvarez hut you meet the Boulderites. Leopoldo is there too. He has just arrived with yet another load of climbers. From Boulder. You wonder how much the direct flight from Boulder to Tlachichuca costs.

You will ride down the mountain in the back of Leopoldo's truck with the Germans. They are dressed in white tracksuits. They look victorious, like Olympic athletes. You wish you were German.

Leopoldo starts the truck. You drive away and the Octavio Alvarez hut disappears in a swirl of dust. You wave goodbye. Then the glacier disappears in a swirl of dust. You wave goodbye. El Pico de Orizaba disappears in a swirl of dust. You wave goodbye. The gate of the truck disappears in the dust. You wave goodbye. The Germans sitting next to you disappear in the swirling dust. You wave. They wave back.

In Tlachichuca the dust settles. The Germans come back into view. Their white tracksuits are black. Their teeth are black. Their hair is black. Their eyes are black. They don't look victorious anymore. You are glad you are not German. Instead, you are dirty and tired. You ride three buses to Mexico City and then a fourth to Guadalajara. You pass out in the aisle because there are no empty seats on the bus. The Guadalajarans think you are a bum. You are.

Four days later you cross the border from Tijuana to San Diego. Now, in San Diego, you have no money. Only a quarter that you found stuck in some gum on the sidewalk. You have a headache and Montezuma's Revenge. Badly. It is the middle of the night.

You stick the quarter in the phone and it gets stuck. You beg for another one. A passerby throws you a coin and runs away. He thinks you are a bum. You always have been.

You dial Paul's number. You hope Paul will come and pick you up. You hope he will let you stay at his house and that he has food and drink and a nice soft couch. You and Paul will laugh until late in the evening. Tomorrow, Paul will offer to drive you home.

You listen to the phone ringing. It rings a long time. You imagine his nice soft couch. The phone keeps ringing. You picture fine food. The phone keeps ringing. You think about you and Paul reminiscing until late in the evening about your mountain climbing adventures in Mexico, and how the two of you will make future plans. The phone keeps ringing and ringing. You picture this story have a completely different ending. It doesn't.

You hang up the phone, unroll your sleeping bag in the grass near the bus station, and lie down. You are an idiot.

But at least you have a book that you can start a campfire with.

A Family Hot Potato in Idaho (1991)

There is so much climbable rock in the western United States that even when one of my neighbors suggests we all go off climbing and carousing for the weekend, no one knows where to start (and really, whether to start at all, but that's another discussion).

Unclimbed rock is especially extensive in the northern western states—Montana, Idaho, and Wyoming—where jackalopes (a mythical cross between an antelope and a jackrabbit that stands eleven feet tall) outnumber developed crags and climbers ten-to-one.

For many years, Idaho seemed the least developed, at least to outsiders like me. A state better known for huge potatoes and white supremacists, it had, until recently, a scant two guidebooks: Dave

Bingham's ever-evolving guide to the City of Rocks and Randall Green's *Idaho Rock,* which is not about *all* Idaho rock—just bits and pieces of it around Sandpoint, a town in the panhandle where Randall lived for a number of years. And honestly, these two books didn't cover much, considering there are at least thirty-nine subranges of the Rockies in Idaho and that the total land area covered by the two old books was likely in the range of a few thousand acres.

In the late 1990s, Tom Lopez published a massive compendium of Idaho peak-bagging and adventure climbing in a new four-hundred-page tome, *Idaho: A Climbing Guide.*

"A lot of Idaho is *terra incognita*," Lopez wrote. "The adventurous will find that Idaho is far from 'climbed out'—there is still room to explore, still time to create your own climbing history."

I know what Tom means. In the early 1990s, I had the chance to explore Idaho and to create a little of my own climbing history. (Today, it's called "family history," and it's something of a black eye in an otherwise virtuous life.)

As it was, my new girlfriend Ann and I had just moved to Montana to work on a book about mountaineering in California's Sierra Nevada with my coauthor, Steve Porcella. We rented a shed on the outskirts of Missoula, and I began hammering at the keys while Ann spent her days at the local animal shelter doing good things with beat-up pets. Several mornings per week, Ann would remove the hammer from my hands and we'd head off to the local climbing gym, where Ann learned to climb and I honed my Fabio-like body before her appreciative eyes. The one thing I taught her was to never let go with her belay hand, her *brake hand.* Of course, weighing about one hundred pounds, Ann became so good at catching Steve's and my falls that she spent the better part of her summer dangling about near the top of the University of Montana climbing wall while Steve and I bounced on the other end of the rope near the floor.

One day in late August, I suggested we drive over to Idaho and do some *real* climbing, some *outdoor* climbing. I suggested a new route on Chimney Rock, in the Selkirk Mountains.

"Sure," Ann said. "Think I can do it?"

"You bet! When you're with Fabio and his hammer, everything is okay."

A few hours' drive later—interrupted only by a visit to the hauntingly titled Cam's Ladies Apparel in the town of Wallace—we arrived at the trailhead. We hiked the roughly three miles to the rock. When we got there, I began looking for unclimbed lines, and I soon learned a lot about Idaho climbing.

Chimney Rock is a stunning chunk of stone. It's essentially a vertical dagger of granite thrusting straight up into the sky, a sort of high mountain version of the Old Man of Hoy or Castleton Tower. The fact that there were dozens of unclimbed lines on it proved to me that jackalope hunting was a more popular local pastime than mountaineering.

Although some well-known climbers (such as Ed Cooper, David Hiser, and Fred Beckey) passed through the annals of Chimney Rock history, most of the notable climbing on Chimney Rock belongs to a younger generation that includes John Roskelley, Chris Kopczynski, Dane Burns, and Randall Green. Throughout the '70s and '80s, these four contributed a raft of excellent climbs, many of them first free ascents of old aid routes.

Amid the swirling mists of history, I pieced together a continuous line on the north face, and we set out. Ann found a comfortable rock in the sun, and I clasped the rope. Two pitches later, we were both ensconced on a ledge below a bulging wall offering a crack stuffed with moss and brown dribbles. I switched into étriers and began a long slow afternoon's worth of soggy gardening.

Of course, this being Ann's first outdoor climb, she had no reason to suspect that an active summer day in the mountains could become a freezing day in the shade on the north face of Chimney Rock (elevation 7,100 feet). She stayed true to the "never-let-go-of-the-rope" lesson better than anyone I've ever seen, so by the time I'd reached the top of the tower, set up an anchor, and asked if she was having fun, it was too late. She had turned blue and her teeth were clattering (uh-oh, Fabio make big dumb mistake). In the excitement of a first ascent, I'd forgotten all the gentlemanly skills I'd never properly learned to begin with—e.g., take care of those you love.

I rappelled down to her, then lowered her off the wall. She was hypothermic, and she looked at me with big eyes, wondering if she had had a good time, and wondering if all men were as rotten as me.

We headed for a hotel in Sandpoint, and—even though it was a hot summer day—Ann climbed into a steaming bath, where she eventually warmed up. In the days that followed, we talked a lot about what had happened, about my lack of planning on her behalf, and about our future adventures together or absence thereof.

"Climbing history," "family history," "romance gone awry"—call it what you will.

The Fabio body is long gone, we are now with children, and Chimney Rock seems a lifetime ago. And yet, every time I forget my manners, let the kid's diaper get so full that poop runs out the arms, or fail to make breakfast for anyone but myself, I'm reminded of Chimney Rock. Funny how when you "create your own climbing history," as Tom Lopez suggested, you have to live with it.

Charlie French checks out the cragging potential on Eleuthera.

2004

Bahamaramadingdong: American Sea Cliff Climbing with a Strange Genetic Secret (2000)

Question: What's wrong with the coastline of the lower forty-eight?

Answer: Besides the outrageously expensive, privately owned estates that clog access to beaches so blue-collar schmoes like me can't go surfing, it's got almost no sea-cliff climbing.

Sure. You can argue that there are a few crags right on the coast. There are a handful of ocean cliffs in Maine, a few crappy crumbly boulders at Mickeys Beach and other places in Northern California, and supposedly some seaside bouldering in Florida. But in all honesty, these cliffs are miniscule and generally as rotten as a raw egg stored in a camel's underpants. None of those gaping zawns or limestone-walled harbors such as found throughout Britain, none of the atmospheric sandstone voids such as found along the New South Wales coast, and certainly none of the wild walls of Baffin, or Newfoundland, or even Quebec.

So when spring break 2000 rolled around and my old pal Charlie French said he wanted to sail through the Bahamas and look at a cliff or two, I volunteered my wife, Ann, and myself quicker than a male porn star can say "noooooow" to the cameraman.

The Bahamas, I knew, might yield some superb sea-cliff climbing, and though they're technically not part of the lower forty-eight—or even North America for that matter—hopefully, none of you will put that into your online book reviews at Amazon.com.

The Bahamas sit upon a gigantic limestone shelf that lies a mere ten to one hundred feet under the surface of the water. This shelf— regarded by some geologists as the biggest hunk of limestone in the world—is estimated to be twenty thousand feet thick. On its upper side, it is so incredibly uniform that almost everywhere one travels in the Bahamas, the bottom of the "ocean" is no more than about thirty feet away. The captains of Spanish galleons were so impressed by the nature of Bahamian waters that they coined a term for the ocean here: *baja mar*, or "shallow sea." It makes for fabulous snorkeling.

On its eastern edge, the giant limestone shelf butts up against the fantastically deep Atlantic Ocean. The water drops off from a depth of thirty feet to something like six thousand feet. Along this strange natural border between the shallow ocean and the deep sea are a handful of long, thin, north-south oriented islands (Eleuthera, the Abacos, Cat Island, Long Island, and others).

What is most impressive, and virtually unknown to the climbing world, is that the eastern edges of these islands have fantastic limestone walls that in some cases seem endless. Certainly, some of the cliffs are only forty feet high, but in other places, they appear to be a ropelength or more.

When Charlie, Ann, and I stumbled across the three-hundred-yard-wide island of Eleuthera and gazed down on these endless untouched walls, we were floored.

"It's just like Go Garth!" Charlie yelled in the wind.

"Go Garth Brooks?" I asked. "What's that?"

"It's a crag in Wales."

"It's what we yell at country music concerts."

Gazing up and down the coast, we realized that here was the potential for five thousand routes. Even more. Maybe ten thousand or fifteen thousand. There were some cracks, some flakes, and edges that would take gear, but mostly it would be tied-off slings in the holey limestone.

"It really is like Go Garth Brooks," Charlie assured me.

We wandered over to an odd formation sticking out of the flat-topped island like a mushroom riding an Oregon cow pie. We grabbed hold. The limestone was strong and riddled with holds that felt like suitcase handles. It was so juggy that we could pull thirty-degree roofs in flimsy rubber boat shoes. And this limestone was solid. Even the tiniest arches seemed capable of supporting us members of the FBI (Fat Bastards International) Climbing Team.

"This is absolutely fantastic," Charlie yelled over.

"Go Johnny Cash!" I yelled while spiking my knee on a roof.

We bouldered until the sun set, vowing to return. We were hooked.

Why this isn't a story about Charlie French, Ann Zee Wife, and I climbing all these cliffs over the course of a month and being heroes in our own BVDs has to do with fate. We had ten days to get to Eleuthera and climb, but a broken propeller shaft, lackluster winds, and a distance of about five hundred miles to cover gave us about three hours for climbing when we finally reached the place. The other big distraction was genetics.

During our eight-day, epic approach to Eleuthera, we decided to spend some time in a town called Spanish Wells. It's on St. George's Island, a small island near Eleuthera.

Spanish Wells is a delightful place. The streets are small and neat; the people are friendly and the houses colorful. A gentle breeze blew constantly off the Northeast Providence Channel, and the beaches were stunning. We parked the boat at the local marina and wandered into the village to buy groceries. On the way back to the boat, a local woman gave us a ride in her golf cart, just because she wanted to. We liked Spanish Wells so much that we decided to stay two nights.

We soon learned, however, that the village has something of a secret. Wherever we walked around town, we saw the same two or three people. They seemed to be everywhere. Charlie was totally mystified.

"I saw that woman on the other side of town a minute ago," he said, scratching his head. "On a scooter. Now, there she goes on a bike! And there she goes driving that purple and mauve Vauxhall lorry!"

We scanned our Lonely Planet guide.

"The village dates back to the days of the Eleutheran Adventurers (of the late seventeenth century)," the book states. "This deeply religious, somewhat reticent, lily-white population follows a midwestern U.S. lifestyle, with a surprising level of sophistication, side-by-side with Swiss clean orderliness and undaunted quaintness. Intriguingly, generations of isolation have concentrated the gene pool, reflected in prevalent inbred traits. Half the island is named Pinder."

We thought we'd found paradise, but honestly, the fact that everyone was related and looked like Herman Munster's brother was kind of spooky, especially since every Pinder descendant had a serious overbite. When they spoke, it sounded as though they had lisps and their mouths were full of clam shells.

Sure, Spanish Wells had cut short our time on the sea cliffs of Eleuthera, but that's okay. I believe it would've been disastrous to the Spanish Wells gene pool if we'd found those cliffs first, then reported the cliffs to the Pinders. Heck, they might've taken up climbing. And, knowing that gene pool, I doubt they would've lasted long.

Anyway, it's out there. Endless, untouched sea cliffs yearning to be explored. And if you go, don't forget to bring along a notepad. You might pick up some potentially saleable data from your own Spanish Wells Genetics Study.

Right: Belaying on the Nose of El Cap.
Left: Our Woolly Wedgies bivouac
(note poo bag on ledge above).

Long Hauls and Hernias on El Capitan (1993)

These days, if you haven't climbed El Capitan at least seventy times you are not really a climber (you are a *something else*). Two years from now, to achieve real climberhood you will have to have climbed the Captain two hundred times, and free, and in fewer than three minutes per route. I wish you luck.

I'm not really a climber. I've only climbed El Cap once, which, in the climbing world, is sort of like being an axe murderer in normal society: it's very illegal. The route my friends and I climbed was a special "remedial" route, we were enormously slow, and—after I mellowed out a bit about the water supply—I had a really relaxing time.

The way I see it, everyone on Earth should climb El Cap once—the same way everyone on Earth should build an eighteen-hundred-foot-long French drain. Climbing El Capitan has some kind of weird status in the climbing world that is wholly unwarranted. In truth, I'd argue that nearly all types of climbing are harder than climbing any of the popular routes on El Cap. Sure, it's a bit like flossing a farmyard's worth of teeth, but it's not particularly tough (try getting a collection of bad writing published).

Nope, climbing the thing isn't too bad; *hoisting a load of heavy junk up the thing*, however, is.

My single ascent was in 1993, with two guys from Montana: Steve and Bruce. Bruce was a very good wall climber and he was very serious about it. You could tell just by looking at Bruce that he was all business. He never smiled—at least he never smiled at me. He never spoke to me either, but then again most people don't. I had heard reports about Bruce's wall climbs in Montana, and they were very scary stories. I pictured Bruce as the star of many comic books: he wore a cape, his balls were made of platinum, and he buffed them so they'd glint in the sun. Steve was just a guy I hung around and drank beer with. Steve was like me: relatively normal (relatively speaking).

Anyway, we planned our ascent of the stone for that September. On a Friday after work, I loaded up piles of old, mangled climbing gear and drove across Utah to a rendezvous with Steve in Ely, Nevada.

"Where's Bruce?" I asked Steve.

"He's already in the Valley."

"Polishing away?"

"Probably."

The next day, we drove the rest of the way to Yosemite, where we parked our vehicles and began staring at the Captain. El Capitan is very big, and when you stare at it for a while, you go insane. You need to be fairly crazy to want to lift commodious heaps of cargo up the side of a big rock.

That evening, we manhandled several enormous bags to the start of the climb, where we immediately found a small crowd of people pottering about the boulders and leaning against the trees in the thinly wooded area at the base of the wall. Apparently, these people were waiting to start the climb, too. None of them looked entirely happy about being there—actually, it was rather glum, like the scene at the guard's office when you go to visit a relative in prison.

"Perhaps we should make up a number," I suggested eagerly.

Bruce and Steve didn't laugh. No one said a word. It seemed we were destined to languish in an austere silence. We took up comfortable positions in the dirt, and fiddled with twigs, rocks, and scabs.

Now, I'm not quite sure what happened during the next few hours, but the composition of the crowd at the base of the cliff changed several times—people came, people went, people sat about with gear looking like they were going to climb something while others wandered past with backpacks. The starting point of one of the most hallowed rock climbs on Earth (the Salathé Wall) is a bit of a mecca for the maladjusted (clearly explaining our presence there, but at least we had the excuse of pretending to be climbers). What everyone was really doing was beyond my estimation.

After several hours of sitting, the crowd thinned to just us, and we started up the climb. Our plan was to fix a couple of pitches, then hump our luggage up to the high point, then descend for a night on the ground. Steve loaded up with gear and started up the first pitch. Curiously, there was a fat, red static rope dangling down from the first belay.

"What do you think that's for?" I asked.

"No clue," Bruce said.

"A handrail? A route marker of some kind? The remains of a tricky rescue?"

"Hmmm." Bruce said. Steve ignored us and kept climbing. He quickly reached the anchors and announced that he was ready to begin lifting. I clipped our luggage to a thin white rope, and Steve started hauling.

Hauling is a term used by climbers to denote a period of extreme physical pain, the ultimate goal of which is a hernia. (Actually, the word *haul* has the same Latin root as the word *hernia*.)

Haul bags—more commonly known as *hernia bags*[1]—are at the heart of the sport of hauling. Haul bags are curious devices. They are long, cylindrical bags made of the same tough, treated fabric that policemen use for bulletproof vests. They are sewn together in such a way that every flap, seam, and buckle catches on every edge, flake, and crack on the side of a mountain. Worse, haul bags are designed to hold immense loads of stuff, so if you're a pack rat or an ambitious collector, you tend to throw everything in. On El Cap, it's possible to cart more stuff up the cliff than you can fit in a standard tractor-trailer. Steve mentioned this as soon as he started hefting the bags up the low-angled rock.

If you have never tugged a haul bag up the side of a mountain, I suggest you try it now. In fact, if you're thinking about climbing a big cliff like El Cap, I recommend you haul several hundred tons of useless items a dozen miles before you attach yourself to the stone itself.

Here's how: Take a cylindrical bag made of stiff fabric, and place your peanut butter and jelly sandwiches in the bottom of the bag. Fill the remaining space with concrete cinder blocks. Now, tip the bag over onto its side, and drag it across a vast parking lot several hundred times—the parking lot at Disney World is perfect for this. So far, so good.

Retrieving lunch from the bottom of the haul bag requires the assistance of your fellow adventurers, but it's an important skill to master, so I suggest you practice it, too.

Have them stand very close to you in the parking lot—so close, in fact, that you cannot move. This might be a good time to take a jumbo roll of high-quality duct tape and bind all three of you together— preferably with at least *one person standing on top of you and the bag.*

Now, start removing the cinder blocks. Hand each of your partners as many cinder blocks as they can hold (no one is allowed to drop any cinder blocks) until you reach the sandwich. When you eventually do, the sandwich will likely be mush. At this point you should suggest that you just skip lunch, to which your partners will definitely agree. It's a safe bet that about this time one of your partners will wriggle to a scratch an itch, and all the cinder blocks will go *thunking* onto the tarmac.

While your baggage-diving techniques are not quite ready for El Cap and you have just failed this specialized test, you have at the same time proved that your mental condition is perfect for the job. Now, repeat the entire process until you can do it without dropping *any* of the cinder blocks. Or at least until Disney World security sees you and arrests you.

Although I have characterized pulling unnecessary junk out of a haul bag at a belay as the toughest activity on a big wall, it is not. And since you're already in Florida for spring hauling training camp, it might not be a bad idea to also practice the ultimate big wall–related challenge: going to the bathroom.

This challenge has, obviously, two distinct components, labeled (of course) Number One and Number Two. Let's start with peeing first.

Go to the nearest Ace Hardware store, buy a six-foot-tall, ten-megawatt, high-velocity blower fan, and position it on the ground next to the three of you (still duct-taped together) in the parking lot. It should be pointed straight up (to simulate the massive updrafts you'll encounter). Turn it on. Pee into it. Mission accomplished—congratulations.

Now it's time to practice Operation Number Twos.

At some belays on a big wall, you'll have ample room to hike about and squat in comfortable positions. At many other belay points, however, this is not the case, and you must do your business cheek-to-jowl with your climbing partners—flexing your forehead muscles while they try to politely look the other way (which is impossible because you can imagine the view).

To practice for such situations, do the following: Move to a quieter, less conspicuous spot in the parking lot. Re-duct-tape yourselves tightly together, more tightly than you were for baggage diving. Include everyone you might climb El Cap with—the more people the better (and *at least* one person must be standing on top of you). Turn the fan up to full bore—you know, so it can blow carabiners out of your hands.

Now, one by one, all of you go to the bathroom, doing Number Two. If anyone gets sprayed, spattered, nauseated, or even slightly disgusted, you have failed as an El Cap team, and you are destined never to climb the Big Stone. I suggest you take up bouldering, along with the thousands of other people who did last month.

Anyway, with Steve straining to yank our three bags up the slab, I suggested we remove several cinder blocks once we reached the bivouac that night. He agreed that this was a good idea. I led the next pitch, then pulled our three bags up. Then, Bruce led a pitch, and so on. Within a few pitches, it was apparent that we were drinking more water than we were winching up the rock (the temperature, we later learned, had gotten well over one hundred degrees that day).

The fixed red ropes continued upward next to each pitch we climbed, and after we'd burned off roughly twenty thousand calories dragging our haul bags around in the heat, I decided to take the heaviest of the three bags (filled with eight gallons of water) and jumar up the red ropes with it dangling from my belay loop. This worked out splendidly, and within no time I had a very big hernia.

The section of the climb we were on is called the Free Blast by most climbers. The golden rule of wall climbing in Yosemite is that you never transport cargo up the Free Blast. What you're supposed to do is go left a bit and heft it up a series of ledges below a giant heart-shaped feature on El Capitan called (surprise) the Heart.

The Heart is well-named. It's about the most obvious thing on the entire mountain, and it's more or less in the center of the southwest face, which seems appropriate when you first learn about it. Indeed, all over El Capitan, there are features named for parts of the human body or things related to the human body: the Nose, the Heart, the Ear, the Cyclops Eye, the Molar Traverse, Lung Ledge, the Tonsillectomy Traverse, the Highbrow Bivouac, and so on. What's confusing is that these features are not in the places you'd find them on a real human. The Ear is above the Heart, and the Heart's arguably where the Right Cheek should be. And there are bits missing, like the Spine, the Tongue, and the Femur. Climbers really should get organized when they name things.

Anyway, if you drag your crap up the cliff below the Heart, it doesn't get stuck as easily. So, as we lumbered our way upward, swearing like sailors, new names came to mind: the Almost Free Blast, the Not-At-All Free Blast, the Almost Okay Drag, and the Blasted Drag. We finally settled upon the section's new title: the Goddamned-Pain-in-the-Ass-Blast, which I recently submitted to the U.S. Park Service. After we had reached a ledge system called Woolly Mammoth Terraces, an area of archaeological ruins, we called it a day. I was quite concerned about our water situation (we had drunk roughly half our supply on the first full day), and I suggested that I rappel down the ubiquitous red ropes (which were also strung down the Esophagus to the Buttocks) and get more water. So that's what I did. Steve came with me. While we were down there, we hitchhiked over to Curry Village, stopped in at a restaurant, and ate two hamburgers apiece, the warm meat juice dribbling down our forearms.

"This hauling El Cap stuff is pretty weird," I suggested.

"Mmmph," Steve said, chewing heavily.

"The climbing's okay. All that heavy lifting, though, sucks."

"Mmm."

We hitchhiked back to the base of the cliff, jumared up the right leg, past the Anus to the Crotch, and found Bruce sitting around on the Woolly Mammoth, polishing his balls and smoothing out the wrinkles in his cape. He had good reason to feel proud: while Steve and I had been languishing on the Valley floor, Bruce had soloed a pitch and fixed a rope. Soloing a pitch and fixing a rope—while straightforward in most places—is more than enough reason to have a serious buff session when you do it in Yosemite Valley, where generally you're already a thousand or two thousand feet off the deck.

"But now we better get some sleep," Bruce said in a heavy tone. "We've got a big day tomorrow."

No kidding, I thought. Another five hundred feet of manual labor.

The thirty-two-pitch Route for Remedial El Cap Climbers climbs the first ten pitches of the Salathé Wall, nine pitches of the Muir Wall, and thirteen pitches of the Nose. If you ascend this stretch of rock with thirteen gallons of water, you are putting out a fairly large effort. In fact, I recently did the calculations of pounds of water multiplied by the height of El Cap and deduced that every person conveying that much water up El Cap is expending an effort roughly equivalent to the amount of energy required to light up New York City for five hundred years . . . or thereabouts.[2]

We crawled into our sleeping bags and pointed our feet over the edge of the Woolly Wedgie for photographs of them dangling in dark space.

Then came the *pht* sound.

Pht-pht-pht-pht. Pht-pht-pht-pht. Pht-pht-pht-pht. Pht-pht-pht-pht. It sounded like tree branches gently scraping the side of a slowly moving car or a broken wagon traveling down a street several blocks away. It was, we soon ascertained, a brown paper bag. Or rather, many brown paper bags. Lunch? Not quite. A grab bag of fun surprises from the county fair? Not exactly.

I already knew what was in the bags, as I'd encountered dozens at the base of El Capitan before we'd begun hoisting. They were bags of human poo, neatly folded around the rim (so that they wouldn't collapse during the user's brief intimate time with them) and hucked— undoubtedly with a moment's reservation—into the night.

As we lay (then sat up) there on Woolly Wedgies Ledge, we began to realize that we were in something of a poo-bag firing range, and as our evening progressed, a half-dozen such bags *pht-phted* down to us, and past us, to other recipients below. One paper bag, I noticed, had clung to a tiny ledge of rock fifty feet away from us. It was a bit miraculous, sitting there, out in space as it were, and I photographed it. I remember being genuinely surprised how talented paper bags could be at attaching themselves to inappropriate points on the rock. Looking around, I noticed there were bags clinging to nubbins in every direction.

"Well, this *is* El Crap," Bruce said.

"Incoming!" Steve said.

Pht-pht-pht-pht. Pht-pht-pht-pht.

The evening reminded me of Christmas Eve, except instead of singing "Jingle Bells" and "Good King Wenceslaus," the carolers on El Cap were chanting "Mortar!" and "Incoming round!" and other non-musical utterances. But then again, in 1993, this method of human waste removal was the way people were dealing with their poop.[3] (Today, of course, climbers have to haul all their output up and out with them.) The less noble way of dealing with poop—that is, crapping into cracks on ledges—was also in high fashion in 1993, and every bivouac, every belay ledge, and every crevice on the Spazzos' Route was completely filled with feces.

I flicked a paper bag off a small crystal near my sleeping quarters on Archaeological Terraces, and said good night to my ropemates, who were already snoring.

In the morning, the heavy lifting began early. By breakfast it was about one hundred degrees. By lunchtime I was ready to take a nap. By dinnertime we had drunk half our water again. We finally stopped for the day at a place called Gray Ledges, where we learned what the red static ropes had been for—besides cafeteria access. A well-known Colorado climber named Charlie Fowler and the late Xavier Bongard were in the process of doing a clean ascent of the Shield for a film, presumably to be titled *Legends of the Haul* or *The Big Pull* or *Lawrence of Ahernia*, or something appropriately fitting.

Hauling legend John Middendorf was doing the rigging for the film crew, and with the help of Rolando Garibotti and John Wason, Middendorf had strung the entire Shield route with a big, fat static rope. The enormous, thick red rope crested over El Cap's headwall, then snaked down the Shield's Triple Cracks, and hit the Gray Ledges. It then cascaded down to Mammoth Wedgies, where it split into two. One set of ropes continued down the Pain-in-the-Ass-Blast, while the other set of ropes went down the Colon to the Kneecap. It was all rather impressive.

We awoke the next morning and continued hoisting.

Pht-pht-pht-pht.

* * *

One of the more useful pieces of equipment available to anyone schlepping luggage in the mountains is a device called a Wallhauler. Back in
1993, it was a fairly new contraption, and we were just getting familiar with it on El Capitan. A simple pulley-ratchet type device, it allows
one to pull downward on a rope running through a pulley so that the
load on the other end of the rope goes upward, then it automatically
locks off at the highest point to which one lifts the load.

Because the bags were so incredibly weighty, much of the challenge
was creating enough force on the "pull" side of the hauling system.
Steve and I regularly used our bodies as counterweights (an activity
called body hauling), but when the specially designed "edge catcher"
seams and "flake-grabber" straps on the haul bags hooked on parts of
the cliff as their designers had intended, we had to work together,
acting as one big and very spastic counterweight. We got so good at
lifting stuff—and proud of that fact—that at the end of every heaving
session, Steve and I also began polishing our balls.

It seems odd, but I've read that hauling is becoming a sport in its
own right. Like the world of climbing itself, professional hauling has
its devotees and champions. There are regular meets on El Cap, and,
I recently read in *Hauling Life* magazine, the National Outdoor
Leadership School and Outward Bound plan to start offering masters'
degrees in wall hauling.

Climbing equipment makers already know that dragging hernia
bags across acres of rock is a proud living in its own right, and they
have invented a raft of devices for expending many calories in the
hills. There is the Wallhauler, made by a company called Rock
Exotica; there are several devices (the Ural-Alp Hauler, versions A
and B; the Hogwauler; and the Hauler) made by a firm called
Ushba; and there are two devices called the Mini-Traxion and the
Pro-Traxion, made by Petzl. Then there are the RSI Rescue Hauling
Pulley; the RM2 and RM22 Rescuemates; and the CMI Uplift—

these latter devices designed for rescue but available for pulling large heaps of crap upward in a pinch.

And, if you're not quite committed enough to take up hauling as a full-time career, a company called Kong-Bonatti makes a thing called the Kong Block Roll, a big, flat-looking device that attaches to a regular Kong-Bonatti jumar and turns it into a device for hefting cargo uphill.

You think I'm kidding, but hauling really is serious business.

Just a quick search of the Web pulls up dozens of websites on hauling, including a site in which a chap actually comments on all this gear, to wit: "The Pro-Traxion is very light for a man-rated hauling pulley. It looks flimsy beside the large monsters like the CMI Uplift, RSI Rescue Hauling Pulley, and SRT RM22 Rescuemate, but apparently it is strong enough to pass European safety standards. The cam teeth are aggressive, but don't seem to do any rope damage unless one is stupid enough to rely on it to catch a dropped load. The front faceplate is barely held closed by a tiny lip on the cam axle; however, with a carabiner in place it can't open far. The thumb-activated cam latch takes some getting used to. Within sixty seconds of receiving my Mini-Traxion, I managed to catch my thumbnail on the frame, which tore the corner of the nail loose. Still, all things considered, for its size the Mini-Traxion is impressive, and it deserves a star."[4]

Although I can't read Greek, I suspect I would agree with this review: Scraping oneself slowly up the side of El Cap the way a postman scrapes dog poop off his shoe was causing me to shred thumbnails and see stars. Why someone hasn't simply designed a bag that moves up the wall with ease is a tremendous mystery to me.

Pht-pht-pht-pht.

We turned a corner and started traversing to the right. Traversing while hauling is possibly the most fun you can ever have on a big rock, and we swaggered through the series of sideways pitches like soldiers on R&R. After every ropelength traveled, I would lower a sack of heavy stuff we were now clearly not going to need sideways, and Steve or Bruce would yank it until his forehead glowed red. Then we'd switch places and repeat the process.

"Maybe we could have a yard sale on top?" I called over while we wrestled a bag off a snaggle-toothed flake.

"Or a bonfire," Bruce called back.

That afternoon, the Remedial Route brought us to some ledges, where we spent another long night nursing aching backs and severe sunburns.

Our fifth day was much the same: haul-snag, haul-snag, haul-snag, haul-snag, haul-snag, haul-snag . . . the thrum of the Wallhauler and the steady scrape of the bags made a kind of background percussion while the occasional finger jam, rope burn, or testes crunch offered the music some highlights. At least we were finding a rhythm. Steve and I now shined our nuts publicly—we were actually getting good at this stuff. Bruce smiled.

Eventually, the Route for Substandard Climbers joined up with the Nose (the most famous rock climb on Earth), and we headed for Camp VI. *Pht-pht-pht-pht.*

I distinctly remember the pitch before Camp VI, our Pitch 26. It was supposed to be a 5.8 but, indeed, it was considerably less because it was so sticky.

At Camp VI, a bunch of very popular routes all converge, and it's where a lot of people spend their last night on the mountain. All the human waste from Camp VI washes down onto Pitch 26 and adheres to the rock. Climbing this section of the cliff in the one hundred degree late afternoon heat was like climbing a freshly tarred roof. My flesh stuck to every hand jam, and my rock shoes adhered to every foothold. I could easily have been climbing up a pile of those revolting Rice Krispies marshmallow desserts that a lot of people make. And it stunk. It is the worst place on El Crapitan, and it's the most prominent memory you'll ever have of climbing in Yosemite. I still get the willies thinking about it.

Like everything else, it was just part of the game. We spent a final night at Camp VI, a cozy platform of rock, snuggled up against one another and nursing multiple hernias. The stars twinkled in the Sierra night and the smell of feces wafted across the platform, thick and chewy in the back of our throats. The really relaxing thing about Camp VI on the Nose is that you don't need to stay roped up to sleep there. It is so incredibly sticky that all you need do is lie down and you are anchored more solidly than in any tangled-rope belay. It's a bit like pressing yourself into a batch of chemical preservative or onto a pan of shellac. *Pht-pht-pht-pht.*

The next morning, we loaded up our peanut butter and jelly sandwiches and concrete cinder blocks and prepared to leave Camp VI. Before we did, though, we went to the bathroom—luckily, Bruce had remembered to pack the duct tape. Anyway, after we'd done the business, we realized we still had a gallon-and-a-half of water left. Steve and Bruce looked at me with slitted eyes, ready to kill. It was, I admitted, a terrible miscalculation.

"Well, we could use it to wash the crack [filled with human waste] behind the ledge," I suggested.

"No, let's leave two bottled quarts and take the rest," Steve said, turning his frown into a smile. "Someone will be thankful to find a half-gallon of water here."

We flew up the last few pitches, enjoying the first breeze we'd felt that week and marveling at the views. The bags were as unruly as ever and performed magical feats of entanglement like possessed macramé projects. We pulled the top of the cliff, stumbled over to flat ground, and sat down.

It had been a fabulous experience, and we were all proud of our effort. Steve and I sat contentedly polishing our balls while Bruce watched like a proud father (as I obviously need not point out, it was a very weird scene). We then loaded up the remainder of our crap, so to speak, and hoofed it quickly down the trail to the Valley floor.

Like I said, I'm not really a climber, but one of these days I must go back and do another route, or at least have lunch at the café. That is, of course, if I can drag myself away from the Disney World parking lot and my newfound love of polishing things.

---

1 The term pigs has long been conferred upon haul bags. I disagree with this application of the cognomen. Pigs are smart, sexy beasts. Haul bags are not.
2 One gallon of water weighs 8.345 pounds. The energy required to lift the water is equal to the weight of the water multiplied by the number of feet it is lifted (in this case, about 3,000). Simply then, lifting 13 gallons (or 108 pounds) up 3,000 feet requires (108 pounds of water x 3,000 feet of lift =) 325,455 foot-pounds, and since 1 horsepower equals 33,000 foot-pounds per minute, we were about equal to a 10 horsepower engine—had we climbed and hauled El Cap in one minute. Okay, I won't go any further with this line of reasoning . . . .
3 Although I must admit, I'm not sure it was allowed even then.
4 See http://storrick.cnchost.com/VerticalDevicesPage/Misc/HaulingPulleyPages/HaulPulley731.html.

Legendary mountain photographer Galen Rowell in Kootenai Canyon, Montana.

Galen Rowell: American Mountaineering's Renaissance Man (2002)

As you've read by now in dozens of magazines, Galen Rowell and his wife of twenty-one years, Barbara Cushman Rowell, were killed in August 2002, when a small aircraft they were traveling in crashed near Bishop, California. The fact that Galen and Barbara died in a plane crash is ironic and sad. Their entire lives centered on calculated risk-taking, and this particular crash was, by most accounts, fairly mundane.

What you probably haven't read yet is a clear explanation as to why Galen Rowell *mattered* to American climbing—and mattered in a way few other men ever will. He climbed as much as Beckey; he explored as much of Asia's mountains as Bonington; he traveled as much as any modern sport climber; he was as eloquent as Winthrop-Young, Robbins, and Ament combined (and arguably better); he understood every aspect of climbing *and* excelled at it in all its forms; and he was a brilliant artist, speaker, imagemaker, writer, technician, naturalist, athlete, conservationist, and aesthete. Yep. This will sound silly, but it's true: he was one of climbing's few ever Renaissance men.

What's that you say? You've never heard of the man? Or you know the name but you're not sure why? First, he did new routes. By the age of thirty, he'd pioneered more than one hundred new climbs in his native Sierra Nevada—from Grade II rock climbs to Grade V walls. He began climbing in Yosemite early, at age sixteen, and was as involved in major ascents there as almost anyone.

In 1962, aged twenty-two, he and a friend climbed the northwest face of Half Dome (Robbins's 1957 "world's first Grade VI"), a major ascent for the time.

Between 1967 and 1983, aged twenty-seven to forty-three, Galen did more mountaineering than most of us in a lifetime. A highly shortened hit list of adventures I've just tacked together using only one book as a reference includes the following: the fourth ascent of the Nose, with Layton Kor, in 1967; he attempted the Great White Throne in Zion with Beckey and Callis; climbed the south face of Half Dome, with Harding, in 1969; in 1972, he attempted the Mooses Tooth's forty-five-hundred-foot south face and climbed the west face of North Howser Tower in the Bugaboos; in 1974, he climbed the south face of Mt. Dickey, likely the biggest wall in North America; in 1976, he free-climbed Keeler Needle in California; in 1977, he made the first ascent of the Great Trango Tower; he made first ascents of several Himalayan summits, including Cholatse in 1981; and in 1983, he led an expedition to Everest's west ridge.

But Galen didn't just stop at ascents of every type of rock on Earth, of ice, of high mountains, of big walls. He ran, hiked, skied, and climbed on every continent, establishing new routes, finding new areas, and succeeding in a litany of geographic adventures that rank up there with the accomplishments of Burton and Speke, Scott and Peary, and Shipton and Tilman. For example, while Galen was doing the things I've just listed, he was also involved in a 1974 winter traverse of California-Nevada's White Mountains; a 1975 traverse of the Nevada's Ruby Range; a 1978 ski circumnavigation of Denali; a 1978 attempt on K2; a 1980 ski traverse of the Karakoram; and a single-day ascent of Denali from the ten-thousand-foot level. Throughout the 1980s and '90s, Galen continued to push himself in every mountain arena available to him. He teamed up with Skinner and Piana to free-climb Proboscis, Mt. Hooker, and Half Dome's Direct Route, for example.

And Galen really was a phenomenal climber. In 1990, I had the opportunity to camp with him and climb near him on the east face of Mount Whitney. Steve Porcella and I were attempting a new route, while Galen and Dave Wilson were completing a route Galen had tried in 1989. At one point Steve and I watched Galen worm his way up a huge, leaning offwidth, asking Dave for tension on the rope. The crack looked awful, but I always wondered if it really was 5.11, as Galen reported it later in *Climbing* magazine (it's called Left-Wing Extremist). The following spring, in Montana, I went out with Galen and Steve to climb a 5.11 route in Kootenai Canyon. Steve led the pitch, then I followed him. I was in great shape at the time, but totally confounded as to how to do the crux—a very weird boulder problem. I hung off small holds for several minutes trying to figure it out, while Galen scrambled all around taking photos. Finally, I got it. Galen was next and without even looking at the problem, he fired it off without hesitation. I was twenty-four at the time; he was fifty-one.

If Galen's climbing was impressive, turn your attention now to his photography and writing. When Galen was twenty-four, his Aunt Marion gave him a copy of Tom Hornbein's *Everest: The West Ridge*.

Back then, wilderness photography books were black-and-white and the images were mostly landscapes, shot by fellows who needed cars to get the equipment to the scene. *Everest: The West Ridge* "had the same lavish reproduction that had been used for the works of Ansel Adams and Eliot Porter," Rowell noted in an article about his early photography. "But *Everest: The West Ridge* featured compelling color images by amateur 35mm photographers of the entire spectrum of experience of a Mount Everest expedition. Native people, natural scenes, camps, climbs, and comrades were all eloquently rendered."

By the late 1960s, he had become a regular contributor to several small mountain magazines. But his big move came in 1971, after he saw *The Creation,* a book by Ernst Haas. "It firmed up my resolve to become a full-time freelancer the following year," he wrote. Until then, he had worked as an auto mechanic at a Berkeley garage he owned.

Galen's big break came quickly. In 1974, Robert Gilka, *National Geographic's* Director of Photography, hired Galen to photograph an ascent of the northwest face of Half Dome. This time, however, he, Doug Robinson, and Dennis Henneck would climb the route "clean"—without the use of rock-scarring devices such as pitons.[1] Galen shot only a few rolls of film (compared with the thousands used by *National Geo* photographers of today), and his modest article about the ascent was meant to be a sidebar to a bigger feature by David Brower on Yosemite in general. When Galen's images arrived on Gilka's desk, the magazine had a new cover story.[2] Galen was thirty-four.

In 1974, Galen's knowledge of and appreciation for the walls of Yosemite Valley and the incredible climbing history made there prompted him to compile and edit a book, *The Vertical World of Yosemite.* Although the material was mostly written by other climbers, the compilation was so well organized and produced that it remains arguably the finest book on that subject matter. By 1980, Galen had produced a string of mountaineering narratives, detailing impressive mountaineering activities all over the world. Some of these books, such as *High & Wild, In the Throne Room of the Mountain Gods,* and *Many People Come, Looking, Looking,* have since become classics of the genre. In 1984, he received the Ansel Adams Award for his contributions to the art of wilderness photography. In 1986, he released what many consider one of the finest books about photography ever written, *Mountain Light: In Search of the Dynamic Landscape.*

Galen was also a media watchdog, a freedom fighter, and a conservationist. In the mid-1990s, he began writing a column for *Outdoor Photographer* magazine, which would soon become one of its most popular. In his December 1996 column, Galen wrote, "Despite the first amendment, America has anything but a free press. Despite the ever greater power of the media in America, truth and freedom seem less apparent. Special interest groups, including, but not limited to, the big corporations that own most mainstream publications exert direct and indirect pressure over the images and words that appear."

For example, in 1995, Galen wrote and shot a feature on California peregrines for a major environmental publication. The article described reproductive problems resulting from DDT exposure. At the time, the Department of the Interior was considering delisting the peregrine falcon as endangered.

"My text was edited to greatly minimize the problems, and phrases that I never wrote were added, such as: 'This bodes well for the Endangered Species Act (ESA) at a critical time in its history,'" Galen recalled. "I was willing to compromise some, but not to negate carefully researched facts. The story was summarily canceled with a revealing explanation. The organization that publishes the magazine was lobbying hard in Washington for reauthorization of the ESA. They had a vested interest in using the peregrine as a success story to convince Congress that the ESA works."

Such convictions about right and wrong led Galen often to Tibet, where he argued for the rights of Tibetans under Chinese rule. Indeed, in a 1994 interview for *Rock & Ice* magazine, he told me how his photograph of a Tibetan holding an image of the Dalai Lama to her forehead had been published and noticed by Chinese officials. Galen was subsequently tried in absentia for sedition. Worse still was the censorship. In one famous 1982 incident, a photo by Galen of a Tibetan boy wearing a soldier's hat was selected as the cover image for an edition of *National Geographic*. *National Geo* editors showed the cover layout to Chinese Embassy officials, and the editors were told that American journalists would be restricted in China. A photo of the Egyptian pyramids went on the front instead. "The positive result of word leaking out was that the editors resolved not to alter content again without disclosure," Rowell later wrote. His work in Tibet eventually led to a major book project with the Dalai Lama, *My Tibet*.

Galen never compromised. He sought the truth, personally and professionally, and often found a lot more. His was a keen mind, a keen sense of all the world's complex connections. He showed us how to be inspired by the big view, but he also taught us to look a little deeper—to notice the subtle things in nature and in ourselves. And, to my way of thinking, that's why he mattered.

1 *Although they used fixed pitons and established bolts.*
2 National Geographic, *June 1974.*

Drag racing in the Valley of the Gods, Utah.

The Paris-Dakar
in the Valley of the Gods (1999)

Being a longtime American desert bumbler, I often hear my peers complain about the best-looking towers and walls having been done, and how there's nothing left "to do."

Well, have I got a spot for you.

It's called the Valley of the Gods, and it's located in the very southeastern corner of Utah, about two hours south of Moab. The Valley of the Gods isn't really a valley; it's more a sort of flat area of washes and canyons, punctuated by some of the coolest-looking towers and buttes around. The towers and buttes sit atop these three-hundred-food talus cones, so that for every four-hundred- to five-hundred-foot tower you climb, you end up a good seven hundred to eight hundred feet off the "valley" floor. It's a pretty cool view.

Added to the fact that the place is almost totally devoid of visitors (you see about one car a day, max), this makes it one of the prettiest, most spectacular climbing spots in the desert Southwest. And, most important of all, there's a twenty-mile-long dirt loop road that weaves among the towers. Covered with about two feet of fine dust, it's just perfect for high-speed, off-road rally racing and offers plenty "to do."

In January of 2000, my old pal Jesse "The Body" Harvey (no relation to the former governor of Minnesota) and I drove the six hours or so from Colorado to Bluff Utah, thence to the "valley." We met up with another friend, Jon Butler, and toured the compact area: Jesse and I in my truck, Jon following in his. As I drove, an enormous plume of red dust rose behind my truck, completely obliterating Jon. The dirt was so fine that it rose thirty feet into the sky before it began to settle.

It reminded me of African dust, the all-consuming, all-nostril-filling dirty brown stuff that seeps into every cell of your brain, making you think you'd prefer a visit from Bill Harzia. I floored it, watching a red, boiling wall of dirt creep along the road behind us. Jon was obliterated again. We could hear his screams of terror.

"That doesn't sound good," Jesse said. "Jon's totally disappeared. You think he's okay?"

I pulled over, and Jon climbed into my vehicle. Then we all toured the area together, creating one single unified dirt plume, a beauty that would put the Paris-Dakar racers to shame. While I drove, Jesse thumbed through the pages of Eric Bjørnstad's 1988 book *Dessert Rock* (no recipes included), trying to figure out what tower was what.

Although the first climb ever done in the Valley of the Gods was North Tower, by Bjørnstad and Ron Wiggle, it was mountaineering legends Bill Forrest and George Hurley who put Valley of the Gods on the map.

During the mid- to late 1970s, they made the first ascents of most of the major landforms, including Tom Tom Tower, Eagle Plume Tower, Petard Tower, Lady in the Bathtub, and Hidden Tower. They also climbed a new route on North Tower.

Ironically, Fred Beckey, that most prolific of pioneers, had driven past Valley of the Gods many times in the '60s and '70s, but he had never stopped there. "I couldn't get Fred interested in going in there," Bjørnstad told me recently. "He was only interested in doing towers in Monument Valley." The same was true of legendary Colorado climber Layton Kor; he just drove straight by it numerous times, never once climbing a thing.

After a couple of trips around the valley's somewhat circular loop road, Jesse located two major towers right next to the road that seemed to be unclimbed.

"Cam, look at those," he said, pointing at a particularly pretty formation out my side window. "We gotta do 'em."

I pulled over and we climbed one tower in about half a day, in absolutely bone-chilling temperatures. We then drove into the town of Mexican Hat to eat Taco Hell food and get warm with the Navajos at the local gas station. Then, we drove around some more—around the loop road, that is, bouncing and skidding all over the place, eagerly watching the massive plume rise as I pushed my old green Toyota up to sixty.

"You know," I said as we careened through a bush, "this beats the hell outta climbing."

The next day, Jon left. And Jesse, who was coming down with a severe case of brown lung, demanded a few days rest in his Grand Junction bachelor pad. We made a fast pact to return.

After The Body had spent a few days recovering (he spat up a four-inch dirt ball one night and felt better) we returned to "da Valley" with two trucks and spent the following two days picking off another nice-looking tower.

We reached our impromptu base camp and, since time was up, we began packing. The civilized world was, surprisingly, calling our names.

Of course, we couldn't just leave like that. I wanted to see if we could break our time record around the loop road, and I needed Jesse as a ballast. "Please!" I begged, scooping up a handful of dirt and stuffing it in my mouth to show my sincerity.

"Okay, Cam. But just one lap. I gotta get back to school."

He hopped in and we sped off, the great dust cloud snaking along the road behind us as we bounced hither and thither, helter-skelter, and up and down. We flew along the straightaways and screeched around corners and through the dry washes. Red dirt flew in through the ventilation system, and we each took long, unhealthy breaths.

Of course, we forgot to set our stopwatches, so we can't be sure of our exact time. We both agreed, however, that we would've beaten the pants off Juan Fango, Mario Andretti, and Michael Schumacher.

Jesse got out of my truck and drove off, and I sat in my cab for ten minutes while the dirt settled. With a bounce, a bump, and a grind, I said farewell to the Valley of the Gods.

Although Forrest and Hurley had done some good climbing there and far outdistanced us in that department, they missed the valley's real attraction: balls-out, thoroughly demented, high-speed danger on its now infamous loop road. In that department, we were kings.

Who says there's nothing left "to do"?

The Gore Range of Colorado from Eagle's Nest peak.

Gore Blimey: What's in a Name? (1997)

I love names in America.

Every proper noun in the United States is so wonderfully and weirdly appropriate, I sometimes think that I'm living in some sort of strange Dickensian fantasy. I grew up in Australia, where everything is Waggawagga or Boomaboomaboom or Didiliomumabah or Grundyfidgety, or pretty much anything with a genuinely native sound to it. It's not like that in America.

Britain's much better, but I hear Bill Bryson is in the process of cataloging Farting Cesspool, Belching Buttocks, Grunting Roddy, and other fun municipalities in his newest book—*Notes from a Bunch of*

Towns with Oddball Names, or something or other—so I won't repeat that process here.

In my opinion, the best town name on earth is Canada's Headsmashedinbuffalojump, Alberta, where the natives used to herd the beasts over a cliff. (I'm not kidding; it's a real place.) Just up the highway from my home in Basalt, Colorado, are Fairplay, Colorado, and, a few miles later, Climax, Colorado. Further north of here, there are three towns in a row called Maybell, Lay, and Craig—or Craig-Lay-Maybell, if you're coming in that direction. (Note to self: Have a poke around Intercourse, Pennsylvania, one of these days, but avoid Blue Ball.)

Even better are climbers' names, both here and elsewhere. Conrad *Anker*—is that real?—must be really good at setting up solid belays. Jimmy *Dunn* has done it all, including the first solo new route on El Cap (Cosmos, in 1972). Steve *Roper?*—gotta be a pen name. *Jack Tackle?* (Jack Tackle the big mountain, I reckon.) *Micah Dash?*—sounds a tad like an Australian rushing to the top to me. Kelly *Cordes*—doesn't *cord* mean rope in one of the European tongues? Mike *Libecki?* (Mike, *lie becki* up that dihedral. . . .) How about *Juan Espuny*, apparently belonging to a Latino climber whom I recently read about in the *American Alpine Journal?* (The obvious answer is: No thanks, I'll just use my fetid fingers in those baked beans again.) And Banny Root—which although it doesn't sound very mountainy, is just the coolest name a climber ever held. (I always thought surfer *Damian Hardman* should've been a climber.)

The Gore Range is perfectly named, too, although very few American climbers have ever heard of it. As William Bueler noted in *Roof of the Rockies: A History of Colorado Mountaineering*, "although they are only sixty miles west of Denver, the Gores are as little known as any major Colorado mountains."

Gore Blimey: What's in a Name? (1997)

Sir George Gore was an Irishman who came out to Colorado in 1855 to hunt in Colorado's three most famous "parks": North, Middle, and South Park (after which the intellectual American children's animated program is titled). A typical big-game hunter of the nineteenth century, Gore hired the legendary scout and beaver trapper Jim Bridger to show him around, and he brought with him some fifty servants. Although he didn't really do much in the Gore Range—in fact, there's little evidence he actually went into the mountains—during his hunting trip he bagged forty grizzly bears, three thousand bison, and many thousands of deer, elk, and antelope. History books on the Gore Range don't say exactly what he did with all this meat; suffice it to say, he probably had fifty servants and one guide in need of the mother of all colostomies by the end of the trip. (And, weirdly, of the several dozen subranges of the Rockies in Colorado, the Gore Range is one of only three named for a person . . . I believe the others are Larry and Moe.)

One of Colorado's great nineteenth-century explorers, Ferdinand Hayden, called the Gore Range a series of "sharp-pointed peaks, crests, and obelisks" when he climbed the range's highest summit, Mount Powell, in 1873. "Great masses of snow, like glaciers, lie on the almost vertical sides perpetually, though they abruptly descend forty or fifty degrees."

The Gore Range is not really as dramatic as Mr. Hayden wrote, and it's definitely not got any big walls. Rather, it's an area of rounded stone mountains with weird rocky pinnacles and gargoyles sprouting out at various points on many of the bigger peaks. The view from Silverthorne, Colorado—where, during the past twenty years, the ugly native trees and prickly shrubs have been razed and replaced with lovely stuccoed strip malls—has so many of these gargoyley-type towers in it that, from a couple of viewpoints, the Gore Range looks a tad like a real mountain range.

The range also boasts a lot of long snow and ice couloirs, all of which offer great ski mountaineering and couloir climbing. A few peaks, though, have genuine climbing.

A couple years back, Benny Bach (full name: Bernhard Wilhelm Bach, II—descended from the eighteenth-century fiddler) and I decided to investigate a "wall" we'd heard about, "a sort of great big granite dome," as one of the local climbers had called it. After much research, much driving around and stopping at the strip malls (underpants were on sale at the Hanes outlet!), and an exploratory jaunt up a peak named Eagles Nest, we figured our goal was the north face of Peak C.

The reason things like faces on Peak C go unclimbed for so long is that the Gore Range, unlike most Colorado ranges, was never developed for mining, so there are almost no roads going anywhere near the mountains, and every mountain requires a serious tromp to reach. As Bueler wrote, because of the lack of a mining history, "much of the Gore has long been classified as a primitive area, preventing construction of major roads." Also, the range is exceedingly rough, "making travel more difficult than in most other mountain ranges."

A few weeks later, loaded up with ninety thousand kilos' worth of climbing and camping gear and food, Benny and I learned how rough the joint was firsthand. We trudged, heavily laden, up some of the steepest tracks I've ever muled; and after a full day, we seemed to be nowhere near our objective, unless our objective included dementia (which I'm almost certain it didn't; nevertheless we achieved it admirably). We spent the following day wandering round in the rain, finally realizing that we were camped on the south side of the peak the north face of which we hoped to climb.

That second afternoon, as a rain pummeled our camp, we were surrounded by dozens of mountain goats—the extremely snotty kind that are prone to goring stray mountaineers. We figured they wanted to get out of the rain and into the tent, but we're strictly sheep men. Weird farmyard fantasies kept me up much of the night.

On our third and last day, we arose early, humped over a high pass, and found the face we were looking for. Not as wall-like as we'd hoped, but at least we'd found it. In our rock shoes we skated up ice slopes to the base of the face—a sort of Tonya-Harding-goes-berserk routine—then climbed six pitches of what should've been great, easy rock—except it had monsooned all night, so it was slick, wet, mossy, disgusting rock. It wasn't as impressive as we'd hoped, but still, it was likely the biggest face in the range.

We topped out as electrical charges raised our hair into weird dancing halos, and we quickly ran down the backside of the peak. At camp we paused for an hour, packing up while simultaneously gorging ourselves on sodden leftover paste that in a past life had been a respectable packet of crackers.

A few weeks later, when the 1997 *American Alpine Journal* was released, we learned that we hadn't been the first up this face: we'd been beaten by a year (and who knows how many there'd been before that). Still, we'd done a new, though exceedingly wet and sloppy, route—and I reckon wet and sloppy things are always cause for celebration.

Blimey, core blimey, caw blimey, and other derivations of the Anglo term, I've read, are expressions that come from "God blind me." Sir George Gore may not have invented the textile that bears his name, but his namesake mountain range certainly is blindingly pretty and definitely worth a look. Don't forget to bring some meat.

International escapades in the
Cordillera Blanca of Peru.

*Touching the 'Roid
(2000)*

Ponder this simple question a moment and see if you can come up
with an answer: What is an *expedition*?

Is it an event? That doesn't seem quite correct, as expeditions can
encompass any number of events all strung together.

Is it an action? There are many actions and subactions in an expedition: walking, sitting, traveling, eating, climbing, and humping loads.

Is it people? I've been on expeditions with people who have split off
from our group and gone climbing with members of other expeditions,
thereby negating the idea that a specific group is key. (Then again, I've
been on expeditions with guys who have split off from humanity and
joined the ranks of the Sasquatch, thereby negating the term *people.*)

I think expeditions are a little bit of everything. The word is a noun, to be sure, but it's a kind of fourth-dimensional noun—one that involves process, movement, characters, and places. A bit like a traveling circus or a drifting ship, going somewhere, taking time to do it, and leaving behind another world.

Of course, in this day and age, the word *expedition* sounds a little heavy. With cut-rate plane fares to every airport on every continent, online video examination of every peak, pass, and puja from here to Timbuktu, the word *expedition* seems far too formal. It sounds very serious—like something British Everesters were doing in the 1920s. *Trip* is a much better word. It's lighthearted. It sums up your attitude when you're on an overseas climbing excursion. *Expedition* sounds like you're planning to sit around in wooden camp chairs swatting flies on an elephant's bum and drinking tea from a silver tea service while the underpaid locals you've hired cook up seven-course meals. *Trip*, on the other hand, sounds like you've fallen down and are trying to get back up. I'd rather go on a trip.

There is nothing quite like a big climbing trip, especially a big international climbing trip. And, predictably, the best big overseas climbing trips always turn out to be the ones to places you've never been, where you can't speak the language, where the mountains are wild-looking and have exotic names, and where the political situation is in disarray. Pop open your typical atlas, and many such places come galloping to mind—Kashmir, Afghanistan, the Faroffistans of the former Soviet Union, and most South American nations. The choices are many and varied.

In early 2000, Peru was going through the political equivalent of dry-heaving. In May, under then-President Alberto Fujimori, the nation held some supposedly democratic elections, but many Peruvians questioned the authenticity of the vote count. They had good reason, given the president's history. Fujimori had come to power in 1992, and with the support of the military he had dissolved the Peruvian Congress and courts and seized dictatorial powers. He quashed various left-wing rebel factions, which were blamed for thousands of deaths and bringing the country to the brink of chaos.

"To his supporters, Mr. Fujimori is the man who saved Peru from the twin evils of terrorism and economic collapse," reported the British Broadcasting Corporation (BBC) in November 2000. "To his opponents, he is an authoritarian strongman who has ridden roughshod over the country's democratic institutions in order to preserve his hold on power." Whether you liked or hated Fujimori, his own tough form of democracy appeared about to be replaced with something else— probably, in typical South American style, via a revolution or a coup.

Thus it was that my dear friend Jordan Campbell thought a quick climbing trip to Peru made a lot of sense: We hadn't been; our little group of friends could barely speak Spanish; there were wild mountains and nutty politics. And, Peru was a hell of a lot cheaper than Kashmir, Afghanistan, and the Faroffistans of the former Soviet Union.

Jordan's plan was simple: nip down and back in three weeks, bag a few twenty-thousand-foot peaks (Alpamayo, Quiteraju, and Artesonraju, for example), and be home in time for summer rock climbing in the high country. This seemed quite an ambitious goal. All the big mountain trips I'd been on up to that point had required at least a week's worth of travel just to get to the mountain, then another week's worth of acclimatization at the very least.

I didn't really know that much about Peru before our trip, but Alpamayo sure sounded lovely—like a creamy topping for dog food, or a high-altitude ruin. I pulled open an atlas and delved further. I was immediately struck by the names of the mountain ranges in Peru.

There's a range called the Cordillera Vilcabamba and another called the Cordillera Huayhuash (pronounced "why wash?"); there are ranges named Tunshu and Raura; Huallanca ("wallanka") and

Huagaruncho ("wagarunko"). These names were so instantly appealing and lyrical, it seemed to me that Peru's mountain cartographers must be moonlighting as salsa musicians.

Likewise, the individual mountains are a magical harmony of *rajus* and *alcas:* Taulliraju, Artesonraju, Chacraraju, Quiteraju, Pucaraju, Uruashraju, Tumarinaraju, Tullparaju, Juchuraju, Huamashraju, Palcaraju, Mururaju, Tocllaraju, Vallunaraju, Paqcharaju, Ranrapalca, Ocshapalca, Cajavilca, Pucaganga, and Cancaraca. There's Tuco, Pisco, Santon, Cashan, Choco, Copap, Churup, Copa, Vicos, Cayesh, Pastoruri, Contrahierbas, Huandoy, Chopicalqui, and Carhuallun. Who could possibly turn these lyrical names down? That'd be a sin—like comparing Julie Andrews to Snoop Doggy Dogg.

"Perhaps the most famous mountain in Peru is Alpamayo," wrote British mountaineer John Cleare is his popular book *World Guide to Mountains and Mountaineering.* "From the northwest it appears a steep pyramid of ice. From the southwest, it is an immaculate trapezoid of tapering ice flutings and has been likened to a white cathedral." Hmm . . . ice flutings? Is that safe? Wasn't it somewhere round there that Joe Simpson had his little *Touching the Void* ordeal? Is this advisable?

Alpamayo has an interesting history. In 1948, a Swiss expedition attempted to make the first ascent of the peak—it failed. In 1950, a few years after the Swiss attempt, a book called *Cordillera Blanca: Peru,* by two climbers named Kinzl and Schneider, was published showing the still-unclimbed Alpamayo. After the book came out, a Swiss mountaineering magazine held a contest to see which mountain on Earth was "the most beautiful." The resounding response—Alpamayo, even though it had only been properly photographed a few years previously. That an unclimbed mountain in the Cordillera Blanca—which looks very similar to all the other mountains in the Cordillera Blanca—beat out such peaks as Switzerland's own Eiger and Matterhorn is quite remarkable.

The first ascent of Alpamayo came in 1951, when the creatively titled "Franco-Belgian Expedition to the Andes" traveled to South America for a summer's climbing. The group consisted of Georges Kogan and his wife, Claude; Maurice Lenoir; Jean Guillemin; Jacques Jongen; Raymond Leininger and his wife, Nicole; and André and René Mallieux.

While four of the men (Lenoir, Jongen, Georges Kogan, and Raymond Leininger) made the first ascent of Alpamayo, the two women, Claude Kogan and Nicole Leininger, spent several days exploring possible routes to the top of Quiteraju. A day after the four men returned from reaching the top of Alpamayo, the group turned its attention to Quiteraju. Several "three-man" rope teams climbed the peak, including the rope team of Claude Kogan and Nicole Leininger. The two women reached the summit around 3:00 P.M. "It is the first time a purely female party has climbed a peak of twenty thousand feet," Leininger later wrote. Quiteraju later became known as Lady's Peak. The cool thing is, Quiteraju, Lady's Peak, is taller than Alpamayo.

A few weeks before our departure, Jordan convened a small meeting of our group's members (Jordan, Rick Leonidas, Ace Kvale, and myself) in Telluride, ostensibly to discuss our trip to Peru and to get to know each other better with a one-day ski traverse from Ophir to Telluride. Discussing the trip to Peru was pretty easy after Jordan produced several six-packs of beer. In fact, the only real discussion centered on a name for what we were doing, and somehow the word expedition crept back into things. Ace came up with the fanciful "Touching the 'Roid Expedition" in honor of Simpson's book,[1] yet with relevant overtones to the extreme gastrointestinal distress that accompanies every journey to Latin America. We all liked that name, but Jordan felt we needed a proper, more publishable name, free of quasi-scatalogical references, so he hit on the "Condor Expedition to

Peru." The word *expedition*—it is easily argued—makes a trip sound official. With that difficult business completed, we focused on the beer and an enjoyable videotape of Jordan's last big climbing trip to Thalay Sagar in the Garwhal region of the Indian Himalaya with a group of British climbers. Ironically, the best portions of it were filmed in Scotland because the BBC wanted close-ups of people standing about in the rain.

The Ophir-to-Telluride ski traverse the following day turned out to be less than perfect, and I wondered if it was a harbinger of things the Touching the 'Roid/Condor Expedition to Peru might suffer once lost in South America. After we'd all climbed a high ridge above Ophir, I learned I had grabbed my wife's skis by accident, and that they could not be adjusted to fit my boots. I was forced to return to Ace's Ophir cabin while the rest of the guys skied happily off toward Telluride. Still, I had just created the surely-destined-to-be-popular Ophir-to-Ophir Ski Traverse—which can even be done without skis. Certainly, without brains.

A month later, Jordan, Rick, and I assembled at the airport in Denver. Ace had had to drop out (some minor magazine called *National Geographic* had called with an assignment) so we had enlisted Charlie French, an English climber Jordan and I both knew well. We loaded up the United Airlines jet with several hundred duffel bags of unnecessary stuff and flew south, into the night. The Touching the 'Roid/Condor Expedition was officially underway. (Drum roll, please.)

If you've ever been to Latin America by plane, you know one iron-clad rule: arrival is always at night. Our plane coasted to the terminal, and we stood in a line of tired, frustrated, anxious, pissed-off, and half-drunk people before disembarking into the blackness. (Remember, this was before September 11—in that age when airline passengers were perpetually belligerent.) We wrangled our herd of duffel bags through customs, and before long, we were standing on a dark pavement below some five-foot-tall blue words that said "something-something-something-*aeropuerto.*"

When you arrive on a late flight in a Latin American city, the taxi drivers know you're tired, frustrated, anxious, pissed off, and half-drunk. So, in what appears to be a genuinely well-intentioned effort to make you feel welcome in their city, they grab your luggage and start dragging it off in different directions, across toothy concrete, filthy gutters, and fetid street debris. I don't know if the Lima Tourist Board promotes this sort of activity, but as I watched our thin, soft nylon luggage dragged away in six different directions across several types of hard, gritty surfaces, I imagined myself in an interview with one of these raucous taximen:

"So, dragging tourists' luggage across rough ground is good for business?"

"Si, Señor!"

"Even though this tourist has no desire to ride with you and even less so now that you've ripped his luggage to shreds?"

"Si, Señor! No problemo!"

"Why do you drive a taxi, anyway?"

"No work in rocket science today, Señor!"

Hmm . . . of course. If the Lima Tourist Board expanded the local university of rocket science, hundreds of tourists might be spared shredded luggage. I decided then and there that I'd write a letter to someone about it.

Of course, with Fujimori's political heaving set to crack Peru apart, Lima was a little scary at that point in time. Painted red and white with political slogans and party endorsements, the city seemed ready for something revolutionary, something crazy. We spent the night at a small hotel by the airport, and in the morning we jumped on a bus bound for the mountains. As we rolled out of Lima, we shut our minds and stared into our books, least we be associated with any rabble of U.S.-supported rebels.

Mountain climbing expeditions (trips) are all about camaraderie. You pick the personality combinations you like; you decline the potential time bombs. If you're lucky, as I was, you're just swapping partners. Jordan had been with Charlie on Thalay Sagar, a wild peak in the Himalaya. I'd been with Charlie in Patagonia. Rick had climbed fourteeners in Colorado with me. Jordan had rock climbed with Rick in Boulder. We knew each other's girlfriends and wives. We knew each other's underwear colors and farting styles. It was—as it always is—a mix of people drawn together by a common, if distant and unseen, goal.

After you've put your desired group together, climbing trips are still a three-dimensional experience, somewhat like ships at sea. They float around, like the *Minnow* in *Gilligan's Island,* occasionally bumping into other ships that are also lost, bobbing here and there on an ocean of humanity, transportation, and tilted geography, before hopefully finding a solid mooring on the side of a mountain. At least, that's one lyrical way to look at it. Our bus rolled north and east, through the Cordillera Negra, a small range that parallels the Cordillera Blanca. At the village of Conococha, we entered the high, wide Rio Santa Valley on the east side of the Cordillera Blanca. Suddenly, there were many big, white, scary-looking mountains frowning down at us.

If you've never been to Huaraz, go now! Jump down offa that seat and roll before it's all messed up by the popularity of trekking and mountain climbing and people like us, who are just like you and think we're so darned unique because we climb mountains. Huaraz is a small, rough-edged city of eighty thousand people, sitting at ten thousand feet in a valley between the Cordillera Blanca and the Cordillera Negra. Huaraz looks like an adolescent who's been beaten up—in a way, it is.

In 1941, an avalanche fell into a lake in the Negra, sending millions of tons of debris flowing down onto Huaraz. Five thousand people were killed and the center of town was flattened. In 1970, a massive earthquake shook much of Central Peru, wiping out an estimated thirty thousand Huaraz residents and destroying 90 percent of the city. When you walk around Huaraz, two things come to mind: one, this is a climbing town (there are more equipment shops than in Boulder and Denver combined), and two, the buildings look like they could collapse in a light breeze. This place is rough.

We *did* Huaraz. We bought those pointy Peruvian wool hats that were such a Boulder/Aspen/Park City/Taos/Jackson/Sonora/Santa Fe/Vail/Mammoth/Sun Valley/Missoula/Breckenridge status symbol in the early 1980s. We drank beer in the pubs. We shopped for vegetables and rice and bartered with burro drivers (*arreiros*). We took photos of ourselves doing expedition things, and pretty soon . . . we had wasted craploads of film.

The next day, we drove up to the village of Cashapampa and headed into the Blanca.

The Cordillera Blanca is gorgeous and dramatic. Consider these dimensions: the range is barely fifteen miles wide (in many places it's fewer than ten miles wide), it rises from valleys on either side that are anywhere between six thousand and ten thousand feet in elevation, and its tallest peaks are over twenty-two-thousand feet. The Blanca is, for all intents and purposes, one big fin made up of smaller, fin-shaped peaks. When you wander into the Blanca, your neck is constantly craned back to a point where your chin becomes the apex of your head.

"Is that our mountain?"

"Nope."

"That?"

"Is that it?"

"Nope."

"Man, my neck hurts."

"Mine, too."

And so you end up watching your feet as they patter into base camp. That's what I loved most about this trip: I got to see my feet in this wild and exotic mountain range. Maybe I'd get to see some mountains, too—my neck would just have to suffer.

Base camp was quite civilized. It was nestled in the crook of a high valley at fourteen thousand feet, just below the point where treeline becomes rockline. There was grass and flat spots for tents, and we quickly set up our own little nylon village. Base camps are the best part of climbing trips, but also the strangest. Think about it: dozens of people living in temporary shelters no thicker than a pair of Speedoes, located in areas of the globe with potentially deadly environments. Now, I'm not one to complain, but didn't our ancestors— Cro-Magnon man, for example—bust their butts to evolve from this sort of existence thousands of years ago? And if you really think about it, wasn't Cro-Magnon man smart enough to live in a cave? Dwelling under flimsy nylon seems a sizeable step backward.

Speaking of Cro-Magnon man—in recent times he's been given a pretty good boost by anthropologists. "They were skilled hunters, toolmakers, and artists," wrote one anthropologist. "Their upper Paleolithic culture produced a markedly more sophisticated tool kit, using a wider variety of raw materials such as bone and antler, and containing new implements for making clothing, engraving, and sculpting. They produced fine artwork, in the form of decorated tools, beads, ivory carvings of humans and animals, shell jewelry, clay figurines, musical instruments, and polychrome cave paintings of exceptional vitality."

Gazing around base camp, I saw bedraggled men in underwear laboring over steel pots with handfuls of streambed gravel. Periodically, each looked upward at the sky with a strained, uncomfortable squint that indicated pure bewilderment. While I was wistfully reflecting on base camps and the history of human development, a loud "whap" sound echoed through the air above our heads—the sort of sound a large piece of fabric makes when it has been caught by the wind and flopped in a new direction. Apparently, a camp stove had exploded, taking with it the dark, furry brow of a climber from Argentina. Clearly, our generation hadn't mastered fire.

Base camps are also the places where you check out who's going up the mountain. Most folks in base camps, you quickly learn, rarely set foot on any mountain. 95 percent of them are trekkers, not climbers. Of the other 5 percent, half are so bewildered by their new environment, they seize up with the sudden realization they have very little experience and absolutely no clue as to what the individual steps for reaching a mountaintop are. A German team camped near us. They were running low on food and were on the verge of self-destruction. We needed water purification drops, so we traded for a big salami.

"Das ees gud ya!" one of the Germans said while waving the huge cylinder of meat around in the air after I'd handed it to him. "Ya!"

Okay, buddy. Just put the salami down and no one gets hurt. . . .

Some young Irish lads arrived late on our second night, full of big talk. They were trying to do Alpamayo in three days from the trail-head. They carried no tents or sleeping bags, and lay down on the wet grass to sleep, their Gore-Tex shells, fleeces, and duvets their only protection from the cold. It began raining around midnight, so they crawled into the official Parque Huascaran toilets—poop-spattered concrete stalls with holes in the floor.

There was a big commercial guided group led by Willie Benegas, a powerful Argentinean guide who'd climbed Alpamayo ten times. Then there was a small group of Chileans, strapping lads with loads of energy. There were teams of climbers from all over the world, many of whom seemed to know very little about climbing, or even, in fact, that they were in Peru.

We spent a couple of nights lounging around base camp, playing Go Fish with a deck of pornographic playing cards, sampling the local food, and enjoying life-altering bouts of diarrhea (that explains those concrete stalls), but most of all sucking in lungfuls of that clean, thin air. Then we began the serious business of carrying gear up the mountain and acclimatizing.

At sixteen thousand feet, Camp One was just above the point where the treeline meets the rockline, on a moraine. It wasn't as comfy as the grass, but at least we were getting some exercise in the breathing department. The Chilean lads camped nearby, as did the Germans who were brandishing several more huge salamis. Just as we were getting ready to go higher, it stormed. In fact, it stormed day and night for the better part of a week—apparently rare for Peru. As we ate most of our mountain food, other groups ran out of food entirely. The Chileans turned back. The German team imploded after one of the group's members made a solo attempt and apparently ended up eating *all* the salami.

Low on food, we decided (of course) to go up higher. We spent a highly entertaining night climbing steep snow and ice by headlamp and looking for Camp Two among some very deep and very dark crevasses. We reached a flat area we thought might be Camp Two about 2:00 A.M.

Camp Two, at eighteen thousand feet, is where you put on your running shoes, so to speak. From this point, it was just a two-thousand-foot sprint to the top of the mountain. We spent one night at Camp Two, our heads swimming and our bowels cranking. The next morning, we crunched out of camp and stomped through fresh snow, wondering whether it would be the blue or the white patches of sky that would dominate our day. Struggling up steep, snowy slopes at eighteen thousand feet, our chests heaved and our heads throbbed. Then it was on to the route.

Our chosen line of ascent was called the Ferrari Route, named after Casimiro Ferrari, a bold Italian climber of the 1970s. The Ferrari Route sounds sporty, like a wild time in Monaco, but it's not. It's a lot more on the moderate side of things than it sounds—a bit more Volkswagen Beetle than flashy red sports car. We reached the top and sat around the summit tied to a complex maze of alpine climbing gear that reminded me more of tangled fishing gear than anything else. We rappelled off Alpamayo in the ever-present clouds. There was no argument, little frustration. We were in awe of the beauty of the mountains.

We got back to Camp Two and plopped into some chairs we'd carved in the snow. As we cooked up crunchy pasta and cold sauce, many new arrivals came stomping into Camp Two. A group of three climbers crested the nearby col, between Camps One and Two, and descended to the flat area where our tents were pitched. They said hello, then erected two tents. Behind them were four more climbers who did the same thing. Then came a group of three, followed by another group of four. Before the sun set, we were in the midst of a small city.

The crowd at Camp Two wasn't that bad. Its effects on the local environment, however, were. As night descended, it became apparent that the meager restroom facilities that had served us thus far (i.e., a small pit in the snow) would have to be enlarged for the masses. Before we could even fathom the drudgery that would involve, some eager fellow with heaps of energy had already done it—a series of pits and holes the length of a Roman bath. The title of our expedition was looking uncannily appropriate.

There was a terrible omission, however, in the new facilities: the builder had supplied no walls. Every time a climber went over to use it, the rest of us in Tent Town were treated to a series of blow-by-blow facial expressions. Some people looked like they were being strangled. One thing that's always bothered me about mountaineering is how well you get to know your fellow climbers' restroom habits and facial expressions.

In the morning, Camp Two had morphed from Tent Town into Tent Megalopolis. We watched about thirty climbers cram onto the Ferrari Route and knock bits of ice and other debris down on each others' heads. While we ate oatmeal and packed up to leave, more people arrived for a try at the mountain. Camp Two bulged. Those already there and waiting saw they would have less of a chance as more and more people arrived. In the commercial guided groups, many guides declined to go for the summit, making their clients very angry. Tempers flared and the f-word made multiple colorful and flamboyant appearances. It was like the stuff I'd read about Everest, yet here it was on a very modest but beautiful mountain—that still sounded like a creamy topping for dog food—in the middle of the Cordillera Blanca. Peaks just next door had no one on them. We knew Alpamayo was popular, but we had little idea that, along with Aconcagua, Huascaran, and a couple of other peaks, Alpamayo is probably one of the top five most popular mountains in South America among climbers.

Unfortunately, the lengthy storm precluded us from climbing another mountain. Like so many, our time had been gobbled up with sitting in tents playing pornographic Go Fish and waiting for the weather to clear. We didn't have enough time or food to make up for the deficit. We descended to base camp and hoofed it out to Huaraz.

Back in Huaraz, I began photographing the locals. The traditional Peruvian women with their colorful skirts and big top hats, sitting on the sides of the narrow streets selling oranges and potatoes, were a fascinating subject. It turned out they don't like having their pictures taken. "Most people resent having a camera thrust in their faces and people in markets will often proudly turn their backs on pushy photographers," wrote Rob Rachowiecki in his travel guide to Peru. (Yeah, no kidding, Robbo. But I wasn't pushy, and I certainly wasn't thrusting.) In fact, they liked it so little that they began throwing potatoes and oranges at me. This was unique—not too many cultures have a tradition where you toss fruits and vegetables at tourists—but then again, this was better than the game of Newly-Arrived-Tourist-Luggage-Thrashing going on down at the Lima airport. I had to wonder what the Peru Tourist Council was teaching the good people.

Anyway, being a sports fan, I threw the potatoes back. I tossed them gently, so the women could catch them. Then I hung around waiting for a full-blown game of something to develop, but it didn't. The top-hatted women simply ignored me. I wandered off to look for other sports involving airborne tubers and fruits.

If you've had a good trip, going home can be hard. Especially if you've had fun with your friends, didn't kill each other, and didn't die, and *especially* if you've climbed something. It means putting an end to this trip, this noun, this experience, this *thing*. Whatever it was, and however you felt about it, doesn't matter anymore. It is winding down and ceasing to exist. Nothing can revive it. Gone, dead, kaput! For us it was, so to speak, the end of the 'Roid.

Everyone gives different reasons for going on climbing trips. A lot of people give some pretty high-minded philosophical reasons: inner peace and reflection, challenge and excitement, experience and camaraderie. I've heard big wall climbers explain that they go climbing because they were getting too comfy on the couch. They beat themselves up on a wall, then come home to the couch for a spell. They get too lazy, so they go out again—a vicious cycle thing. I've heard non-outdoorsy folks discuss how they go on trekking trips to see if they can meet certain specified challenges, to see if they can put up with ten nights in a tent and camp food, to see if they have the mettle to complete a challenge. Climbing trips have made me realize something much more simple. They've made me realize that there's a whole wide world out there of interesting people and cultures, mountains and geographic regions, fruits and vegetables, and international headgames involving salamis and potatoes.

In the end, everyone will have his or her own reasons for journeying halfway around the globe and spending thousands of dollars to sleep in nylon domes and eat crunchy pasta. I go now because I simply want to see it. No pictures in any book ever do the mountains justice. They don't do the sunsets or the smog justice either, and never has a photo properly caught the spirit of a moment. After I skimmed through a pile of books on South America, Peru's mountains looked so darn cool that I figured they'd be fantastic in real life. Any hassle to get there would be worth it. Even if I was just walking past, or riding a bus up the Rio Santa Valley, that would've been okay. The main thing was, I wanted to go and have a look. And to me, that's what a trip is all about.

---

1 *Joe Simpson's first book, describing a climbing trip to Peru in which, after summitting a steep, twenty-one-thousand-foot mountain, he falls into a crevasse and breaks his leg. His partner, Simon Yates, leaves him. During the next three days, while Yates is overcome with guilt and grief in base camp, Simpson manages to crawl down the mountain and save himself. Recently released in movie form.*

Fred Beckey in his element. Inset: Famous '80s sportclimber Christian Griffith talks shop with Fred.

The Unbearable Greatness of Fred (2004)

"Why don't these fucking people learn English?!"

Mike Baker stares across the table at me; I look back at him. In perfect unison, our eyebrows creep up our respective foreheads and head for the smalls of our respective backs. We remain silent as a waitress brings a pot of coffee and refills our cups. Our companion doesn't. "Why don't these fucking people learn English?!"

Fed up with Mexican service, Fred Beckey stands up, grunts, farts, and heads for the door. Taken aback, Mike and I stare at each other. Beckey, a personal hero for both of us, is proving anything but a hero. It is February 1991. We are two days' drive into Mexico and about a thousand miles south of the border. Fred Beckey wants to climb a new route on the west face of Cerro Blanco. Mike and I are there for two reasons. One: we like climbing. The second—and perhaps the real reason for our mind-numbing, fifteen-hundred-mile jaunt—is that we think climbing with Fred Beckey will make us better people; we think it will add a feather to our caps; we think it might rub off, even though we have no idea what *it* is. Because despite the fact that we soon learn to hate him—and that he's as odd as a three-dollar bill—Fred Beckey is probably the world's foremost pioneering mountaineer. Period.

Shouldering our way through a crowd, Fred and I enter customs in Juarez. Fred is wearing a pair of blue jeans and an ugly-as-all-hell, dark brown, knitted polyester shirt—like some kind of retro-'70s couch fabric. He's got a blue and white baseball cap on that reads "Gore-Tex." It doesn't look right. Never having been one to commercialize climbing, Beckey with his ugly clothes and a big blue label on his head is a strange sight. Somehow, he fits perfectly in Juarez.

"Fred, back in the early '60s, liked to go to St. Vincent de Paul's and buy gaudy neckties," said Eric Bjørnstad, a well-known desert climber and writer who was Beckey's most enduring partner, during a 1994 interview. "He'd tie these neckties under overhangs or in impossible places so that somebody else coming up would suddenly see this necktie. He stopped doing that when I cussed him out one time. He led a pitch on the Rain Shadow route on Castle Rock and tied the rope into a piton underneath an overhang (with the necktie) and then went out over the overhang and on up. I was coming up under another overhang below and the necktie broke and I swung way out into space. I thought the rope had broken. I thought I was falling. It scared the hell out of me. I cussed Fred out so severely I never saw him use a necktie after that."

* * *

Inside customs, Fred and I get in line to get our visas stamped.

"So, Fred, how old are you?" I asked naively, the first attempt at conversation with Fred in two days.

"Mmmmph." He waves my questions away with his hand.

"All you do is climb, right? How do you support yourself?"

"I don't want to talk about that," he says.

We ante up to the counter and Fred pulls out his visa. I crane my neck and peer over his shoulder, catching sight of the word *teacher* under the heading "Occupation." With that one stealth move, I've learned more than people who've known Fred for thirty years.

"Teacher, huh?" said Doug Leen, a regular Beckey partner during the late '60s, and someone who's been as close to Beckey as a climbing partner can. "That's a new one on me."

Leen's surprise is perhaps expected. Fred Beckey's past is probably the second-most-guarded secret in American mountaineering. The first is what he plans to climb next.

"One thing you find out very quickly when you climb with Fred is that he very rarely talks about the past," said another Beckey friend and climbing partner Don Liska, in the mid-1990s. "He's got more experience and more know-how, and he's done more than probably any other climber in the world—not just this country, but the world—and yet it's very difficult to get things out of him. He especially doesn't like to talk about the accidents and the close shaves, things of that sort, you know."

Reports vary on when and where Wolfgang Gottfried Beckey was actually born. And if you ask him, he won't enlighten you. He ignored my questioning in Mexico thirteen years ago.

In his book *The Mountaineers: Famous Climbers in Canada*, Phil Dowling states that ". . . Beckey was born in 1923 in West Seattle." Most other historians believe Beckey to have been born in Germany.

Harvey Manning wrote "Zulpich." Jon Krakauer, in an early 1990s *Outside* magazine article, wrote "Dusseldorf in 1923."

Whenever and wherever perhaps doesn't matter because within a few years, the Beckey family was in the United States—the Pacific Northwest, to be exact. In Seattle, young Wolfgang was raised by his German parents (an opera singer and a doctor) and saw for the first time the mountains that would dominate much of his life.

Young "Fred," as he became known, was introduced to the mountains via car camping trips with the family. In 1936, he first showed his proclivity for the mountains by wandering off to climb Boulder Peak, alone. The ascent alarmed the parental Beckeys, and young Fred was soon enrolled in the local chapter of the Boy Scouts, where hiking was encouraged.

Beckey took to scouting, and by the time he signed up and joined the Mountaineers in 1939, he had already tromped across hundreds of miles of virgin scrub and scree and scrambled up several dozen peaks in the Cascades and Olympic Mountains. In the Mountaineers, he learned a new craft, something as strange and perverse as his sense of humor was shaping up to be: mountaineering.

"Climbing appealed to me right away," Beckey said in a 1986 *Climbing* magazine[1] interview. "I seemed to do as well as the average guy, and it just seemed to turn me on. I had found an activity which to me was an art—something I could do that was creative and just plain enjoyable."

Although 1939 was his first year at true mountaineering—with the prerequisite clutter of ropes, equipment, and funny jargon— Beckey was a natural. With Clint Kelley and Lloyd Anderson (the founder of REI), Beckey picked off the first ascent of Mt. Despair in the Cascades—a peak labeled unclimbable in a Mountaineers publication—followed closely with a trip to the Tetons and ascents of six peaks, including the Grand.

The summer of '39 was far from over. Beckey, outside the regimented order of the Mountaineers and with a few young friends, muscled his way through the inhospitable Cascades. From Snoqualmie Pass north, he and his pals bagged first ascents of Bears Breast and Little Big Chief, besides repeating over thirty other peaks. It was truly rough country.

"People couldn't get their rucksacks of pitons to the base of the faces because it was such a bushwhack," said Leen of Cascades climbing in the late '30s. "I went in with Fred to Dome Peak once. We Tyrolean-traversed rivers, got chased by bears; Fred almost died. If Roger (Johnson) hadn't pulled him out of the river, he would've drowned."

But the summer of 1939 was not when Fred Beckey became *Fred Beckey*. Nor was it in 1940, when—at the ripe old age of seventeen—he made first ascents of the Cascades' Forbidden Peak, Crooked Thumb, Phantom Peak, and Inspiration Peak.

Fred became *The Fred* on Waddington.

By 1942, Mt. Waddington held an awesome status. It had seen sixteen attempts spread over two decades. Fritz Weissner—who nearly made the first ascent of K2 in 1939—and partner Bill House conquered the "Mystery Peak" in 1936. The two-hundred-mile hike was a thrash through the wilds of thickest British Columbia—across rivers, rocks, and glaciers; on skis, foot, and all fours. Beckey's willingness to persevere in country where many others would have turned back would later became a trademark of his style.

So, too, was his apparent willingness to just leave the weaker members of a party behind.

"There is a report on the Waddington trip back in the 1940s that he and his brother did, in fact, have to leave one guy behind because he just wasn't able to keep up with them," recalled Liska. "He had to sort of more or less fend for himself."

The third soldier was a fellow by the name of Eric Larsson. Larsson couldn't keep up with the Beckeys' high-speed backwoods pace, so the much more athletic Beckey brothers left him.

As Krakauer noted in his article, the Larsson incident underscores Beckey's deep drive. At times, it has given him a reputation for recklessness and insensitivity toward partners.

Sure, concede some, "But here's a tough, strong guy, he was a poet in his field," said Liska. "He expected other people to toe the mark, too. He wasn't particularly kind to weakness or lack of condition, or reticence to continue on when conditions were okay. A lot of people are that way. Harvey Carter was the same way."

Despite the bad-boy reputation, the Beckey brothers succeeded on Waddington and turned the mountaineering world on its ear. Two mere children—boys named Beckey, whoever *they* were—had climbed Weissner's Mystery Peak. It is a route comparable to the north face of the Petit Dru, and an achievement comparable to the Sourdoughs dragging a wooden pole up Denali. Fred Beckey, *climber extraordinaire*, had arrived. He was just nineteen.

Mike Baker, myself, and an aging climber extraordinaire arrive—in 1991—in the town of Peñon Blanco, a charming backcountry village in the mountains of Central Mexico. Dust is everywhere and on everything. It adds emphasis to the massive lines on Fred's face.

Our first stop is to find a rancher Fred knows who owns Cerro Blanco. We spend a frustrated few hours ambling around town, relying on my pathetic Spanish vocabulary and all its dozen words to relay that we need to find Señor So-and-So. Cerro Blanco rises invitingly behind town.

Late in the afternoon, with all three of us drooling over the granite dome, we drive out of town with Mike at the wheel. Scoping out the massive Cerro Blanco is far more important than niggling details like permission.

Motoring through cornfields in the middle of Mexico below a Tuolumne-like dome might not sound risky, but when we hear a grass-hidden stump rip the bottom of the Rabbit to shreds and feel the seats drop about four inches, we know the shit has bounced off the fan blades and is now raining down upon us.

The car, you see, was borrowed. When a young bike technician named Aaron Miller heard we were going climbing with Fred in Mexico—and because neither Mike nor I wanted to take our own cars—he offered us his. He was such a Fred Fan (one misdirected youth in a cult of thousands) that he simply said, "Take it."

Mike, Fred, and I get out to examine the damage. The borrowed auto's frame is snapped—literally—into two separate pieces. The whole thing sags to the ground. Obviously the car had seen a lot of winter salt in some northeastern state and was rusted to the bone, but that information didn't help us in the transportation department. Tempers flare, harsh words are exchanged, and a thoroughly disgusted Fred, rolls up in his sleeping bag in a bush—no kidding.

Despite Fred's proclivity for new routes and despite his tenacity, Mike and I were to learn many things on our jaunt to central Mexico. Number one: No one who climbs with Beckey remains friends with him during the trip. Number two: The climbing doesn't matter.

Hundreds of climbers who've roamed through the Cascades—and other ranges—with Beckey already know this.

"Fred has falling outs with people at all times," said Bjørnstad. "I had a falling out with him after twenty days on Shiprock. My girl-friend and I hitchhiked back to Seattle. Fred would drive by and just kind of taunt and wave to us.

"He had a falling out with Charlie Bell years ago in the Cascades and dumped Charlie out of his car and drove off. He still had all of Charlie's gear in the trunk. Charlie got a hold of a highway patrolman that stopped Fred and made Fred wait for Charlie to catch up and get his gear back."

Most mountain ranges have a so-called golden age, a period when the biggest, most impressive routes—which later become classics—are climbed. The Cascades are no such range. Fred Beckey has been such a predominant player in the history of the range that about any decade Fred's been alive could be counted as golden. First, there were the pre–World War II years, when Cascade mountaineering was invented by the Beckey brothers and their pals. Then there were the early '40s, when a lot of the still-remaining blanks on the map got their names: Crooked Thumb, Phantom Peak, Inspiration Peak, Nooksack Tower, Big Snagtooth, Willow Tooth, Cedar Tooth, Red Tooth, the Fin, the Tomahawk, Kangaroo Temple, and Big Kangaroo, to name a few.

Fred, inspired and energetic, climbed them all.

Part of what Fred and Helmy were doing in the Cascades back-country was important in two ways: First, they were really exploring, seeing mountains and walls other people wouldn't really know about until years later. Second, and perhaps why Beckey would remain such a force in the climbing world, is that the brothers were delving into the limits of physical endurance—seeing how far they could push themselves in rough country and bad weather.

"That trip Helmy and I made into the Pickets in 1940 was one of roughest," Fred told Chris Jones in a 1973 *Mountain* magazine interview. "We traversed the Pickets, just the two of us. I think we were very bold doing our first major climbs in such desolate country. We were taking chances on really bad rock, with broken 'streetcars' of ice hanging above us, and the glaciers were heavily crevassed. I gained a lot of confidence on that trip . . . I tend to think at the time we had an aura of braveness, or maybe we just lacked fear, but in any case we didn't think about it as much as we would now . . . we became good at making our own preparations and fending for ourselves. If it stormed for three days, you got soaking wet, but you knew you could survive."

In the mid-1940s, brother Helmy "retired" from mountaineering. Although Helmy was Fred's most trustworthy and able-bodied partner, he had other objectives in life. Not Fred. In 1946, he made his second expedition to Canada and climbed Kate's Needle and the Devil's Thumb, both firsts.

Besides straightforward rock routes, by the mid-1940s, Beckey was becoming attracted to full-blown expeditions. In 1947, he spent two months in British Columbia, climbing with a Harvard University expedition. The group made first ascents of twenty-four unclimbed peaks, including Asperity. Beckey was on twelve of them.

In the late 1940s, Beckey also began dabbling in writing. In 1949, the *Climber's Guide to the Cascades and Olympics of Washington* was published, the first of nearly a dozen subsequent books.

Like many climbers today, Beckey's "career moves" were primarily centered around keeping as much time free for the mountains. He had done a stint in the army in the early 1940s, where he trained troops in various mountain-related activities, including a month of ice climbing and crevasse rescue on Rainier, but he also wrote manuals on mountain warfare. During this period, he met David Brower, Raffi Bedayn, and other noteworthy climbers of the day—all of whom had been assigned to the mountain-related branches of the army.

Some of Fred's other jobs were with in the publishing world, with paper companies. In the early 1950s, there is a noticeable lull in the action on major peaks and routes as Fred was "forcibly localized" by one situation. "I was working full-time as a display advertising salesman in Seattle," he said in an interview, "and didn't have a vacation for three or four summers in a row."

"One of the other jobs he had when I first knew him was selling paper to publishing companies," Bjørnstad recalled. "I don't think he was involved in publishing; he was just a paper salesman. He had a company car and he'd use that car for climbing. . . . His brother sold drugs to drug stores. That's why a lot of notes from Fred are written on weird [drug company] stationery."

The company car was always important to Fred, and his weekend forays into the Cascades during the '50s became legendary *tours de force*. "There were good weekends during those years—mad dashes to the mountains," he said. "In Seattle, we used to plan to leave on a Friday night, and not worry how late we got back at the end of the weekend as long as it was in time for work. I sometimes wonder how we did it, keeping up those night hikes at both ends—in on Friday night, out on Sunday. They were incredibly tough, but the drive home was the worst."

A return from the first ascent of the south buttress of Cutthroat Peak in 1958 was typical: Fred and Don Claunch climbed the route on the weekend days, hiked back over Twisp Pass (in the early part of Sunday night), then drove for six hours (in the late part of Sunday night) back to Seattle in an old 1947 Ford, arriving home at 4:00 A.M.—"...just in time for a quick shave, a change of clothes, and maybe a shower."

Beckey's tricks for staying awake through such a drive became well-known in the Seattle-area climbing community. "I knew a whole bag of tricks for making myself stay awake, all sorts of self-inflicted tortures. One of the best was to make the car terribly cold. Roll my sleeve up and hang my arm out of the window till I couldn't stand it any more. For about half an hour you feel really great. Then you find some rock 'n' roll on the car radio, take your shoes off—better yet, takes your socks off—and then there's the sensation of your bare feet on the pedals. You need a continual series of things. Best of all, stick your head out the window. It really works at fifty miles per hour. That's good for a couple of hours."

The fifties saw other major ascents. In 1954, Beckey made the first ascent of the northwest buttress on Denali, the third route on the peak, as well as the first ascents of Mt. Hunter and Mt. Deborah, in a team that included Heinrich Harrer (of Eiger *Nordwand* fame).

In 1955, Beckey's climbing career—and his life—dive-bombed when he participated in a big, international expedition to Nepal. The peak was 27,939-foot Lhotse, at the time the highest unclimbed summit in the world. According to reports of the day, Beckey got as high as 24,500 feet. Due to high winds, intense cold, and unstable snow, Beckey and his companions—two Sherpas and Swiss climber Bruno Spirig—couldn't move. Storms kept them pinned in their Camp V.

". . . The next morning we tried to move up," Beckey said in *Mountain*. "But the tracks were all blown in. The conditions were abominable . . . The night spent in that tent was pretty unrewarding. Spirig was affected. I don't know what it was, it may have been oxygen starvation, or it may have been psychological."

The next morning, Beckey and the Sherpas helped Spirig down to Camp IV. There were no sleeping bags in Camp IV; they had been left at another camp.

"It seemed a pretty untenable situation," Beckey said. "I didn't know whether to stay in the tent or go down and get help. I don't think there was a question of personal survival involved; I felt it best to get help. On the way down, the others saw me coming, and those in Camps II and III went up in the morning to get Spirig. There was some criticism because he had spent the night alone. What I could have done for him other than to help him keep warm, I don't know."

At base camp, expedition leader Norman Dyhrenfurth was none too pleased. He and other members of the expedition rescued Spirig, but Beckey's reputation had already been tarnished. Bjørnstad knows the event well, and what it did to Beckey.

"It's something that Fred will never live down, and that he shouldn't have ever done," said Bjørnstad in a 1994 interview. "That's basically why he wasn't invited on the [famed American] '63 Everest expedition because of his reputation after having left that guy." The '63 American Everest expedition saw Jim Whittaker become the first American to climb the world's tallest peak.

Although Lhotse was a failure, Beckey managed to pull off several other noteworthy achievements. Among them were the world record for high altitude skiing (twenty-three thousand feet on the Khumbu glacier), the first ascents of Kantega IV, Langcha, and the south summit of Lobuje. An attempt on Ama Dablam with Dick McGowan and George Bell failed due to lack of support from Dyhrenfurth.

Beckey recalled the moment: "He said, if you want to do something, go ahead. Good luck. Take what food you need. Then he turned his back and walked away."

After hearing Beckey bitch at Mike for the hundredth time about the busted car, I have to walk away, too. I wander across open sage and scrub and gaze up at the peak we've spent four days getting to. It's just five miles away, and its clean white granite walls glow warmly in the sunset.

In the near-distance, I can hear Fred: "Goddammit, Mike. Why didn't you get a truck!? You knew we'd need a truck to get around down here. I spent all that money flying to Albuquerque and you don't even have a proper vehicle."

"No, Fred, I didn't know," Mike replies. "You're the one who knew about this place. I've never been here before and you know it.

Maybe you should have brought a car. Besides, I'm the one who has to tell Aaron his car is fucked!"

Beckey can definitely get on your nerves. Mike and I have paid for every hotel room and every tank of gas—a couple of hundred bucks—thus far, and now it looks like we're going to have to pay for a car. Fred keeps saying he'll pay us back for all the expenses at the end of the trip, but somehow, it comes out like a lie.

"We'll settle up at the end," he says repeatedly. "We'll settle up then."

Yeah, right.

I have not yet entered the argument in which Mike and Fred are engaged—one which will last several days as we try to resume our expedition, and a few more days as we quit Mexico—but I'm getting warmed up. My own Beckey blowout is on the back burner. Fred has just bumped the setting from simmer to medium.

Whatever Norman Dyhrenfurth thought about Beckey in 1955 didn't matter to Fred. At least not for a few years. Beckey kept climbing as he had for twenty years: hard and fast.

In 1957, Beckey and photographer Ira Spring went roaming around the roads in the Cascade foothills, looking for a location to photograph a Canadian Club whiskey advertisement. They discovered a cliff that would later become one of Canada's premier rock climbing centers.

"It was on that particular trip that I really noticed the [Squamish] Chief," said Beckey. "It dawned on me that we were running out of weekend climbs in the Cascades, so next morning I got together with Hank Mather and we agreed to do one of the buttresses."

The climb the pair did was dubbed the Squamish Buttress, and was the first big wall on the Chief.

Oddly, in the late '50s the *Seattle Post-Intelligencer* newspaper printed reports of first ascents, giving an aura of legitimacy to climbing. Bjørnstad remembers the period.

"He was infamous," said Bjørnstad. "He was in the newspapers weekly for first ascents. . . . He made his living in the early '60s, when I first met him, showing John Jay and Warren Miller ski films. He would rent the projector and rent the hall, then get the tickets and posters made up. Warren Miller or John Jay would fly into the town, Fred would go up on stage and personally introduce John Jay or Warren Miller, and then he'd be out the back door, going climbing. Warren Miller or John Jay would then narrate their ski films."

Through the late 1950s and early 1960s, Beckey continued climbing in the Cascades and Canada, but it was in the Bugaboos where he made the contribution of the period. Beckey had bagged the first ascent of the north face of Pigeon Spire in 1948. But in 1959, he and Hank Mather pushed the limit on Canadian big-wall climbing with their ascent of the east face of Snowpatch Spire, the first Grade VI in the range.

The first half of the route overhangs, and it is separated from the glacier by a deep bergschrund. Only by using Yosemite-style wall tactics, Beckey figured, could they do the climb. On July 26, Mather—laughing about the difficulty with which the climb started— lowered Beckey into the bergschrund where he began climbing. It wasn't until the end of the day that he had reached Mather's height on the glacier. Over the next three days, they managed only four overhanging pitches. Knowing they'd have to commit to the wall sooner or later, they bailed off and rested for a few days. On August 5, they re-ascended to their high point, and after seven exceptionally tough days, seventeen leads, 160 piton placements, and eight bolts, they topped out.

"In some ways," said Beckey, "it was more committing than anything I'd been involved with before. . . . We only had soft steel pegs and homemade angles . . . that slowed us up a bit."

Over the following four years, he climbed the most demanding routes in the Bugaboos, including the Beckey-Greenwood on Snowpatch Spire; the west face of Bugaboo Spire; the Beckey-Chouinard and the northeast face on South Howser Tower; the northwest face and the southeast buttress of Pigeon Spire; and the west buttress of North Howser Tower. Several of the routes are now considered all-time classics.

In 1961, with Yvon Chouinard and Dan Doody, Beckey made the first ascent of the north face of Mt. Edith Cavell—at the time, the biggest mixed route (thirty-eight hundred feet) in Canada.

"I was very happy we did it," Beckey said in an interview. "And very happy we got off it. We were pretty scared by rockfall."

While he had been continually picking up his pace in the early '60s, in 1963, Beckey went wild. He had not been chosen for an expedition to Everest's west ridge, even asked. The leader of the expedition was none other than Norman Dyhrenfurth.

Lhotse, it seemed, was coming back to haunt him. Jim Whittaker became the first American to summit Everest—and his photo graced the cover of various popular magazines. Beckey's stomach must have been turning.

His response was to put all his energy into climbing on this continent, and to many climbers of the day, what Beckey achieved in the mid-'60s makes Whittaker's repeat of the south col route pale by comparison.

Flip through American guidebooks and the "Beckey" routes come up in 1963 more than any other year. From the Cascades to the Sierra Nevada, from Alaska to the Wind Rivers, Beckey was out there making a tremendous mark in American mountaineering.

"I met Fred in the early '60s," recalls Liska. "He already knew he was not going to be invited to join that [Everest] team, even though he was one of the most qualified climbers. In the '60s, he did go crazy. He was doing thirty to forty trips a summer—major, major climbs. He had this book full of objectives. Most climbers that were active would have given two or three fingers of their right hand to get a hold of that book. Fred was very active. He really, from an alpine achievement point of view, made up tenfold in activity and achievement in that period for a mere ascent of Everest.

"After all, looking back, what does an ascent of the south col route on Everest really mean? Very little except in the eyes of the uninformed public. But in terms of mountaineering achievement, it doesn't mean much. The things Fred achieved are still of outstanding value. But, of course, at the time, you couldn't look at it that way. At the time, Everest was the big nail."

By the time Fred, Mike, and I are rescued by the mayor of Peñon Blanco and a dozen of his gauchos, I am ready to drive a big nail through Fred Beckey's head. Mike won't even talk to Fred. We wander around the suburbs of Peñon Blanco for two days. I am still eager to climb something, but with every passing hour—living out of a hotel room and with no transportation whatsoever—it's looking like a pipe dream. Fred refuses to stop hammering Mike, and it destroys any semblance of "team" that is left.

However, things change when the mayor learns that I'm a journalist. He thinks I might be of some kind of value—via potential articles in American magazines attracting tourists to Peñon Blanco. We are chauffeured everywhere and suddenly have Mexican helpers at our beck and call. Fred notices the shift and tries to take command of the situation.

"We'll try the climb," he declares a day after the Rabbit dies. "I think we only need gear for three or four days."

Mike shakes his head: "I'm not tying on a rope with him. What if things really got bad?"

Mike has a good point. Seeing Fred's dramatic change from hounding critic to cheerful, able-bodied leader once the sun is shining, is mind-boggling. I decline, too. We retreat once more to Peñon Blanco. Mike and I rent a hotel room and leave Fred—who has not yet paid a dime toward mutual team expenses after a week and a half—standing outside. He creeps in while we shower, and curls up on the floor. Mike and I leave and go out for a *cerveza* and a meal.

If anyone knows how to get comfortable on a $2-a-night hotel room floor, it's Beckey. Money, or lack of it, has kept Beckey stateside most of his years. It's one reason his massive route list stretches from Alaska to Baja, Moab to Ketchikan, but no farther.

"Fred was always a poor climber, living out of his car, eating out of cans," noted Bjørnstad. "He lives very inexpensively. He likes McDonald's because he saves the coffee cup and reuses it for months and gets free coffee."

However, Bjørnstad admits, there's more to McDonald's than coffee: "He just goes up to women in McDonald's. He was very successful at it. He was charming, he had a good approach. He liked showgirls. I had a coffeehouse at the end of the Seattle World's Fair on Show Street, next to Backstage USA, a kind of a strip joint. Fred and I dated a lot of the showgirls.

"I remember one particular striking one with long, blonde hair and long, long fingernails. She couldn't open any doors because she was scared of breaking her fingernails. Her name was Lisa. Fred stayed in touch with Lisa for years afterward. He had another girlfriend in the early '60s that he almost married. He went with her for many years. I think, because of Fred's procrastination, she ended up marrying some older person that Fred called a 'sugar daddy.'"

And despite a healthy appetite for women, "he's never smoked and he doesn't drink," according to Bjørnstad. "He'll go to a tavern to pick up girls and be social, and he'll order a beer, but there'll be three-quarters of it left by the time he leaves."

In the *Mountain* interview, Fred described the nature of his love life: "There were a few of those [affairs]," he said. "You get involved with somebody and follow it up temporarily, but this doesn't disintegrate your interest [for climbing], it simply mitigates it. You just don't spend every weekend climbing. For a couple of years I was pretty well involved. I didn't climb for a month, maybe." Although a few women nearly entrapped Beckey into domestic bliss, none did, and it left him free to do his thing.

By the mid-'60s, Beckey's hoboesque climbing life had drawn him to the great southwestern desert. Beckey faired well on the crumbling towers of the desert, and, as he has done everywhere else on the continent, he was soon driving a thousand miles for weekend climbing near Moab, only to turn around after an ascent and drive up into Canada to climb something else.

Except for summitting on the second day during the first ascent of the Priest, in Castle Valley, Beckey's first big spire was the biggest: Shiprock, in 1965.

His two-thousand-foot route, climbed with Bjørnstad, Alex Bertulis, and Harvey Carter,[2] took thirty days. It was one of the first Grade V climbs done in the Southwest and, with the exception of the Nose in Yosemite, probably the most time spent on a route anywhere on the North American continent. Certainly, the "Beckey Buttress" is the most impressive line on *Tse'Bit'ai*, as the locals used to call Shiprock.

The following year Beckey created another record when he made the first ascent of Echo Tower in the Fisher Towers, with Bjørnstad and Carter: seventy-one bolts over seven pitches. Beckey has returned ever since to make some of the finest contributions to desert climbing. Although former Colorado climber Layton Kor is generally regarded as having plucked the best cherries, Beckey's list is every bit as impressive. It includes first ascents of Moses Tower, Owl Rock, Echo Tower, the Throne, Middle Sister, Eagle Rock Spire, Zeus, the Bride, Chinle Spire, Jacob's Ladder, Sewing Machine Needle, and the Great White Throne in Zion, guessed by some[3] to be the longest sandstone route in the world.

Routes, it seems, have only interested Fred Beckey if they haven't been done before. No one is quite sure when first-ascent fever really grabbed Beckey, but it has never let go. If it ain't new, it ain't going to be Beckey.

No exact numbers exist, but most American climbers agree that Beckey has climbed more new routes than anyone in the world. In fact, in the 1970s, the editor of one mountaineering magazine speculated that Fred had pioneered over ten thousand new routes. But the significance of Beckey routes isn't the quantity, it's the quality. All Beckey's routes are long, impressive, and very worthwhile.

"If it has been done, Fred will just turn around and go home," said Doug Leen, remembering a jaunt in the early '70s. "We ended up going off for about a week in the desert, climbing all these pinnacles. We climbed Dark Angel, and I got up to within twenty feet of the top and I said, 'Fred, there's a sling up here.' Fred would literally pull me down the pinnacle. He'd say, 'Let's just get out of here, we're wasting our time,' and he'd just tie me off and I couldn't finish the climb. It had been climbed before and he wanted a first ascent."

On some climbs, if the first man in a two-man climbing team has made it up, that's enough for Beckey.

"For instance," recalled Bjørnstad, "I made the first ascent of Zeus, and Fred said: 'Oh well, you've reached the summit; why should I come up?' It would still be written up as Fred and Eric's first ascent of Zeus, even though Fred didn't lead any of it. He just belayed me the whole distance. He would do that a lot, not go to the top. He'd just say, 'It's a waste of time. The climb's been done.' It would be written up, and a lot of times it would become known as 'Beckey's route' when he didn't even touch the rock. He didn't reach the summit of the Sewing Machine Needle either."

Down and out in deepest Mexico, the nadir of my relationship with Beckey is reached in the little hotel room late in the evening before we come home. Mike and I pay for a room, then Mike goes off to find a phone while I lug some gear into the room. Fred silently follows me in—like a scolded child or a dirty shadow, or rather, like the cloud that follows Pigpen around in the *Peanuts* comic strips. He picks one of the two beds, lies down, and is soon fast asleep.

Mike arrives and shrugs—and says he'll leave Fred there on the bed while he goes to take a leak. "I'll get him off in a minute," Mike says.

Not me. Mooching ropemates are my biggest pet peeve on any climbing trip. I simply tell Fred that if he doesn't get off Mike's bed, I'm going to toss him out on his can. I wander around the room giving Fred serious looks. He unfurls a sleeping pad and gets on the floor. Admittedly, mine is a wildly ridiculous display. What kind of person would threaten a poor old man, who even then at sixty-eight is permanently bent from a lifetime of toil? Who's revered among men of action and whose writing is as eloquent as Shakespeare's and as learned as Attenborough's? Well, me for one—because that's what Fred does to you.

Over the past few days I've generated a "default mode theory" about climbing trips with Fred. On every climbing trip, there are defaults waiting to happen. Bad weather is one type of default; a climbing accident is another type of default; transportation is another possible default. Then there are personality disorders, location and direction confusions, language hurdles, food shortages, gear failures, natural disasters, and plain old bad luck. On most climbing trips, one or two things can default and you're still okay—even three things sometimes. On trips with Fred, everything defaults, starting on the first day, and it all goes downhill from there. A trip with Fred is a bit like beating yourself over the head with a two-by-four while simultaneously jogging in step atop a heap of broken glass and being sprayed with hot tar: it feels really good when you stop.

Over the next three days, things get better. The mayor of Peñon Blanco buys the borrowed-but-now-destroyed Rabbit from us for $80. Mike and I forget about Fred, pack up all the gear, and load it onto a bus headed north. Not knowing a word of the local tongue, Fred hovers in the distance: getting on buses when we do, eating meals when we do, and generally taking on the role of dirty cloud.

However, he keeps his distance the entire way. An unhappy, sweaty Burns, grunting at Fred in a grimy hotel room, has given him a nasty scare—as it would any civilized human.

Throughout the "adventure," Fred has promised to "settle up" with expenses at the end of the trip. That doesn't happen, even when we *ask* to settle up. The final straw—for me, at least—comes while we're loading our bags onto a bus in Guadalajara. Fred watches while I dig through my empty wallet looking for a few pesos for the extra baggage. Finally, I tell Fred he needs to chip in because I'm completely out of money.

He thumbs through his stack of untouched bills, hems and haws. Having wrangled a heavy haul bag containing all of Fred's gear across Mexico, I boil over: "Gimme that!"

I snatch his wallet, take out five thousand pesos, and hand it to the bus driver. I give Fred's wallet back to him, smile, and tell him to shut up and get on the bus. Getting Fred to pay was, some say, one of the more challenging feats in American mountaineering. It goes at the top of my questionable list of achievements.

On our way back through Mexico, we stop at the café where Fred asked, "Why don't these people learn English?" This time, however, he complains that the chili is too expensive: it costs 70 cents.

It took me a while to learn that Fred says a lot of things simply to shock people—to see exactly how far he can go.

"Fred liked making statements like that," Bjørnstad later told me. "He enjoyed being obnoxious. He'd be eating cheese and salami and French bread and he'd say, 'Pass the horse cock.'"

"Fred's a real character," added Leen. "There's a dimension to Fred that's very difficult to perceive. In some ways he was very advanced. In other ways he wasn't."

Fred Beckey continued at his hell-bent pace through the 1970s, and 1980s, focusing much of his attention on the same ranges that have made him a living, breathing legend: the Sierra Nevada, the Canadian Rockies, the Wind Rivers, the Cascades, and the desert.

In 1982, he led a successful expedition to China. Throughout the 1990s and well into the new millennium, Beckey continued traveling across the continent in search of routes and partners.

"After that [1986 *Climbing* magazine] magazine article came out on Fred, I was so impressed that I sent a long letter and a copy of that article to Jimmy Carter," said Liska. "I asked Carter if there was any way the nation could award a person who did things in this area, like climbing and climbing achievement, which inherently doesn't get much in the way of awards. Unfortunately, I haven't gotten a reply back. That's the level of my respect for Fred."

On January 13, 2004, Beckey turned eighty-one. He still gets out there, climbing, traveling, and having fun. And he still proves on a daily basis that the best life is a life of action. It isn't necessary to understand him, or love him, or even like him—hell, you don't even have to get along with him most of the time. All that's required is that you understand that Fred Beckey's mountaineering career has never, and *will* never, be surpassed by any American mountaineer. Period.

Postscipt: 1994–Present

After our disastrous 1991 Mexico excursion, I never thought I'd talk to Fred again—but was I wrong. In 1994, I was hauling ski gear from the slopes at Snowmass to my car when, passing an après-ski joint, I recognized a face inside. I stared at the older man. He was fairly neat, obviously in good shape, and was half-bent over the bar, talking to a waitress. It was Fred. I went in, walked over to the bar, and said hi. Fred shook hands and immediately started talking machine-gun style about this and that and places he wanted to go climbing. It was as if we'd never met—or rather, as if we were old friends, but had never climbed together or been on a trip with each other. Years later, I was to learn that the early 1990s were a bad period for Fred, and that he'd been living— extremely unhappily, according to several reports—in Los Angeles.

Regardless, this brief encounter kicked off the second half of my relationship with Fred, which lasts more or less to this day.

In the summer of 1997, Fred invited me up to try a new route he'd been eyeing in the Wind River Range, where we climbed a minor new route after being rained out and running out of time. During that trip, Fred was polite and considerate, and he offered to pay for every- thing—in fact, he did pay for gas from Jackson, where we had stayed with a guide named Wes Bunch, to the trailhead. On the trail, he wanted to carry more than was appropriate, and he asked me constantly if everything was going okay. He was a different guy entirely. We agreed to meet the following spring, in Zion—I had a project he might be interested in.

That winter [1997–98], however, Fred came and stayed with my wife and me during a ski trip to Colorado. Everyone knows about Fred's climbing; few people realize he is one hell of a skier, too; and we spent one day at Snowmass and a second day on Huntsmans Ridge, a wooded hill near Redstone, cutting turns through some seriously heavy mashed potatoes. I have never seen anyone in his or her mid-seventies ski so well in such poor conditions.

That night, Fred asked if he could use my computer to type an expedition report for Lindsay Griffin, at *High* magazine in Britain. I set him up in my office and went downstairs to fix dinner. I pointed out the various facets of a basic e-mail application, and in his typical style, he grunted a caveman response, acknowledging that he understood. Hours and hours later, when Fred had finally finished the e-mail and dinner was cold, he announced he was ready to send the thing. I went upstairs, logged on to the local Internet service provider, and waited while the squawking connection established itself. While I was waiting, I took a look at what Fred had written. It was, to say the least, some of the most eloquent writing I've ever encountered. The piece, which would have been several pages long on paper, was structured perfectly. It touched on the finer points of the range into which Fred had traveled and climbed, and it described some very detailed aspects of the climbs he'd done, and the climbs he'd tried. It was floral where appropriate and curt where it needed to be—in short, one of the finest trip reports I've ever read.

"Fred, this is fantastic," I said. "You are a brilliant writer."
Fred grunted and shooed my praise away: "Aww, it's just an article for Lindsay. It's nothing."

I read the entire document twice—it was that good. In fact, it was somewhat eerie, as if someone else had sneaked into the room and done the typing while Fred stepped out. The incident made me appreciate every one of Fred's written pieces a great deal more (I had occasionally wondered if they'd been ghostwritten).

In April 1998, we met again in Beaver, Utah. Fred had driven down from the Northwest with Pete Doorish, a Seattle-based climber. We headed into the park, hoping to scope a few lines. I pointed out my proposed route—an oft-discussed line on Red Arch Mountain— to Fred and Pete, and they agreed to try it. Then, the weather turned sour. The three of us spent the next week or so dodging storms and trying to find a dry place to sleep. We eventually broke into John Middendorf's Hurricane house and established a base camp in his living room. Sitting in the house while it rained, Pete and I got to observe Fred's typical nonclimbing routine, likely the first time for both of us. Every day, Fred would sleep late, get up, eat a piece of bread or something for breakfast, read the *Wall Street Journal,* then get on the phone to his broker. Over the last few days of our visit, we managed a few pitches on the climb, but then we ran out of time and left the project uncompleted.

About a month later, I returned with Fred (sans Pete). At that time, Fred was more interested in climbing either the Touchstone wall or Prodigal Son, for a book he was working on. He had no interest in try-ing to complete the route we'd started a month earlier. After a couple of days' rain, Fred suggested we travel out to Red Rocks, Nevada, where he wanted to try Crimson Chrysalis, another route for his book. A young climber named Andrew Nichols came along. We humped a load of gear into the base of the route, camped, and awoke the next morn-ing. Andrew and I were eager to get on the climb because it's often crowded. Fred, however, had a sore back, and wanted to wait another day. We repeated the process, and on the second day Fred felt too unrested to climb anything. We retreated to Zion, where the next morning, Andrew and I sneaked out and climbed Prodigal Son while Fred slept late. We attempted Prodigal several times with Fred—even walking out to the climb the long way (along the west side of the river)—but Fred just wasn't in the mood. Fred and I left Zion a few days later. He flew back to Seattle; I drove back to Colorado.

Clearly, Fred is slowing down, and he's losing a bit of his energy and bravado. And certainly, during these half-dozen or so other climbing trips, we didn't do a whole lot of climbing. But I'm incredibly glad I went with him. He is a genuinely great guy, and he deserves a prominent position in every climber's pantheon.

I haven't been out with him for several years because of my work and family commitments, but every few months, I get a frantic e-mail: "Cam, Chile this spring?" "Cam, Iryan Jaya next winter?" "Cam, Zion this fall?" "Sierras?" "Rocky Mountain Park?" Sooner or later, I know I'll hook up with him. He is, after all, Fred Beckey.

---

1 *February 1986, No. 94.*
2 *Carter told me in a 1993 interview that the south ridge was his idea, and that Beckey "commandeered it."*
3 *Who were obviously wrong.*

Right: Shiprock, New Mexico. Left: Cove, Arizona, resident Curtis Benally points out Luke Laeser and Jon Butler on the first ascent of Down Tower.

Coming to Grips with Climbing on the Big Rez

In the late 1980s, I began traveling through the Navajo reservation on a regular basis. I was working in the film industry as a *grip* (someone who holds things very tightly) and a *gaffer* (someone who pokes metal flaps on hot lights), I was living in Hollyweird, and visits to my parents' place in New Mexico made life on the so-called "Left Coast" sane-ish. Whenever possible, I drove through the various Indian reservations sprinkled across northern Arizona and eastern New Mexico. These were interesting places, and I enjoyed visiting them because the landscape—as anyone who's ever been there can tell you—is surreal: wild cheese-snack-shaped towers, bread-loaf-square buttes, and strange, pulpy-looking volcanic plugs.

One of my first "up-close-and-personal" experiences on Navajolands was photographing Shiprock in 1989. For some reason, I'd decided to drive out to the beautiful monolith and take pictures of it. A young Navajo in a Thriftway, the local convenience store, told me it was no problem camping out near the enormous stone—which I had planned to do. He even said I could climb the spire if I wanted, noting that several climbers had been spotted on the tower that day. I bought a can of beans, thanked him, and declined. After all, I didn't have a partner. I didn't think any Navajo could offer me the use of the land like that, but I wasn't sure—I had no idea how recreation on the Big Rez worked. I returned to my campsite and quietly went to bed, gripping my can of beans tightly.

During the next few years, I made a handful of nonclimbing visits to the reservation (as well as one climbing trip, the Regular Route on Shiprock). In general, none of the Navajos with whom I spoke minded us visiting the reservation and recreating. Recreating tourists were the least of their problems.

In 1992, Luke Laeser, Trevor Lucero, and I made a longer, more extensive auto-tour of the reservation and, after climbing a virgin plug half the size of Shiprock,[1] we visited Todilto Park, near Window Rock, Arizona. We had stopped our vehicle for only a few minutes to admire Venus Needle, one of the better-known pinnacles in the desert, when a Navajo woman driving a small pickup pulled along-side my truck. The dust slowly settled, and she rolled down her window. Before she could say a word, Luke and I had blurted out the explanation that we were "just looking," nothing more. We knew—at least we *thought* we knew—that climbing was off-limits on the reservation. At least that's what we'd gleamed from every reservation-related climbing article ever published.

The woman ignored our clearly simple message and suggested we go and talk to an older gent sitting on the front porch of a nearby mobile home. She pointed up the hill to him: "He's my dad. Go tell him I said it was okay."

We wandered up the driveway.

"Said *what* was okay?" I muttered to Luke as we wandered up to the trailer home.

"You think she thought we were going to go out there?" Luke asked.

Thus it was that we found ourselves standing before Leo Watchman[2] as he sat on his front porch, explaining that we were climbers, certainly, but that we didn't intend to climb Venus Needle ("we were just marveling at it"), and that some woman in a blue Chevy pickup had told us to come and say hello to him. Again, we said, we were just looking.

Mr. Watchman introduced us to "Junior," his son, sitting next to him, then asked us if we'd like to climb the lovely red tower. We nearly flipped. Only later would we learn that Leo Senior was a highly respected Navajo politician as well as former director of Navajo Health Care Services. He lived in Todilto Wash and his family held the "grazing permit" to the area.

Mr. Watchman told us he had the ability to let us do the climb. But, since it was late on a Sunday afternoon, we decided to return later, when we could wangle a bit more time.

Two weeks later, we were back—Luke, my wife Ann, and several friends. Leo Senior met us and told Leo Junior to move a couple of cars so we could park our vehicles in the family compound, and we pulled in. Mr. Watchman then told us that we could stay overnight, and as long as we wanted, in a second house on his property that was currently unoccupied. We unloaded our junk, beans and all, and settled in.

That night, we hung out with Junior and talked about this and that—nothing important. It was just three white guys, two white girls, and a Navajo youngster hanging out—as you do—in a borrowed house on the Navajo reservation. The next day, a monsoon hit. Although Junior had been assigned to transport us and our gear back and forth across the wash in his Jeep (an assignment he clearly loved), the weather was worse than is appropriate for climbing up soft rock, and we spent more of that soggy, fall day wandering around Window Rock than we did climbing.

Leo Junior told us of his desire to open a Pizza Hut franchise in Window Rock, an interesting goal for a young Navajo but certainly a better life plan than I had (i.e., gripping things tightly). Day Two was about the same: rain, wind, and a little bit of upward progress. By the time we departed late on a Sunday afternoon, Luke and I had fixed a rope—a pathetic one hundred sixty feet of upward progress mocked by a subsequent twelve-hour drive home.

We returned another two weeks later—with a pair of rock shoes for Leo Junior, donated by Boreal—and, after showing him the basics of rock climbing on a crack up a slab near the family home, finished the first route on the east side of Venus Needle. We spent another evening with the Watchmans, bid them adieu, and left for home.

The Watchmans appeared to have enjoyed our visit. They told us they were simply happy that we'd spent time with them. Many climbers had come to their land over the years, ignored them, and climbed the tower. No polite "hellos," no "may I's," not even a thank you—just a lot of climbers being, apparently, pretty rude.

Leo Senior also explained how tribal lands were set up, and they suggested that climbing was okay if we got the local landowner's permission. Even though Mr. Watchman was high up in the government and well respected by his people, I decided to call around and find out if what we had been told was correct.

In a 1993 interview, Nathaniel Boyd, a right-of-way agent with the Navajo Tribal Parks and Recreation Department, told me that while climbing is prohibited in certain places, such as Canyon de

Chelly and Monument Valley, it is not prohibited elsewhere. If a person is interested in visiting the reservation for climbing, Boyd recommended the official route, which is to ask for permission from the grazing-permit holders wherever the climbing objective is located: exactly what the Watchmans had told us. "A permittee," said Boyd, "has domain over that land and is the person to ask for permission when seeking a climbing objective."

Operating under that assumption, Luke and I went all over the reservation. We asked for and received permission from grazing-permit holders to climb a spectrum of virgin towers, including the Tombstone, an untouched pinnacle nearly as big as Moses Tower in Canyonlands National Park.

We had a great few years and spent considerable storm-bound time hanging out with various locals, from shepherds to kids.

Our best experiences were arguably with the Benally family, out near Cove, Arizona. Luke and I, with Jon Butler, had intended to climb the virgin Down and Out Towers over the course of a February weekend, but after climbing the taller of the two, Curtis Benally's family invited us to dinner in their home, where we ate sheep stew and hung out with Curtis's family. After dinner, the Benallys asked us if we'd like to watch a Ye Bei Chei ceremony and promised it would be good because we'd be the only non-Navajos there. The ceremony didn't start until about 1:00 A.M., and we stayed up most of the night watching the painted dancers gyrate in the subzero desert air. In the morning, we were far too tired to do any climbing, so we went home. A few months later, we returned to climb Out Tower, explaining to Curtis the intricacies of rock climbing while we belayed.

Our friendship with Curtis lasted for many years, and he visited Luke and me at our Colorado homes several times (at one point with his girlfriend from New Jersey, Hertha, who, ironically, was Kurt Diemberger's niece).

In May 1994, Luke and I found ourselves at the base of Tse'Bit'ai (Shiprock) itself and looked up a stunning, natural line on the east face. We went to work on the enormous buttress that lies just left of the Honeycomb Gully. The route had been attempted by Colorado Springs climbers Art Howells, Don Doucette, and Steve Wilman in 1969, when they climbed five pitches before being blown off by a storm.

We were certain that Shiprock couldn't be part of any Navajo's grazing permit as there are no houses for miles around it, and the Parks and Recreation Department's Boyd had never said anything about Shiprock. It was my blunder not to press him—or someone else—further.

Luke and I whacked pitons for four days. On May 10, while Luke was tapping bird-beaks into Pitch 6, a Navajo man rode up on a horse.

"We have the resolution," he called. "You're not supposed to be up there."

"The grazing permit?" I called down.

"Yes."

We asked the rider if he wanted us to descend and leave. For a few tense minutes, he didn't answer. Then he finally said, "Just meet me here at seven o'clock tonight. We'll talk."

Luke and I descended, embarrassed that we hadn't investigated the ownership of the monolith further. We felt ashamed. Luke suggested that we drive to the rider's home. "This is the formal way to do it," Luke said. "Let's do it right."

We arrived as he was putting his horse away. He squinted, trying to recognize the car. I stopped the engine and we got out. Then we apologized. We apologized and we apologized and we apologized. I must have said "I'm sorry" twenty times. The Navajo man, Brandon Paul, was surprised. People climb Shiprock all the time and no one asks permission,³ and certainly no one apologizes either. Brandon accepted our apologies and, after a few more minutes of discussion, gave us the go-ahead to complete the route. We invited him along on the climb, but he didn't want to go. His biggest concern was that we should be off Shiprock before May 14, when his family was hosting a peyote ceremony. He feared any noise we might inadvertently create.

Over the following two days and nights, we worked on the route, stringing pitches together and then descending in mid-afternoon as massive thunderstorms enveloped the spire. Brandon hung out with us at the base of the wall in the evenings, and he told us all about trespassing onto his land. He said that his own attempts to block off the access road to Shiprock had been stymied by tourists in trucks, who pushed the boulders aside. He said he'd placed signs on the road, warning people away. Nothing had worked. Of course, Luke and I knew that—we were getting really good at trespassing.

Brandon told us about Ted Danson's then-unreleased film, *Pontiac Moon,* shot at the base of Shiprock. According to Brandon, his family signed a contract with the company making the film for a sum to be paid for the use of the land. The company shot the film, then packed up and left. The Pauls never saw a dime. At the time we were there, Brandon's family was trying to bring a lawsuit against the company that produced the film. "The lawsuit," he said, "was going nowhere."

In return for letting us climb, we gave him five cans of beans, a can of motor oil (so he could start his generator and power his television), and $20 so he could drive to Flagstaff to pick up his four children, who would spend the summer with him.

Luke and I decided Brandon's shopping list of goods wasn't enough. We suggested—forced upon him, really—that in return for his letting us do the route, we clean up the hundreds of broken bottles smashed against the rocks at the base of the east face by beer drinkers and that we paint over sexist and racist graffiti. The worst eyesore was Sheila, a twenty-foot-by-twenty-foot nude, spread-eagled woman. Brandon laughed at the nickname—I think because Sheila had a beard and looked a great deal like me—and agreed to the idea.

We finished the route over the next three days, rappelling to the ground each night when electrical storms began drifting around the rock and lightning started striking the prairie below us—one of the scarier things I've seen in twenty years of climbing. From the haven of my sleeping bag at the base of the rock, I remember seeing one lightning bolt blast the south summit of Shiprock, then arc across and blast the main summit, with red light scorching the tips of the pinnacles in between.

Luke and I topped out on Friday, May 13. We had placed no bolts on leads and drilled only eighteen holes, all of which were for bolts at belay/rappel stations. About a dozen bolts had been placed by Howells, Doucette, and Wilman, mostly on the first pitch.

Saturday was spent driving around Farmington, buying paint and garbage bags. My parents drove four hours from Los Alamos to help with the cleanup. We picked up seven huge bags' worth of broken glass, fast-food wrappers, and other trash, and after four hours' cleanup left Shiprock the most satisfied we've ever felt after a climbing trip.

As far as climbing on the reservation goes, I must admit I'm now not entirely sure what's right and what's appropriate—except that every article on the subject is completely screwy. Almost every story about climbing on the Navajo reservation is written by a fellow who has bagged various towers and then, having done his thing, suddenly gets religion and suggests that reservation climbing is very wrong, *very* unethical (whatever that means), and highly disrespectful. Several of the most prominent U.S. mountaineering journals have published such articles, and they are utter codswallop.

In the late 1980s, Gallup climber Bob Rosebrough[4] had begun a search that Luke and I heard about midway through our own reservation adventures. It paralleled our own research for the true regulations. Rosebrough, a lawyer, dug into Navajo annals to find that the basis for a "ban" on climbing on the reservation seemed to be a letter written by Charles Damon, director of Navajo Parks and Recreation Department in the early 1970s. Damon suggested a ban after the death of two climbers on Shiprock in 1970. However, Damon's directive was only that: a letter expressing that "it is the policy of the tribe to prohibit anyone from climbing any . . . monoliths."

Rosebrough conducted several interviews with lawyers in the Navajo Department of Justice, only to learn that the letter was never backed up by any kind of legislation and that no ban officially exists or ever has existed.

Indeed, in an interview with Damon himself, Rosebrough learned what Luke and I had discovered through our own investigations. Damon suggested to Rosebrough that if he wanted to pursue climbing on the reservation, he seek permission at a local level rather than from the central tribal government.

And this is where the subtleties of tribal governance get difficult to negotiate for anyone interested in climbing on the Rez. There appears to be a fairly sizeable rift between the central Window Rock government and the local governments. What each told us differed, depending on when I asked and whom I questioned.

Ban or no ban, Luke and I (and other climbing buddies) have found that honesty and diplomacy are the best approach to everything on the reservation, from camping to trying to find stores that sell beer. And for us, the best aspect of this approach is mixing with the locals. Many climbers show up, climb, and leave without so much as saying hello. Some don't even acknowledge the existence of the *Dineh*, or people, living there. Some climbers even try to hide (always unsuccessfully) from their curious hosts. They don't know what they're missing.

In 1992, Leo Watchman Junior told us the story of one famous American climber—a guy who's graced the covers of the major American magazines—and his ascent of a monolith near Window Rock. This fellow kept trying to hide from passing Navajos, in cars and on horses, by flattening himself on ledges and ducking into chimneys. All rather pointless, of course, with an SUV sitting at the base of the climb.

In the late 1990s, a famed mountaineering journalist wrote an article about climbing on "native" lands and rock formations (notably Devils Tower) and tried to pit my "approach" against that of a climber who runs a guiding operation and was outspoken against climbing bans there. When I was interviewed, I tried to point out that I was no saint—I'm as selfish and self-centered as any climber—and that my "approach" was not the result of some bogus ethical gyrations.

I explained that I liked cruising around seeing the reservation and meeting Navajos and that I got a huge kick out of hanging out with them, talking to them, and learning about the culture—eating sheep stew, too. Climbing was always secondary to having a good time—hell, climbing is secondary to *everything* on the reservation. My "approach" simply appeared more politically correct than those of other climbers visiting "tribal lands," and the author wrote a commensurately skewed article.

My take on climbing on the reservation, though, seemed okay with the locals and that's really all that matters to me. At a journalism conference in 1993, the renowned Navajo writer Valerie Taliman pointed out the obvious to me: the Navajos are as curious about us as we are about them, and they hold many of the same values, including respect and common courtesy. "Treat us," she said, "as you hope to be treated."

1 *Bennett Peak.*
2 *He died in 1993.*
3 *The monolith gets many visits from all types of tourists. Most, though, are amateur geologists and mountain bikers.*
4 *Currently the mayor of Gallup, New Mexico.*

Climbing at Chute de Montmarency, Québec, with our new friend François-Guy Thivierge (inset).

Making Friends
en Québec (2003)

One of the things I've always hated about ice climbing is the long approaches. I remember living near Denver in the mid-1980s where, to get to climbable ice, I'd load up the gear, gas up the Mini, drive out along some of the most congested highways on Earth toward some of the orb's prettiest peaks, then sit amongst stationary autos containing young men and women glaring at me as if this was all my fault (which it likely was). After gaining Interstate 70 west, we'd then *pfutter* up into the mountains, park, hike a half-mile up a steep hill, and ultimately join a queue where we'd all stand around hoping that when we reached the head of said queue the ice wasn't all hacked away and lying in a pathetic pile at the bottom of the cliff.

While I've never minded off-gassing with my fellow climbers (indeed, many say it's the strongest part of my game), long queues of such origination tend to offer conversations of very limited subject matter, i.e.: (1) road conditions; (2) automobile repairs; (3) winter driving in Colorado; (4) winter driving elsewhere—say, Florida; (5) "that Norman-Bates-looking hitchhiker" splattered with brown snow near the truck stop; and (6) how many ice climbers there are. By the end of any conversation, all the ice had invariably been hacked away and we'd queue our separate-but-intertwined ways home.

The Province of Québec, in Canada, is not like this. Québec offers civilized ice climbing, ice climbing you can love. During a nice (*an ice*) trip in 2003 to Québec, Luke Laeser and I had a chance to check out *la glâce,* and found that our neighbors to the north have a winter wonderland and a take on the season that rivals Kris Kringle's.

In Québec City (that charming Francophone *ville* dating from 1608 and North America's only walled city, according to the litera-ture)[1], we met François-Guy Thivierge, a wonderfully friendly and flamboyant Québecois, who has been at the forefront of ice climbing in Canada for twenty years. Thirty-eight years old, and at the top of his athletic game (he wants to be the first to cross-country ski across Canada), Frank, as he is known to Anglophones from the south, met us in our small, delightful hotel (the Relais Charles-Alexandre) in Québec's old city. Over breakfast, he told us of Québec City's nearby Chute de Montmarency. It was, he assured, some of the best "in-city" ice climbing in the world. After a brief stop at Frank's rock gym and *centre d'affaires,* we cruised a few minutes to the edge of the city and were presented with a full frontal view of the enormous Chute de Montmarency. Like test-match streakers in a wind tunnel, we were blown away.

The Chute de Montmarency is a waterfall that boggles the mind. About one hundred meters tall, the cascade—which seems to have burst its narrow confines and spills down the cliffs on each side—is about 350 meters wide. Such a wide, wet swath produces an enormous area of climbable ice (indeed, were I a mathematician, I'd call it about 35,000 square meters of climbable surface—minus the odd tree, which is handy for rappelling).

We set to work climbing the falls in various places. There were only a few other climbers (Luke and I met a couple from Poland, and Frank ran into a cop friend), great views of the mighty St. Lawrence River, and fat, thunker ice—the kind that makes some people say "ooohhhh." No lines, no traffic jams, no Norman-Bates-looking hitchhikers hanging about truck stops. Tom Patey would've held a really big Scotch tasting party.

Midway through the day, Frank suggested we climb a new route. This seemed somewhat strange as the ice was in gigantic sheets, like furniture draped with white sheets to keep it clean. What could possibly be considered a new route? He pointed to a thin drizzle of brown ice squirting over a rock buttress and explained that the drizzle rarely formed and, better yet, it had never been climbed. We humped our way to the base of the rock buttress. There, Frank had found a frozen robin near the base of the climb, and he repeatedly suggested the route be named Dead Bird.[2]

Right; off we go then. I attacked a "jungle" pitch—one of those quasigymnastic, quasispastic excursions up loose rock, trees frozen at impossible angles, and unconsolidated snow—and arrived at a comfortable ledge. Frank and Luke, covered with my unconsolidated snow droppings and a few logs that I had let loose, arrived at the ledge and examined the ice above.

"Luuuuk's guud!" Frank announced in his thick Québecois as he launched up the rock. He caught the bottom of the drizzle and began yanking his way up, shouting with enthusiasm and grinning madly. As he climbed higher, the *tick-tick-ticking* of his tools floated down like a kind of metronome. Another happy shout and Frank was pulling on the rope. "Ha ha!" he said. "It's a guud one! We shall call it 'Colorado Vapor'!" I couldn't tell if that was a tongue-in-cheek reference to the hot air emitting from us, or the thick scent of exercise-heavy polypropylene issuing from some location south of my mouth.

Luke and I followed and we gained a small forest on the ice slope where Frank was still smiling happily. This is one of the things I love about Québec—the ice climbing is terrific and the locals know it; they show nothing but total enthusiasm for being out on very cold days and sharing their *glâce* with visitors.

That night we celebrated by dining at Cosmos, Québec City's hottest bar/restaurant, where we shared stories about climbing around the world. Luke and I left the next day and went on to climb at Mont-Sainte-Anne, in the Parc des Grandes Jardins, and at Pont Rouge, the hot new "ice-crag" where, incidentally, Frank had pioneered the first routes in 1991.

Québec is a good place for ice climbing. In fact, for reliability, length of season, and variety of climbs available, I'd take Québec over pretty much any other place on the planet for ice climbing. But one thing cinches Québec as my pick for top ice climbing destination in North America: the friendliness of the locals. The Québecois know how to be nice neighbors, and sharing ice—even 35,000 square feet of it—is about as neighborly as it gets. In fact, next time I go, I think I'll bring Norman from the truck stop—he could use a friend.

1 *The literature writers forgot about Santa Fe.*
2 *Clearly, a better name than the silly philosophical titles given to many climbs (e.g., Revelation, Statement of Youth, Catharsis, etc.).*

Warren Harding, the first man to climb El Capitan (inset).

FIGHT GRAVIT

for the Hard Life (1990)

"Camdaaaaawwwwwwg! Is that Camdaaawwwg?!"

Warren Harding's screeching voice bursts through the screen door of his Moab home. Standing on a square patch of carpet and holding a glass of clear liquid, his gaze flickers between an approaching me and the two barking dogs at his feet. A woman's hand pushes past Warren and opens the door. "C'mon on in, guys," says Alice Flomp, Warren's confidante, girlfriend, and wrangler. I step inside and am immediately overtaken by a feeling of warmth and welcoming. "How was your trip?" Alice asks. "You hungry? I can make you a sandwich if you like."

"C'mon in and have a seat," Warren adds.

In January 1990, Paul Fehlau and I went to live with Warren and Alice in Moab for about ten days. I wanted to quiz the legendary climber because he had done some outstanding mountaineering in the Sierra Nevada, and rather than just answer questions over the phone, he eagerly suggested that I come stay with him.

Warren and Alice showed us to a couple of inflatable beds in the basement, then offered us food and refreshment. We ate and drank the night away. Manhattans—Warren's beverage of choice in those days—flowed copiously. Our heads filled with stories of mountaineering in the Sierra Nevada and Warren's simple but eloquent philosophy ("simple mind: start at the bottom, come out at the top"), we passed out at around 5:00 A.M.

At 10:30 A.M., I awoke to Warren nudging my bed. He was holding another manhattan and announced that Alice had made us breakfast. Paul and I got up, ate breakfast, attempted to go climbing (which ended in a Moab blizzard), and then delved back into the conversation of the night before—it was wildly interesting. It continued through the day (more manhattans) and well into the night. Warren would regularly break out the slides of the first ascent of the Porcelain Wall, his 1989 thirty-first anniversary ascent of the Nose, and all sorts of other slides that forty years of climbing had produced. It was one of the best visits with an old climber—and there have been dozens and dozens—I've ever had.

Warren Harding was best known as the first guy to climb El Capitan, in Yosemite, in 1958–59, but that handy label shortchanges the man's real achievements. He not only made the first ascents of many of Yosemite's biggest walls (the south faces of Half Dome and Mount Watkins, the west face of the Leaning Tower, the Porcelain Wall near Half Dome, and the east face of Washington Column, to name just a few), but his climbing career also included some of the finest routes in the Sierra high country—like the east face of Keeler Needle, the southeast face of Mount Conness, the northwest ridge of Mount Williamson, and the southwest face of Agassiz Needle.

But arguably, Harding's greatest achievement was showing the entire climbing community that it needn't take itself so seriously. Indeed, it was his cutting sense of humor and his ability to poke fun at the mountaineering establishment that made him a hero for thousands of climbers.

Harding was born in 1924 in Oakland, California, and he grew up in Downieville and Marysville. During World War II, he worked at Sacramento's McClellan Field, where he was a propeller mechanic. After the war, and until his retirement in 1988, he was a surveyor for both the State of California and private construction firms.

"He started climbing in 1952 and was a weak member of a Grand Teton ascent, causing someone to remarking on his lack of endurance," wrote George Meyers in his 1987 guide to *Yosemite Climbs*. "This could well be an apocryphal story, for Harding became known as the iron man of Yosemite climbing." A year later, Harding discovered the "Valley."

"I first came to Yosemite in September 1953," he told me in one of our 1990 interviews. "Could you imagine going [there] when nothing had been done on El Cap? Today there are three hundred routes."

Harding started out climbing in Yosemite with whomever he could find. He took to the sport like few others—he was a natural—and was almost immediately climbing new routes, many of which would become classic climbs, like 1954's east buttress of Middle Cathedral, and the East Arrowhead Chimney in 1956. But the things that would set Harding apart were his ascents of the Valley's biggest walls, the giant expanses of vertical granite that became his home on and off for two decades.

On June 28, 1957, a group of teenagers (Royal Robbins, Mike Sherrick, and Jerry Gallwas) climbed the northwest face of Half Dome, a remarkable climb that set a new standard for big-cliff climbing. Harding was originally intended to be part of that team, as he had been part of a 1955 attempt on Half Dome with Robbins. He felt inspired by what the trio had achieved, but he also felt a sense of loss at not being part of the group. It was the first Grade VI climb in the world, and it marked the start of the golden age of Yosemite climbing. None of this was lost on Harding as he hiked up the trail to the top of Half Dome to greet Robbins, Gallwas, and Sherrick. A few days later, he turned his attention to El Capitan, one of the biggest monoliths on Earth.

On July 4, 1957, Harding and his small team (Mark Powell and Bill "Dolt" Feuerer) began laboring away on El Cap via a route later to be called the Nose. A climb of such magnitude had never before been undertaken, and some of the climbing and hauling systems were invented specifically for the ascent. The Dolt Cart, "which looked like a shopping cart with two bicycle wheels," was designed to roll vertically up the wall and carried food and supplies. The Dolt Winch, placed twelve hundred feet up the route, was the point from which the cart was pulled. Powered by the climbers, they were never sure whether the energy expended in hauling food and supplies up was greater than the caloric value of the food they were hauling.

Much of the route was strung with ropes, some of which dangled a quarter-mile down the face at times and far outweighed any supplies being hauled. Tangles were a nightmare to sort out. Left for long periods while Harding and his partners were back at their regular jobs, the ropes wore out in the wind and were chewed on by rats. They required constant replacement. The climbing was mostly aid climbing—slow and equipment-intensive. It was done in stages over an eighteen-month period. Partway through the ascent, in September 1957,

Powell fell (while on an easy climb), fracturing and dislocating his ankle. He and Feuerer dropped out of the climb, and Harding recruited Wayne Merry, George Whitmore, and Rich Calderwood (who also later dropped out).

By the fall of 1958, Harding, Whitmore, and Merry had ascended two thousand feet of rock. The Park Service had given the climbers a deadline of Thanksgiving by which to complete the ascent; so, on November 1, the men committed themselves to the wall. Eleven days later, having spent a total of forty-four days on the monolith, the three men reached the final overhanging section of the route. Using his head-lamp, Harding worked through the night of November 11, drilling twenty-eight bolt holes while Whitmore and Merry huddled half-asleep on a ledge below. It was this effort that earned Harding his reputation as an iron man. He emerged on the summit the following morning, around 6:00 A.M., where a crowd of supporters had gathered. The ascent had required six hundred pitons and 125 expansion bolts.

Harding received tremendous accolades for that ascent: nothing like it had ever been accomplished, and it set a new standard for magnitude and commitment. It was feted around the world. Unfortunately, however, fixed ropes and the use of so many bolts were eschewed by some leading climbers of the day, notably Royal Robbins. Although Robbins and Harding were friends who respected and admired each other (Harding and Robbins regularly invited the other along on their adventures in the 1950s), a handful of Robbins's friends began criticizing Harding's style.

In the years that followed the Nose, Harding climbed most of the other major formations in the Valley that were unclimbed—the Leaning Tower, Washington Column, Half Dome's south face, and other walls. In November 1970, he undertook another major ascent of El Capitan, via the Dawn Wall.[1] Harding and Dean Caldwell spent twenty-seven days on the Dawn Wall and drilled 330 bolts—and they garnered worldwide press coverage when they refused a rescue offered by the Park Service.

The climb went on to become one of the most controversial in history for other important reasons. First, the climb itself saw a record number of bolts for a Yosemite climb (even though Robbins himself had used 110 bolts on the route Tis-sa-ack, on Half Dome, in 1969—at that point a record high for bolting on a big-wall climb). Also, many climbers felt the massive publicity given the ascent was inappropriate. The controversy became even greater when Robbins and Don Lauria went up to repeat the Dawn Wall with the intention of "erasing" the route (by chopping the bolts Harding and Caldwell had placed). After chopping some three hundred feet worth of bolts, the two stopped and climbed the route as they found it, impressed by the quality of the climb.

"For the most part, the climbing was of high caliber," Robbins said in a 1971 interview with Galen Rowell and Allen Steck. "There was one good lead after another; both Caldwell and Harding must have been climbing at a really inspired level. And that, of course, complicated the whole thing enormously—how could one continue to judge it so simply? Essentially it means that Harding won. . . . Everyone makes mistakes. I'm happy to admit this was one."

Others weren't so kind, and criticism of the man was to become a mainstay of Harding's existence, relentless and destructive, for the rest of his life.

Climber T. M. Herbert wrote an article for the *American Alpine Journal* that stated: ". . . amidst helicopters, reporters, rangers and tourists, two climbers came bolting, bat hooking, and aluminum riveting over the summit . . . everyone I met was talking about the two on El Cap. I felt like screaming, 'But they bolted the damned thing and then they sold it to millions on television!'" The events surrounding the Dawn Wall were tough on Harding and Caldwell, and after numerous television appearances, the latter dropped out of sight.

Harding returned a few more times to the Valley—notably to climb the two-thousand-foot Porcelain Wall near Half Dome in 1975—but his activities in Yosemite declined.

Despite Harding's famous activities in Yosemite, he also achieved numerous important ascents in the high mountains. The northwest ridge of Mt. Williamson in the Sierra Nevada is one of the most grueling climbs in those mountains. Harding and John Ohrenschall made the first winter ascent of the ridge during the winter of 1954–55. The two spent four desperate days on the route, bivouacking in the open and generally being miserable.

And the east face of Keeler Needle and the southwest face of Mount Conness, both of which Harding pioneered, are regarded as two of the finest climbs in the Sierra.

One of the significant differences between Harding and most of his climbing contemporaries was the fact that he had a full-time job, as a surveyor. While many others lived the "climbing bum" life and had endless time for the sport, Harding did his climbing on holidays and weekends.

His working-class status made him something of a hero. But most important for many was Warren's philosophy about climbing and life: He did his routes, and never commented on anyone else's. Period.

Although Harding retired in 1988, he did one noteworthy climb after that: the Nose, at the age of sixty-five, becoming at that time the oldest person to climb El Cap. The same year, Harding and Alice Flomp moved to Moab, where they lived through the mid-1990s. Their home there was a haven for climbers from around the globe. In the mid-1990s, they returned to California, where they lived in Happy Valley until Harding died on February 27, 2002, at the age of seventy-seven, from liver failure.

Today, the Nose of El Capitan is considered the single-greatest rock climb on Earth. Thirty-six pitches, thirty-three hundred feet of varied, interesting climbing—men, women, and children from around the globe swarm to it and line up at El Cap's base for the experience. Many have been known to quit climbing afterward. It's a big achievement to get up the route, even for today's gym-trained athletes with fancy gear. In Harding's day, before big-wall climbing had really been invented, it was nothing short of brilliant. And for that, we should all be grateful.

Over the course of those ten days in January 1990, I recorded 270 minutes' worth of discussion. We talked about many climbs that Warren had done and cared about, and the climbers who mattered in his life: Denny, Tarver, Corbett, Bosque, and a whole raft of folks I'd heard of but never met.

Sitting and listening to his stories—and re-listening to them now—I realize there's something greater about Warren than most people will ever recognize, something remarkable about this funny, seemingly simple but stubborn man whom many criticized during his climbing career and well into the years afterward. First, there was his genuine affection for and desire to be with people. And second, there was the depth of his understanding about the human condition—through his own experiences—and his reaction to it.

Everyone Warren had known he referred to highly, from Royal Robbins ("he's a gentleman") to Ricardo Cassin ("he's wonderful"). Warren even thought sportscaster Howard Cosell was a decent fellow "because he did his research" before asking Warren and Caldwell about the Dawn Wall ascent in 1970. And every experience yielded some tidbit of wisdom: "Well, we didn't die. That allowed us to keep climbing the next day."

In the coming years, I suspect there'll be a book or two written about Warren and his adventures—whether devoted entirely to Warren, or simply featuring him as one actor on a vast stage, I don't know. I'd like to offer a few quotes from my recordings—which, although they're very random and out of context, are highly enjoyable and illustrate how much of a fun and original guy Warren was:

- "I was an aircraft mechanic for a while. Can you believe that?"
- "I'm normally locked in a turret."
- "There are some drawbacks to being young."
- "I hate slideshows. I've never seen one that I like, including my own."
- "I am so much smarter than you in this respect." (This after I'd described my poor motorcycle riding abilities.)
- "I like sex. I think I'm pretty good at it."
- "I don't know why I can't retain anything."
- "Hey, I love hippies. I grew up with hippies."
- "Presumably you get wiser as you get older. I doubt if that's necessarily true. Maybe the most you can hope for is, as you get older, you realize what's important. Now I'm not sure what the difference is."
- "That's a good-lookin' rock. And that's the only thing that ever grabbed me at anything—how they look." (Talking about the south face of Half Dome.)
- "Mommas, don't let your babies grow up to be winos."
- "Simple mind: Start at the bottom, come out at the top."
- "I went up a little ways and sank behind a boulder. I don't know how you guys are, but I guess there'd been such an emotional buildup, I just collapsed and cried and cried." (Describing topping out on the Dawn Wall.)
- "I don't even like boiled squigglies." (Describing microbes growing in his water bottles.)
- "It's only a thousand feet of overhanging wall." (Describing the Porcelain Wall.)
- "We got to another screw-ass little ledge. I led up to this thing, got up there, kind of took a comforting grasp on one of these little

towers, about five feet high and a few feet around and the fucker started leaning out on me! I kind of moved it back in. Oooh. I yelled down, 'hey, I'm going to be a while.' I drilled runners around these things and tied these things off. I won't say I was nervous but the thought of these things free-falling maybe 1,000 feet, hitting, sending shockwaves up, a lot of other stuff could come peeling off—so I was nervous." (Describing the Porcelain Wall).

• "Some people say I have a contract that on these first ascents I get to lead the first and the last pitch. Well, that isn't true. It all seemed to work out that way" (Commenting on the Porcelain Wall.)

• "Climbing is an individual thing. I'm not Trotsky or Marx."

• "I stay away from everything Australian." (Talking about the author of this book.)

• "I don't know anything about tennis. I don't even know what they're trying to do." (When a tennis match came on the television.)

• "You probably think I'm really a great person. You know, close to Gandhi."

• "I never thought I'd like this shit [climbing]."

• "I first came to Yosemite in September 1953. It's seems to me I burned up most of my life going to Yosemite, driving. For starters, it was about four hundred miles. Wasteful. I wasn't even youthful. I was thirty!"

Warren Harding's gone, but the world's a better place because he stayed for a while. He was humble, gracious, generous, caring, sharing, and friendly. He didn't give a rat's ass if you'd never climbed the Nose, the Dawn Wall, or the Leaning Tower—he'd take you as you were, and offer all those things humans continually seem to want to deny one another: self-respect, feelings of accomplishment, perspective.

Thanks for stopping by, Warren. We all needed it.

---

1 *Harding told me he called it the Dawn Wall while Caldwell referred to it as the Wall of the Early Morning Light; both names regularly appeared in early 1970s' mountaineering publications.*

Who knew these hills were full of ticks? Drip Buttress, Blodgett Canyon, Montana.

Ticking a Few Routes in Montana
(1991–1997)

What's the most uncomfortable you've ever been while climbing? A hanging belay where you and your eight partners can't move and you quickly learn that Jim and the Twins have been caught in a leg loop? Learning that you have a genuine case of Delhi Belly—not just the funny farts—and that you have to sit out a ten-hour Ecuadorian bus ride in a more-than-already-adequately-sated pair of undies? Sharing a ledge the size of a wired stopper with an evacuation the size of (or rather the volume of) Denali?

I think I'm most uncomfortable climbing in places with a lot of bugs. Climbing in the northeastern part of this country (the USA) is nasty for much of the summer because there are millions of small, biting things that both are invisible to the naked eye and have cheese graters for teeth. After a few hours outside, you're ready to use the garden rake on your legs and battery acid on your arms to get rid of the itch.

I once went hill walking in Costa Rica, a place so buggy that I am now in a cold shiver thinking about the spiders. Did you know they have tarantulas called Tiger Rump Doppelgängers?

And I double over when I see pictures of people climbing *tepuis* in Venezuela—what are these people on? I'd take a quadruple case of Delhi Belly and a two-thousand-hour hanging belay with Jim *and* the Twins skewered between released camming unit springs and pointy nut tools over climbing in Venezuela any day.

Weirdly, though, one of the worst places for insects I've ever encountered is in the arid West of the United States, in a relatively bug-benign state called Montana. Montana is, to put it conservatively, absolutely filled with ticks.

(Strangely, as I type this, my wife has begun leaning over my shoulder for what seems like an extended stay. "Montana means *tick* in Iroquois," she says sarcastically. "And where'd you learn to type? A proctology office?". . . Aren't you supposed to be darning socks or something?)

I went to live in Montana in the early 1990s, while writing a book about some mountains in California with my friend Steve Porcella. I took my then girlfriend—my then *onlyfriend*, really—Ann (aforementioned wife), and we rented a cozy shack on the Clark Fork River, on the opposite bank to downtown Missoula, with a glorious view of the Pacific, a humongous sawmill that was helping turn great big beautiful pine trees into attractive-sounding forest products like *pulp*. (It was likely a Louisiana Pacific sawmill, but we could only see the word *Pacific* from the shanty.)

Climbing-wise, Montana is the best-kept secret in the United States, with the exception of Canada. There are massive Yosemite-like canyons, there are wild alpine faces in remote ranges, and there are sport-climbing crags near every town, trailer park, and dumpster. (And there are very few people, because the ticks have eaten them all. The ticks have eaten most of the grizzlies, too.)

The Bitterroot Mountains are a fine example of just how unexplored Montana's mountains are. The Bitterroots are like a giant, granite loaf of bread that has been carefully sliced, and then every other slice has been removed. The resulting fins of bread in this bad analogy form the walls of each canyon in the range. The dozen-odd canyons in the range have been relatively unexplored by climbers, *relatively* being a relative term.

Blodgett Canyon is the best-known of the Bitterroot's large crevices and a sort of showcase of Montana climbing. A Yosemite-like ditch that has been climbed in for decades, it boasts some of the state's best-known (and most repeated) routes, like the south face of Flathead Spire and the regular route on Shoshone Spire, plus a bunch of others that are considered must-do classics.

The first time I ever heard of the place was back in the early 1980s, while trawling through John Harlin's collection of guidebooks to climbing across North America. Harlin's book, now considered a "rare" book and a "collectors' item," described Blodgett thus—crap, I can't find my copy, so I'll wing it—John wrote something like this: "Big and rad, with some butt-puckering walls."

When Ann and I moved to Missoula in 1991, about the first thing we learned during a Blodgett hike with Steve was: "When it rains, the ticks all climb to the tops of the plants, cling on with their front legs, and wave their back legs around in the air, hoping something will come past." The rest you can clearly imagine. . . .

The first route Ann and I did was Blodgett's Shoshone Spire, an introductory ramble. We were rained off, of course, as you are on every route in Blodgett, and we rappelled through a series of wild roofs and corners. At the bottom, we coiled the ropes.

"Er, Cam," Ann said cautiously. "You have a tick on your leg."

I looked down, found the offending insect, and flicked it toward Alberta.

"One there, too," she said pointing. "And another there. And another there. And another there."

"You better check yourself, too," I suggested.

We pulled a couple more ticks off—there had been about ten on me—and thought we were good to go. Then Ann's expression grew bleak and wintry: "There's one crawling across your face!"

We hiked quickly out and searched our clothes and selves at home, until we were satisfied we'd removed all the ticks.

A few days later, I went to Kootenai Canyon with Steve and the late Galen Rowell and put up a new sport climb (later given a really dumb name by some guidebook author). I removed a half-dozen ticks from my socks but, in all, it was a great day at the crag. A few days later, Ann and I went to Mill Canyon with Steve and the late Rod Sutherland and while top-roping a new route, I was marched on by a small army of hungry ticks.

("Tell 'em I watched a dozen ticks crawl up your shorts while you were climbing," my wife pipes up as I poke the keyboard. "Remember those nasty, tiny Coq Sportif shorts you had? Oooooh. Dunno what was worse: the shorts or the ticks. How's the typing lesson, Cam? Going to ask the keyboard to cough?" . . . Isn't there a bucket of runny slop to be cleaned up 'round here someplace and isn't that your job as heckler? . . .)

Our entire stay in Montana was something of a perennial tick search and it gave me the willies. I have been unfond of ticks ever since birth, and when I was a wee lad, my sister pulled one the size of a plum off one of our horses' ears and squished it between her thumb and finger—a great splitch of blood squirted into my eye.

Anyway, after six months in Montana spent walking quickly, performing awkward belay-stance body searches, and losing several thousands of gallons of blood, we moved back to Colorado, where, a couple of years later, I got Rocky Mountain tick fever and was the sickest I have ever been in my life.

In the late 1990s, Ann and I and two Boulder friends, Robin and Tony Asnicar (who answer their phone "Ants-n-pants-n-car residence," to throw off telemarketers) drove up to Montana to attend a wedding. It was a sort of climbing road trip, with visits to all the bolted roadcuts.

The morning after we entered the great tick-filled state of Montana, we stopped at a roadside café at a small town along the Bighole River (no kidding on the name, and certainly a gathering point for ticks) for breakfast. As I was explaining to Robin and Tony how tick-filled Montana was, one scurried across my face. Ann screamed.

I carefully pulled the trespasser off my face, deposited it on the outside doorstep, and crushed it with a hard Vibram heel. I wasn't as repulsed as I had been about ticks, and I felt quite comfortable about the whole ordeal—perhaps the fever had been more than just a physical reparation.

A couple days later, Tony and I climbed the Drip Buttress in Blodgett Canyon. We swung leads and enjoyed the sunshine. We topped out, hiked off, and found the descent through the forests. Back at the car (I suggested Tony change his name to "Ants-n-ticks-in-car"), the religious tick search got underway: socks, shorts, pants, grundies—pasty folds of flabby skin that haven't been rolled back in years. Gladly, I couldn't find a single one.

I guess the only thing more discomfiting than the size and frequency of the ticks in Montana is that if you climb for more than a few years, every guidebook you own becomes a "rare" book and a "collectors' item."

And that is bringing back my nervous eye twitch, or, as I call it, my Montana tick.

Climber and surgeon Geoff Tabin brings sight to the Himalaya.

The Doctor Is In

Geoff Tabin, a Climber Worthy of Note

One of the truly great pleasures of mountaineering literature is reading about great people doing heroic things (something I've tried to
keep out of my climbing column since its inception by describing my
own exploits). And one of the absolutely best pleasures of climbing as
an activity is meeting the stars of said literature and finding out
whether they really are as great as said literature says.

I can happily report that Geoff Tabin, an American Everester who
was part of the 1981 and '83 attempts on the Kangshung Face, is one
of the greats.

Tabin is the cofounder and chief motivator of an organization
called the Himalayan Cataract Foundation, which treats cataract illness

in Himalayan nations where native populations are susceptible to cataract blindness. Intense ultraviolet light, genetic predilection to cataract blindness, diet (with "chronic big fluid shifts," as Dr. Geoff so delicately puts it), and a shortage of doctors are all factors that cause the indigenous people of Nepal, northern India, Pakistan, Bhutan, Sikkim, Tibet, and other Himalayan nations to have a larger than expected number of blind or semiblind people, as a result of cataracts.

Geoff's life story, recounted in his 1991/2001 book *Blind Corners,* is a wow of a climber's fairy tale. He had his first climbing trip to Europe funded because he was a good Yale tennis player (after he was knocked out of tennis competition, he took a mountaineering vacation labeled "strenuous exercise"—don't ask; just read the book). After graduating Yale, he was selected as a Marshall Scholar to attend Oxford, which he and climbing chum Bob Shapiro soon found had all sorts of money for "gentlemen to explore strenuous holidays in mountains abroad." (My alma mater, the Bumfuck Vocational Shed for Cretins and Losers, only has scholarships "for gentlemen to buy strenuously used socks"—just in case you end up attending.)

Anyway, Geoff got good at climbing and, with it, he took off. In 1980, he went to Mount Kenya and did a handful of climbs, including new routes on Point John, Midget Peak, and the first free ascent of the Diamond Buttress. The same year, he climbed a new route on Carstensz Pyramid (delving deep into, of course, Oxford's funding for gents to "explore strenuous holidays in mountains abroad," as well as sponsorship from *Sports Illustrated,* a dreadfully boring but gigantic-circulation American magazine). The following year, he was plucked by the gods (specifically, Lou Reichardt and George Lowe) to go to Everest, where he reached twenty-one thousand feet before the team imploded. In 1983, he was invited back and, though he didn't summit, he caught Everest fever. During the 1980s, he completed medical school at Harvard (after dropping out twice) and enjoyed all sorts of climbing adventures. In 1988, he climbed the Big E with Peggy Luce, as part of a team that included the first U.S. summittress, Stacy Allison. He also summitted Aconcagua that year, and in 1989 he climbed Vinson, Kili, and Elbrus, becoming the fourth person to do the seven summits.

In 1989, after Harvard medical school and a "climbing" year, Geoff was invited to serve as a physician in Phalpu, Nepal. It was during his time in Phalpu that he witnessed a Dutch doctor doing cataract surgery on an old woman named Dolma, who had been totally blind for three years. The Dutch team did the surgery and a day later she was able to see. Her joy was endless, and, as Geoff said in a recent interview, "I got fired up on the miracle of ophthalmology. I really started to focus on it."

Focus is not just a pun; Geoff delved into ophthalmology with a vengeance, and he did two fellowships in the sport (one in the United States, one in Australia) before devoting himself to cataract surgery in Nepal. In 1994, after working with Nepal's most famous cataract surgeon, Dr. Sanduk Ruit, "we formed a pledge," Geoff said, "to eradicate cataract blindness in the region."

Dr. Ruit figures prominently in Geoff's life. He has revolutionized sight care in the Himalayan countries in which he's worked. In the early 1990s, Dr. Ruit introduced intraocular lens implants—considered heretical at the time—into the villages of Nepal, Himalayan India, Pakistan, Tibet, and other nations. Other surgeons in these countries considered Ruit's lens implants questionable, and they kept a close, scrupulous eye on him for many years. (History would prove his techniques to be more advanced than his critics'.) Geoff—who trained at Harvard, Brown, and Melbourne, in some of the world's finest ophthalmology institutions—came under Ruit's spell in the mid-1990s and realized that Ruit's style of surgery, often performed in high-patient-volume, fast-surgery-speed eye camps in remote locations, was the route to take if cataract blindness was to be conquered in the Himalayas.

Originally, Geoff and Dr. Ruit's organization was run through the University of Vermont, where Geoff has a job as an associate professor. The pair soon learned, however, that the university's systems for paying vendors was hopeless (requiring competing bids, for example, on one-of-a-kind equipment needed for surgery), so they formed their own organization, the Himalayan Cataract Foundation.

Geoff has been somewhat critical of showy goodwill doctors tripping the globe in plush jets, and he has called Project ORBIS and SEE International organizations—two well-known American charities— "very cost-ineffective, producing more flash than actual results." Rather, he has always ascribed to the maxim that teaching local surgeons how to perform cataract surgery themselves is the best thing any doctor could do.

Today, Geoff is still a "gentleman" who likes "to explore strenuous holidays in mountains abroad" as Oxford's A. C. Irvine grant suggests. But that doesn't mean flying to Asia to do huge, churn-'em-out-type surgeries, day after day, in remote villages. These days, he spends most of his time teaching local surgeons to perform the surgeries—teaching them "how to fish," as he puts it. "It varies," he said. "We're really to the stage where there are many good surgeons in Nepal, and for the most part I just teach them. Now, on a typical trip, if I'm gone for three weeks, I'll do 250 to 300 surgeries. Dr. Ruit will do 600, and I'll probably help and supervise on another 150."

Geoff goes three times a year, for about three weeks at a time. His goal is to return sight to as many Himalayan citizens as possible. He's trying to wangle a job that will allow him to spend half the year in Nepal doing eye surgery, but undoubtedly, he'll be looking for some "strenuous exercise" to boot. Regardless, he is devoted to his cause.

"These people have provided me with so many years of wonderful hospitality and so many great experiences that sharing my skills to give them a better life is the least I can do," Geoff said. "If you ever get to see the look on a person's face after they've just found they can see again, it will make your life complete. I've made my life very, very complete, and I hope theirs, too."

As I mentioned, one of the best pleasures of climbing literature is meeting the stars of said literature and finding out they really are as great as said literature says.

I say, "Go Geoff."

2004

Mad Glaswegians on the Peñon d'Ifach (2003)

Question: What parts of Spain are ruled by Britain?

Answer: Any places with climbable rock, Mediterranean views, sunshine, and red wine that are covered in a Rockfax guidebook (which includes the Costa Blanca, Costa Daruda, El Chorro, and Mallorca—in sum, pretty much all of southern Spain).

I learned these facts about twenty-first-century British colonization this summer, when a Glaswegian friend, Jumar Joe Coll, was married to a lovely Spanish lady, Eva, in Valencia. Joe invited me to the wedding, and after a stunningly complex set of airplane flights (Denver-Chicago, Chicago-St. Louis, St. Louis-Toronto, Toronto-St. Petersburg, St. Petersburg-Christchurch, Christchurch-Toronto, Toronto-Madrid),

I arrived in the Spanish capital, where a Yorkshireman named Charlie French met me at the airport. We then drove off toward the Costa Blanca in a rented steel thimble at speeds best reserved for space shuttle reentry and light in a really big hurry.

Glaswegian accents are, to put it politely, a tad thick. When Charlie and I arrived at a seaside crag overlooking Calpé and the magnificent Peñon d'Ifach, several of Joe's Clydeside friends greeted me with welcoming salutes like: "Hae ma donnie don't dock, Cam!" and "Muffwent mon bannie der gump, Cam."

"Urm er dummy und yah," I replied happily.

"Aye!" everyone agreed.

Actually, my response to these sunny Glaswegians was nothing like that. It was more like: "Huh? What? Who, me? Can I possibly be as ignorant as I think those facial expressions are indicating?"

"Aye!" everyone agreed.

After a half a route, I suggested we repair to a villa the Glaswegians had rented ("Aye!" everyone agreed), where I would spend six nights sawing logs at extreme volumes, and nine Glaswegians and two Englishmen would spend six nights wondering how to rebreak my nose—and possibly my entire *heeeeeeeed*—into shapes favorable for the passage of air.

The next day, we attempted some cragging at a place called Sella. It was about 5:30 P.M. when we got started, about the time the temperature was finally dipping below the melting point of cobalt—you know, 1495°C or thereabouts.

At Sella, I immediately realized something about climbing on European limestone (which, of course, Charlie had mentioned to me several times already): that limestone routes have a limited lifetime. That's not to say the rock decomposes after big-boned climbers like myself have upon it trod—no. That's to say the holds slicken out with continued use, and in Spain it takes very little continued use for them to turn to glass entirely. Following Charlie around the crags was a lesson in what not to climb—anything over two years of age, he wanted no part of. He'd scan the second-to-latest Rockfax guidebook for routes, and if the line of bolts he was looking at weren't in there, he'd suggest we climb them—about the most interesting way of using a guidebook I think I've ever seen.

Anyway, we climbed a few Sella routes and after we'd had our asses severely whooped, we retreated to the villa for some appetizers and some aperitifs.

The following day, we wandered around the base of the Peñon d'Ifach, which, not made of cobalt, was not apparently melting. We spied a new "lazy" route (i.e., one not requiring many millions of miles of approach walking) on a block at the base of the Peñon and, by late afternoon, established a bolted line on it—among whizzing plaps of seagull shit.

The day after that, we attempted a big route on something called the *Pug Campaña* (Spanish for "country dog"), a huge canine jutting into the sky north of the small, traditional village of Benidorm. After seven pitches of thorny jungle, we had lost the route and called it a day. We retreated, heads hung, and aimed for the pub in Finnestrat, a place where England's famed Edwardses have a climbing school, or so I'm told. I would very much like to have met Mr. Edwards Senior, having read so much about his climbing activities in Britain and now gazing at a guidebook filled with his exploits in Spain; alas, I only met a man interested in talking about David Beckham and Dental Floss Spice, or whatever her name is, in quick, garbled Spanish—not my first Iberian tongue.

The next day, Charlie and I explored Benidorm. Now, I don't know how fond of concrete you are, but I'm very enthusiastic about the material. I've seen it shaped into all sorts of useless-yet-marvelous-to-behold things. And in Benidorm, no expense has been spared to make the town look like a traditional concrete Roman Villa. Charlie and I wandered the streets for hours, marveling at how concrete can replace: (1) stone, (2) wood, and (3) brains. At that time my wife was expecting a second child and *Concretia* started to have a certain ring to it. . . .

We stopped at a typical streetside café and Charlie handed me a menu, which had no writing in it, only overexposed photographs of various dishes, most of which were too red for my liking. It was, Charlie explained, a "point-and-grunt menu." Because the Costa Blanca gets so many tourists who cannot speak Spanish (or any language, for that matter), restaurateurs there have developed a whole new publishing regime that uses no words, only guttural noises and hand gestures. That seemed quite sensible and I suggested to Charlie that the EU should work on a universal "point-and-grunt" language based on this idea. He grunted happily at the idea. I actually thought about writing this essay in Point and Grunt—to boost EU book sales for Lyons Press—but I'm still learning the difficult-to-master tongue.

The following day we picked up the bolt gun again and headed to Toix North, a lovely crag overlooking the Costa, where we bolted a thirty-meter route. Geoff Der, a Welshman with a half-English/half-Glaswegian accent (if that's possible), pulled off all the loose bits and threw them at my head during the first ascent. Thank you, Geoff—I needed that more than you realize. Geoff just pointed, grunted, and threw more rock.

So, then we went to Joe and Eva's wedding and it was lovely. The sight of many large, pasty white Scotsmen with bright red "suntans" standing next to svelte brown Spanish fashion models was quite the photo opportunity, and I snapped away contentedly. After the ceremony, we ate, drank, made merry, and celebrated a fine week's worth of culture, kilts, and cragging. And it was thus that my Glaswegian friends bid me adieu: "Hae ma donnie don't dock, Cam!"

"Mugfwich mon bannie der donk monk, Cam."

"Urm der dummy und grump den," I replied happily.

"Aye!" everyone agreed.

2004

Woodies Beat Viagra Every Time (2002)

Growing old is a debilitating ailment that strikes a lot of people, animals, and plants. According to statistics compiled by the National
Association Promoting Aging, millions suffer from it every year; some
never fully recover. I'm growing old, and I recently read in *How to Put
Off Growing Old Until Later* by Reg Grundy that home climbing gyms
are one way to stay young, spry, and un-old. And, you can also have
some fun destroying your home while you install one.

Home climbing gyms are pretty common these days, and despite
a world shortage of resin, epoxy, and patience, they show no sign of
declining in popularity anytime soon. A typical wall can cost anywhere between $50 (for a crappy one without holds) to $1,000 (for a

better one, with, say, a cappuccino machine nailed into the roof for bivy practice and really weird boulder problems). In America there are several types of gym construction methods. The most popular, of course, is called the "woody," in which old-growth forests near Seattle are cut down and turned into complicated playthings.

In late 2002, my wife, Ann, announced that she was going out of town for two days, as well as for the night in between them. Our temporary roommate, Luke Laeser, and I decided that might be a good time for some good old-fashioned remodeling—you know, like punching holes in drywall and ramming two-by-fours through light fixtures, smashing her expensive glass trinkets and generally wreaking havoc (and generally reeking).

I called our local building supply store and requested that they deliver half a ton of lumber to our address. I came home from work and found it heaped in our driveway, like straight pretzels that had been stepped on by a giant. So far, so good. We made a few measurements Roman-style (using our thumbs, hands, and forearms), plugged in a circular saw, and began cutting big, expensive pieces of lumber into small shapes of dubious use and even more dubious value. Once we'd dumped these on the Berber carpet in the basement, we had the makings of a really nice bonfire.

Rather than light the pile, Luke suggested we start "framing." Framing, in case you're unfamiliar with it, is sort of like that children's game where you dump the aforementioned pretzels in a heap, then try to extract them one by one without moving any of the other pretzels. Except when you're framing, you do the reverse: stack wood in piles while trying not to knock down other pieces of wood already stacked. By mid-afternoon we once again had the makings of a really nice bonfire. I don't know if the Foundry or Rockreation or any of the big famous indoor climbing venues built their walls like this, but our activities certainly attracted a few local pyromaniacs.

Ann called that night: "Hi, honey. How's the house?"

"Ummm. Good. We're building a smallish climbing wall in the basement."

"Smallish?"

"You know, three hundred square feet of climbing surface or thereabouts."

"Is that smallish?"

"Well, compared to most things . . . like El Cap."

"Is Luke helping you?"

"Well, he knows this stuff. He's in charge. You could say he's giving me a woody in the basement."

"Oh. Thank goodness. Have fun then, and I'll see you tomorrow night."

The following day, Luke and I went back to the local building supply store and bought eight sheets of expensive plywood. No sooner did we arrive home with the four-foot-by-eight-foot sheets than we realized we had no idea how to get them inside. Unfortunately, the only option was to remove an entire window assembly from one end of the house.

This was serious. Removing parts of a perfectly good house in order to build a mini lumberyard in one's basement is an activity for the demented.

We hauled the sheets in and began throwing them against the pile of lumber and screwing them into place. I don't know about you, but I'm not fully developed when it comes to the building arts, so Luke got the adult job of running the screw gun. Meanwhile, I was the supporting mechanism that held up the sheets as they were attached.

Eight hours of toil, cuts, scrapes, sore backs, and minor head injuries later, the lumber heap in the basement had been transformed—we had a home climbing gym! Luke, who's postponed aging for now, began screwing holds into all sorts of impossible positions and was immediately powering out V50 moves and the like. I flapped about on the only "jug" holds we had (called, by the way, the "Burlmaster" set), looking more like laundry on a line than a spry young climber.

Ann came home late that night and descended into the basement.

"Wow!" she said, genuinely impressed. "That's a lot of lumber."

"Don't light a match!" I warned.

Ann put on her climbing shoes and began repeating Luke's problems, minus a hold or two. I flapped and dried in the breeze, the way a Burlmaster should.

The wall has been up for two years now, and I'm finally starting to understand how much fun it is. All my old injuries have returned, and the neighbors are filing a lawsuit because a piece of wood punched through the wall into their fish tank during construction. If these sorts of demanding challenges don't keep one young, nothing will. Yep, my woody sure beats the hell outta Viagra!

Dave Brower (left), with famed desert climber Eric Bjørnstad, at Mountainfilm in Telluride in 2000.

Eating Waffles with Dave (1989)

I ate waffles with David Brower.

It was in the summer of 1989. I was a ripe twenty-four, and Dave, who seemed pretty old back then, must have been a sprightly seventy-seven. Afterward, I got to know many seventy-seven-year-olds. Dave—as I look back and remember it—seemed to be in a lot better health than every other seventy-seven-year-old I've met since. Maybe it was those waffles.

I met Dave Brower almost by accident. It was during a summer when I was running around the Sierra Nevada with Steve Porcella, climbing every route we could get our hands on, some old, some new. I knew the name David Brower, because it was tucked between the filthy pages of my copy of Steve Roper's *Climbers Guide to the Sierra Nevada*. There were descriptions of about seventy peaks that Dave had made the first ascent of, the first winter ascent of, or some other noteworthy ascent. In hindsight, they all blend together. I gazed at Brower's name, along with those of Norman Clyde, Glen Dawson, Jules Eichorn, Hervey Voge, Galen Rowell, Bolton Coit Brown, Andy Smatko, Clarence King, Vern Clevenger, Chris Jones, John and Ruth Mendenhall, Gary Colliver, Claude Fiddler, Bob Harrington, and many other people whom I had met in print and felt I was close to, even if only in name. We all knew the subtleties of the spectacular peaks of the high Sierra.

Steve and I lived and climbed for nearly three months in the Sierra Nevada in the summer of 1989, with occasional trips out to de-crustify our polypropylene long underwear and to restock on lentils and rice (which, as a food group, goes hand-in-hand with recrustifying).

During one trip out of the mountains, we visited San Francisco. While we were there, someone suggested we give Dave a call. We did (his number was listed in Berkeley), and he invited us over the following morning for breakfast: waffles, with strawberries and cream.

We drove up and parked outside the small-but-quaint house overlooking the Bay. A wonderfully friendly gray-haired woman (Anne Brower, Dave's wife) came out the front door, with a tall, solid, gray-haired man (Dave himself) right on her heels. Their heads of silver shined in the clear morning sun. We said our hellos and followed them inside, where some serious waffle making was in progress. These weren't just any waffles. They were chock-full of vegetables, like zucchinis, and served with an array of jams and jellies. Steve and I were in waffle nirvana.

Steve set up the slide projector, Dave pulled the curtains closed, and we started rolling through climbing slides, showing the wild backcountry of the Sierra Nevada.

"Ah, North Palisade," Dave said as the first image appeared on the screen. "I did that in winter."

He knew pretty much every crag and every mountain we showed him by heart, and had some story of his own to relate that seemed infinitely more interesting than our young tales of bravado.

At that time, in 1989, I knew David Brower was an environmentalist, but that was about all I knew about the man. It would take another eleven years—as I traveled across and lived throughout the West—for me to begin to comprehend the length, breadth, and scope of Dave's activities.

David Ross Brower was born in Berkeley on July 1, 1912. In 1933, Brower and his childhood friend George Rockwood undertook a seventy-day backpacking trip through the Sierra Nevada, and made ascents of many peaks. The following fall, the editor of the *Sierra Club Bulletin*, Francis Farquhar, asked Brower to submit a story about his activities. "Far from the Madding Mules" was published in the 1935 *Bulletin*, and as Dave observed: "Our Sierra trip was immortalized and my ego trip had begun."

Throughout the mid-1930s, Dave and numerous friends made a huge number of first ascents in the high Sierra. Because he and his friends were some of the few American climbers that at that time had learned and perfected belayed climbing techniques, they soon found themselves involved with the two "last great challenges" of pre-War mountaineering on the North American continent: Mt. Waddington, in British Columbia, and Shiprock, in New Mexico.

Dave's team's Waddington attempt of 1935 ended in failure, as did a second attempt by a group of Californians in 1936. After Easterners Fritz Weissner and Bill House had conquered Waddington in 1936, every American mountaineer turned his eyes toward Shiprock. The allure of the mountain was heightened by a widespread rumor that there was a $1,000 prize awaiting the first mountaineers to climb the fantastic spire.

In October 1939, Dave, Bestor Robinson, Raffi Bedayn, and John Dyer drove twelve hundred miles from Berkeley to make their own attempt on Shiprock, bringing with them fourteen hundred feet of rope, seventy pitons, eighteen carabiners, two hammers, and four cameras. They also brought a small supply of expansion bolts, items which had never before been used by American mountaineers.

On October 12, 1939—after three days' effort—they reached the summit. In all, only four bolts had been placed, but according to historical accounts, they were the first bolts ever placed for mountaineering in the Americas (a "fact" that I later learned was not quite factual; bolts had been placed on several earlier climbs in the Sierra Nevada).

In May of 1993, after I became involved with Shiprock, I asked Dave about the bolts he'd placed and the irony of his dislike for sport climbing, which relies entirely on bolts.

"I disapprove of rappel-bolting," he said. "I think it takes all the challenge out of climbing. I feel differently about the bolts I put in [on Shiprock]. It took an hour and a half to drill each hole. You don't do very much of that."

Dave's early love of the outdoors and wild places precipitated a long involvement with the Sierra Club. In 1941, he became a member of the club's board of directors, and from 1952 to 1969 he was its first executive director. He saw the club's membership grow from two thousand to seventy-seven thousand, before leaving the club—under a cloud of disagreements—in 1969. The 1950s and '60s saw perhaps Dave's most important work, when he led several major campaigns that halted the damming of the Grand Canyon and several other river corridors. One mistake, which would plague him for the rest of his life, was an agreement whereby he and the Sierra Club wouldn't protest the damming of Glen Canyon and Flaming Gorge in exchange for several other rivers being left alone.

In 1969, he founded Friends of the Earth (FOE), as well as the League of Conservation Voters, and he helped found independent FOE organizations in many countries (FOE now operates in sixty-three countries). After leaving FOE in a dispute over control of the organization in 1982, Dave established the San Francisco–based Earth Island Institute, where he remained as chairman until his death.

Eating Dave's amazing waffles in 1989 seems like a dream now. It's taken me fifteen years to begin to understand the scope of his achievements—and I've been to the Grand Canyon only once. Dave's waffle breakfasts, like everything he did, became well-known among career environmentalists, who studied his life with an electron microscope.

Years after those waffles, I moved to Colorado and met a lot of lifelong environmentalists. Some were young and enthusiastic, eager to do whatever they could to save the planet. Others—the older, been-there-protested-that types—were following in Dave's lifelong commitment and cared little about their public appearance.

Then there were a few who were all career and virtually no environment—in it to stroke their holier-than-thou egos and move up some kind of environmentalist corporate ladder.

When I met these folks, I'd let it casually slip that "Hey, I had waffles at Dave's!"

"What? You?"

It left them wondering how a heathen who knew so little about Dave's policies and protests had made it into the inner sanctum and dined with the archdruid.

I don't quite know the answer to that, but I'll tell you one thing: the more slides of the high Sierra we showed to Dave that waffly morning in 1989, the more excited he became. It got to the point where he was calling out the names of various places the instant the projector dropped the slide.

David Brower became concerned about wilderness in part because of his years as a climber and the mountains he loved. I like to think that for Dave, talking about the high Sierras that morning was a rejuvenating process, a trip back in time to his strongest, healthiest roots. For me, it's something I'll never forget.

Acknowledgments

Bernard Newman, the revered-until-now former editor of *Mountain* magazine, deserves credit—and, the more significant attendant blame—for the creation of the column that mostly comprises this book, and therefore for the book itself. He first egged on my "journalism" career (i.e., harassing famed American climbers) in the late 1980s, when I started doing short articles for *Mountain,* and later he made me an editor of the magazine—Sub-Assistant Editor of Silly Climbing Stories, or something along those lines.

Mountain went under in the early 1990s, but it was resurrected in a way in the late 1990s, when Bernard took over as editor of *Climber.* He called me one penniless day in 1997 and asked if I wanted to "produce" a column on climbing in the United States. He said it paid actual dollars, and the result was a long-running column that has slowly but certainly proved to all Britons why they have not needed colonial types for more than two hundred years.

Ed Douglas was, in a way, Bernard's coconspirator. After *Mountain*'s demise, he asked me to do the same thing—"produce material"—for his now-defunct magazine, *Mountain Review.* Some of the stories in this volume first appeared there (and I am still "producing material"—Ed, need a fresh load of it?).

Others who deserve a tip of a generally askance hat and credit for creating the illiterate tome in your hands include all those who have: (1) climbed with me; (2) edited my "produce"; (3) lived with me; (4) let me stay with them; (5) given me useful items; and (6) given me money.

The people in categories one, two, and five include the lovely chaps to whom this volume is dedicated. Others who variously fit the six categories include: Bruce Anderson, Khuttis Arminarf and Soonil Havaskar of the Hampi Bouldering Squad, Pete Athans, Eric Bjørnstad, Carrie Click, the El Costa Blanca Climbing Team (Barbara, Emily, Eva, Joe, John, Kirsten, Mark, Nigel, and Reggie (Perrin)), Ilene Dover, Daniel Farnbach, Tufac N. Farny, Julian and Elke Fisher, Alice Flomp, Julie Garrison, Jesse Harvey, Leslie Henderson, Madonna Kantsing, Suumartass Klymahtïp, Ariil Kocsarça, Ace Kvale, Dougald MacDonald, Soomril Matafarka, Dan McCollum, John Middendorf, Christina Page, Margaret Quenemoen, Doug Robinson, Donna and Curtis Robinson, Steve Roper, Mykah Sabitrusty, Luke Trihey, Chris Vandiver, Mike ("Hotel") Walker, and Jeff Widen.

The people in categories three, four, five, and six include my parents, Kerry and Mary Burns; my sisters Gillian and Penny and their families (Mike, Glenn, Jessica, Natalie, Katie, Ryan, Kelsea, Jamie); my wife, Ann, and her parents, Bob and Sylvia; and my daughters, Zoe and Mollie Burns—thank you.

Others to whom I owe real gratitude, not just a severe chafing, include: Andrew Davies (of the you-must-stay-at Hotel Capri, St. Lucia), Darwin Mondesir (of the Tuxedo Villas, St. Lucia), and Aly Brown (of the fabulous Stonefield Estate Villas, St. Lucia—which gets a deserving plug herein). Plus, thanks to members of the Polish Skiing Team for their 1999 visit: Geau Digadich, Ive Gotanich, Seau Kanshiski, Noah Kanshiski, Rill E. Hucanski, Ustinki Lycraze, Bellevemi Ucantski, Frank Lee Ustinki, and Popovalium Andropov.

Acknowledgments

Finally, thanks to Susannah Hogendorn (and, subsequently, Jessie Shiers), who rewrote this entire book from the Cyrillic alphabet in which it was submitted to The Lyons Press, and to Tom McCarthy, whose McCarthyistic rules of publishing were a bit like El Cap with penalties (he spanked me severely when he read my Cyrillic script— pleasure's all mine, Tom). Thank you all—I hope you can soon come live with me and we can create something huge and weird.

Yours truly on El Cap.

About the Author

Cameron M. "Cam" Burns was born in Melbourne, and grew up in Sydney. At the age of twelve he was deported by the Australian government to the only country that would take him (the United States), where he has been foisting illiterate scribble on publishers since. His hobbies include dangling modifiers, splitting infinitives, and cutting and pasting plagiarisms into his everyday speech. He lives with his wife, Ann, daughters, Zoe and Mollie, dog, Lefty, and cat, Morrigan, in a small town in Colorado.

Photo Credits